THE DEFEAT OF SATAN

**T&T Clark
Explorations in Reformed Theology**

Series Editors
Paul T. Nimmo
Paul Dafydd Jones

Editorial Board
Christophe Chalamet
David A. S. Fergusson
Angela Dienhart Hancock
Leanne Van Dyk
Matthias D. Wüthrich

Volume III

THE DEFEAT OF SATAN

Karl Barth's Three-Agent Account of Salvation

Declan Kelly

LONDON • NEW YORK • OXFORD • NEW DELHI • SYDNEY

T&T CLARK
Bloomsbury Publishing Plc
50 Bedford Square, London, WC1B 3DP, UK
1385 Broadway, New York, NY 10018, USA
29 Earlsfort Terrace, Dublin 2, Ireland

BLOOMSBURY, T&T CLARK and the T&T Clark logo are trademarks of
Bloomsbury Publishing Plc

First published in Great Britain 2022
Paperback edition published 2023

Copyright © Declan Kelly, 2022

Declan Kelly has asserted his right under the Copyright, Designs and Patents Act,
1988, to be identified as Author of this work.

For legal purposes the Acknowledgments on pp. viii–ix constitute an extension
of this copyright page.

Cover design: Anna Berzovan

All rights reserved. No part of this publication may be reproduced or transmitted in
any form or by any means, electronic or mechanical, including photocopying,
recording, or any information storage or retrieval system, without prior permission
in writing from the publishers.

Bloomsbury Publishing Plc does not have any control over, or responsibility for, any
third-party websites referred to or in this book. All internet addresses given in this
book were correct at the time of going to press. The author and publisher regret any
inconvenience caused if addresses have changed or sites have ceased to exist, but can
accept no responsibility for any such changes.

A catalogue record for this book is available from the British Library.

Library of Congress Cataloging-in-Publication Data
Names: Kelly, Declan, author.
Title: The defeat of satan : Karl Barth's three-agent account of salvation / Declan Kelly.
Description: London, UK ; New York, NY, USA : T&T Clark, 2022. |
Series: T&T Clark explorations in reformed theology ; 3 |
Includes bibliographical references and index. |
Identifiers: LCCN 2021035297 (print) | LCCN 2021035298 (ebook) |
ISBN 9780567698230 (hb) | ISBN 9780567698810 (paperback) |
ISBN 9780567698247 (epdf) | ISBN 9780567698261 (epub)
Subjects: LCSH: Barth, Karl, 1886–1968. | Salvation–Christianity–History of
doctrines–20th century. | Barth, Karl, 1886–1968. Kirchliche Dogmatik.
Classification: LCC BX4827.B3 K39 2022 (print) | LCC BX4827.B3 (ebook) |
DDC 230/.044092–dc23
LC record available at https://lccn.loc.gov/2021035297
LC ebook record available at https://lccn.loc.gov/2021035298

ISBN: HB: 978-0-5676-9823-0
PB: 978-0-5676-9881-0
ePDF: 978-0-5676-9824-7
ePUB: 978-0-5676-9826-1

Typeset by Newgen KnowledgeWorks Pvt. Ltd., Chennai, India

To find out more about our authors and books visit www.bloomsbury.com
and sign up for our newsletters.

For Dermot & Pauline,
who have never tired of reminding me that the resurrected Christ can walk through closed doors

CONTENTS

Acknowledgments — viii
List of Abbreviations — xi

Chapter 1
INTRODUCTION — 1

Chapter 2
ELECTION AND THE DEFEAT OF SATAN — 21

Chapter 3
THE JUDGMENT OF SATAN'S WORLD — 51

Chapter 4
GOD'S COVENANT WITH DEATH — 81

Chapter 5
GOD'S ESCHATOLOGICAL JUSTIFICATION — 111

Chapter 6
CONCLUSION — 139

Bibliography — 147
Index — 161

ACKNOWLEDGMENTS

This book began life as a PhD thesis at the University of Aberdeen. Special thanks must therefore be extended first of all to Paul Nimmo, my supervisor during those research years. He has demonstrated enormous patience and insight in guiding this project through its various twists and turns. His probing questions, rigorous attention to detail, and generosity of spirit have proved fundamental to the completion of this book.

Other members of the Divinity faculty in Aberdeen have also made direct or indirect contributions to the present work. The Systematic Theology seminars with Don Wood, Paul Nimmo, Tom Greggs, and Philip Ziegler, as well as the annual retreats to Pluscarden Abbey, proved deeply formative for my own thinking and writing and provided unique opportunities to participate in rich theological conversations. I also learned much during my regular incursions into the Theological Ethics seminars. Brian Brock always kept us systematicians on our toes and passed on to me an appreciation for Martin Luther's thought that has subtly and not so subtly seeped its way into these pages.

I am also grateful to Jake Rollins, Kevin Hargaden, Taido Chino, David Lilley, and Marty Phillips for their contributions to this project at various stages along the way and to Kevin O' Farrell for his friendship and encouragement amidst those occasional spouts of existential dread that accompany any research that is worth doing.

I would also like to thank Paul Dafydd Jones, co-editor with Paul Nimmo of the series to which this book belongs, for his encouragement and insight, both of which have been invaluable to this project, as well as Anna Turton and her colleagues at T&T Clark for their diligent work in preparing this text for publication.

There are many over the years who have taught me well—William Ford, Scott Spurlock, Cynthia Bennett Brown, Charlie Hadjiev, Graham Cheesman—but one teacher merits particular acknowledgement. Arden Autry did not introduce me to Barth, but I am confident that it is his skill and passion as an exegete that first drew me to Barth. Arden, who led the Emmaus Scripture School in my hometown Galway for several years, teaches and preaches as one whose heart burns within him as the Scriptures are opened. This book owes much to his encouragement and example.

To my family here in Aberdeen, I am grateful for the time they have allowed me to write this book. Raquel's kindness, patience, and humour have sustained me through much of the solitude and doubt that can attend the task of writing theology. And our daughter Alva and son Mateo have enriched my life in incalculable ways. It may seem to them at present that I have wasted my time writing this when I could have been playing with them. But perhaps one day they will pick this book up and read it and then know for sure that I was wasting my time writing it when I could have been playing with them.

To my family in Ireland, I owe untold debts—in every sense of the word. My sister Elaine is the true theologian of our family. Her unflinching curiosity and courage are qualities that I can only hope to imitate, and her feedback on this work has been hugely beneficial. And my brother David is perhaps the reason this book exists in the first place. His willingness to tell me the truth has proved indispensable to this project getting off the ground. Finally, my parents Pauline and Dermot have prayed for me from before I can remember. Hearing their encouraging words after they had read one of this book's chapters meant more to me than I could express. It is to them that I dedicate this book.

ABBREVIATIONS

I/I	*Church Dogmatics*, vol. I, part 1. Peabody: Hendrickson, 2010.
I/2	*Church Dogmatics*, vol. I, part 2. Peabody: Hendrickson, 2010.
II/l	*Church Dogmatics*, vol. II, part 1. Peabody: Hendrickson, 2010.
II/2	*Church Dogmatics*, vol. II, part 2. Peabody: Hendrickson, 2010.
III/1	*Church Dogmatics*, vol. III, part 1. Peabody: Hendrickson, 2010.
III/2	*Church Dogmatics*, vol. III, part 2. Peabody: Hendrickson, 2010.
III/3	*Church Dogmatics*, vol. III, part 3. Peabody: Hendrickson, 2010.
III/4	*Church Dogmatics*, vol. III, part 4. Peabody: Hendrickson, 2010.
IV/1	*Church Dogmatics*, vol. IV, part 1. Peabody: Hendrickson, 2010.
IV/2	*Church Dogmatics*, vol. IV, part 2. Peabody: Hendrickson, 2010.
IV/3	*Church Dogmatics*, vol. IV, part 3. Peabody: Hendrickson, 2010.
IV/4	*Church Dogmatics*, vol. IV, part 4. Peabody: Hendrickson, 2010.
TCL	*The Christian Life. Church Dogmatics*, vol. IV, part 4, Lecture Fragments. Edinburgh: T&T Clark, 1981.
KD	*Die Kirchliche Dogmatik* (13 vols; Munich: Chr. Kaiser, 1932 and thereafter Zürich: EVZ, 1938–65).
RII	*The Epistle to the Romans*. Translated by Edwin C. Hoskyns. Oxford: Oxford University Press, 1968.
GD	*The Göttingen Dogmatics: Instruction in the Christian Religion,* Volume 1, trans. Geoffrey W. Bromiley. Grand Rapids: Eerdmans, 1990.

Chapter 1

INTRODUCTION

And the saving and preserving will of God is not primarily directed against sin. With a higher and deeper aim, it is directed against the nothingness affirmed in sin.

—Karl Barth[1]

In John's first epistle, the apostle declares to his readers the purpose behind the Son of God's coming: "to destroy the works of the devil" (1 Jn 3:8). Modern theology has had a complicated relationship with New Testament declarations of this kind.[2] Are these idiosyncratic descriptions of the Christian understanding of salvation inhabiting the margins of New Testament thought? Do they reflect merely one of several discrete metaphors—one that is neither more nor less important than the others—used by the scriptural authors to convey the meaning of the atonement? Or do they in fact take us to the very heart of the gospel, summing up in a few words the biblical doctrine of salvation? Yet even if we take these declarations to have accurately summarised the New Testament's apocalyptic understanding of the gospel, the question arises of whether, to what extent, and how we can follow John and the other New Testament authors in presenting the gospel as the message of Satan's defeat.[3] As an answer to that question, this book aims to display, critique, and develop the soteriology of a theologian who seeks to be faithful to this peculiar New Testament witness—Karl Barth.

---

1. Karl Barth, *Church Dogmatics*, 4 vols. in 13 pts., ed. G. W. Bromiley and T. F. Torrance (Peabody, MA: Hendrickson, 2010), III/2, 143. References to *Church Dogmatics* in the footnotes will henceforth take the form of the volume/part number followed by the page number.

2. See, for example, Jn 12:31; Acts 10:38; 1 Cor. 15:54-7; Col. 1:13, 2:15; Heb. 2:14.

3. I use the term "apocalyptic" here as a theological term of art signalling the gospel's concern with God's eschatological overthrow of usurping powers, an overthrow that ends "the present evil age" (Gal. 1:4) and ushers in the "new creation."

Theology without Satan

In the middle of the twentieth century, Paul Althaus declared that "the age of a theology without Satan has come to an end."[4] Though Barth is by no means the figure solely—or even primarily—responsible for ending that "age," the theological revolution he spearheaded in the early decades of the twentieth century and to which he gave systematic expression in the monumental *Church Dogmatics* did much to refute the assumption that a "theology without Satan" was the only reasonable option for a discourse desiring to be taken seriously as a science.

"Theology without Satan," and, in particular, a doctrine of salvation without Satan, came to arguably its purest expression in the work of Friedrich Schleiermacher in the first half of the nineteenth century.[5] According to Schleiermacher, the New Testament does not teach us anything new regarding the devil. Rather than deriving the idea from the Old Testament or "Divine revelation," it simply makes use of the popular conception of Satan.[6] This "incidental" way in which the subject of the devil occurs indicates "that neither Christ nor His disciples desired either to give support to the idea or vouch for its truth."[7] Additionally, Schleiermacher finds no substantial New Testament evidence for the notion that Satan is a real "overlord" of humanity and that the coming of the Son of God was intended to break the power of the devil.[8] Alongside this exegetical warrant for rejecting the notion of the devil's authority, he also puts forward a more pastoral or practical reason. He worries that the thought of humanity as being in Satan's grip "gravely strengthens the already strong inclination of men to deny their own guilt."[9] The regrettable consequence of such scapegoating is that "severe self-examination" is replaced by a belief in the "influence of Satan" as an explanation for growing wickedness.[10] The dogmatic upshot is that the Christian doctrine of salvation is threatened by a salvation that "appears to be only a help against an external enemy."[11]

In the end, the question of Satan, for Schleiermacher, has the same dogmatic status as the question of the stars and the planets—which is to say, no dogmatic

---

4. Paul Althaus, *Die christliche Wahrheit: Lehrbuch der Dogmatik* (Gütersloh: Gütersloher Verlagshaus, 1962), 391.

5. Isaak Dorner describes Schleiermacher as "the most acute opponent of the doctrine of the devil." Isaak A. Dorner, *A System of Christian Doctrine: Volume III*, trans. Alfred Cave and J. S. Banks (Edinburgh: T&T Clark, 1882), 94–5.

6. Friedrich D. E. Schleiermacher, *The Christian Faith*, ed. H. R. Mackintosh and J. S. Stewart (London: T&T Clark, 1999), 163, 167.

7. Schleiermacher, *The Christian Faith*, 164.

8. Schleiermacher, *The Christian Faith*, 165–6.

9. Schleiermacher, *The Christian Faith*, 168.

10. Schleiermacher, *The Christian Faith*, 169.

11. Schleiermacher, *The Christian Faith*, 169.

status whatsoever. It is a matter of "cosmology," and has no bearing on the Christian doctrine of redemption, since "that from which we are to be redeemed remains the same (as does also the manner of our redemption) whether there be a devil or no."[12] In Schleiermacher's view, an increased concentration on "our own inner life"—a concentration he takes to be recommended by the Scriptures—entails the increasing impossibility of considering things as "works of the devil." The final effect of such concentration? The conception of the devil would eventually become "obsolete."[13] As a poetic expression, the idea of the devil could (and should) still find a place in the Church's liturgy.[14] But Schleiermacher saw no future for the devil in dogmatic work.

Schleiermacher's "theology without Satan" was bolstered by Albrecht Ritschl's influential contribution to the doctrine of salvation in the latter part of the nineteenth century.[15] Ritschl criticises the "dramatic" doctrine of redemption developed in patristic theology—the idea that redemption involves the overthrow of Satan's power—for being "thoroughly non-ethical."[16] As with Schleiermacher, the issue of individual sin and guilt was the motor driving Ritschl's critical remarks. The dramatic doctrine of the atonement, he contends, represents sin as *"merely a mechanical subjection to the devil,"* and in so doing the relation of redemption to the "human will" is severed.[17] In his recital of the history of the doctrine of the atonement, Ritschl adjudges the dramatic theory to have been thoroughly uprooted by the mediaeval theologians. They achieved this uprooting principally by ethicising the conception of sin. Sin now came to be viewed "in its legal and moral aspects"—a felicitous development from Ritschl's perspective and one upon which he would seek to build.[18]

---

12. Schleiermacher, *The Christian Faith*, 167.

13. Schleiermacher, *The Christian Faith*, 168. On Schleiermacher's concept of the devil as it relates to the question of the origins and nature of sin, see Daniel J. Pedersen, *Schleiermacher's Theology of Sin and Nature: Agency, Value, and Modern Theology* (New York: Routledge, 2020), 17–35.

14. Schleiermacher, *The Christian Faith*, 169–70.

15. See Albrecht Ritschl, *The Christian Doctrine of Justification and Reconciliation*, ed. H. R. Mackintosh and A. B. Macaulay (Edinburgh: T&T Clark, 1902).

16. Albrecht Ritschl, *A Critical History of the Christian Doctrine of Justification and Reconciliation*, trans. John S. Black (Edinburgh: Edmonston and Douglas, 1872), 4. This, it is worth noting, is a judgment shared by Gustaf Aulén, the great proponent of the "dramatic" or "classic" doctrine of the atonement. He asserts that "the classic idea of the Atonement is always anti-moralistic." Gustaf Aulén, *Christus Victor: An Historical Study of the Three Main Types of the Idea of Atonement*, trans. A. G. Hebert (London: SPCK, 1970), 69.

17. Ritschl, *A Critical History of the Christian Doctrine of Justification and Reconciliation*, 5.

18. Ritschl, *A Critical History of the Christian Doctrine of Justification and Reconciliation*, 5.

The Apocalyptic Turn

It would be misleading to describe Barth's "break" from liberal theology as initiating, among other things, a lasting return to the old idea of Satan.[19] He does not ultimately adhere to the traditional view of the devil as defined and disparaged in Schleiermacher's *The Christian Faith*, namely, the view of the devil as a spiritual being "who lived in close relation with God, [and] voluntarily changed from this state to a state of antagonism and rebellion against God."[20] Moreover, Barth would go on to express a certain Schleiermacherian unwillingness to elevate the position of Satan within the dogmatic task. In his formal treatment of angels and demons in §51 of *Church Dogmatics* III/3, he issues a verdict that could derail the argument of the present work before it has even left the station.[21] "It is nonsense," he states, "to talk about God and the devil ... in the same breath."[22] Later, in §69 of *CD* IV/3, he similarly cautions that we should think and speak of the devil "only reluctantly, infrequently, and with great reserve."[23] In light of these comments, Gustav Wingren's criticism of Barth might at first glance seem to be more or less justified: while his "break" with liberalism consisted in a needed reversal of its movement from the human to the divine, its "two-agent" framework of God and human beings was regrettably retained.[24] Expressed more forcefully still, "There is no devil in Barth's theology."[25]

---

19. Whether Barth is best described as having broken away from liberal theology or having redirected and even radicalised liberal theology is an ongoing point of debate. Christophe Chalamet rightly speaks of "continuities and discontinuities" between Barth and liberal Protestantism. Christophe Chalamet, "Barth and Liberal Protestantism," in *The Oxford Handbook of Karl Barth*, ed. Paul T. Nimmo and Paul Dafydd Jones (Oxford: Oxford University Press, 2019), 132–46.

20. Schleiermacher, *The Christian Faith*, 161. It is Barth's mature judgment that we must understand God and the devil as being in "essential conflict" with one another and not as one-time allies who then became enemies. See *CD* III/3, 520.

21. When referencing a particular part-volume of *Church Dogmatics* in the main text, I will henceforth use the abbreviation *CD* followed by the volume/part number, e.g., *CD* II/2.

22. *CD* III/3, 520 revised translation (henceforth "rev.").

23. *CD* IV/3, 261. Mention might also be made here of Barth's dismissive remarks in response to the talk of demons that took place among theologians in Germany after the war in 1945. On these remarks, see Matthias D. Wüthrich, "Das 'fremde Geheimnis des wirklich Nichtigen': Karl Barths einsamer Denkweg in der Frage des Bösen," in *Karl Barth im europäischen Zeitgeschehen (1935–1950): Widerstand—Bewährung—Orientierung*, ed. Michael Beintker, Christian Link, and Michael Trowitzsch (Zürich: TVZ, 2010), 396–8.

24. Gustaf Wingren, *Theology in Conflict: Nygren, Barth, Bultmann*, trans. Eric H. Wahlstrom (Edinburgh: Oliver and Boyd, 1958), 25–8.

25. Wingren, *Theology in Conflict*, 25.

But first glances can be deceiving. Under the influence of the Blumhardts,[26] in the wake of the "apocalyptic turn" in biblical scholarship and theology,[27] and with a keen awareness of the tumultuous times in which he was living and the power of the Scriptures to speak to such times, Barth's sermons as a pastor in Safenwil, and to a lesser extent his lectures delivered at various conferences and events in his early years, become increasingly populated with references to powers and principalities, to a third agent in the cosmic drama that is neither divine nor human.[28] As Barth's friend Eduard Thurneysen would later say of this

---

26. On the influence of the Blumhardts on Barth's theology, see Christian T. Collins Winn, *"Jesus Is Victor!": The Significance of the Blumhardts for the Theology of Karl Barth* (Eugene, OR: Pickwick, 2009).

27. Narrations of the apocalyptic turn and its effects can be found in Theodore W. Jennings, "Apocalyptic and Contemporary Theology," *Quarterly Review* 4, no. 3 (1984): 54–68; R. Barry Matlock, *Unveiling the Apocalyptic Paul: Paul's Interpreters and the Rhetoric of Criticism* (Sheffield: Sheffield Academic Press, 1996); Richard E. Sturm, "Defining the Word 'Apocalyptic': A Problem in Biblical Criticism," in *Apocalyptic and the New Testament: Essays in Honour of J. Louis Martyn*, ed. Marion L. Soards and Joel Marcus (Sheffield: Sheffield Academic Press, 1989), 17–48; Joshua B. Davis, "The Challenge of Apocalyptic to Modern Theology," in *Apocalyptic and the Future of Theology: With and beyond J. Louis Martyn*, ed. Joshua B. Davis and Douglas Harink (Eugene, OR: Cascade, 2012), 1–48; J. P. Davies, *Paul among the Apocalypses? An Evaluation of the "Apocalyptic Paul" in the Context of Jewish and Christian Apocalyptic Literature* (London: T&T Clark, 2016), 3–22; Jörg Frey, "Demythologizing Apocalyptic? On N. T. Wright's Paul, Apocalyptic Interpretation, and the Constraints of Construction," in *God and the Faithfulness of Paul: A Critical Examination of the Pauline Theology of N.T. Wright*, ed. Christoph Heilig, J. Thomas Hewitt, and Michael F. Bird (Tübingen: Mohr Siebeck, 2016), 503–7. Of particular importance to the resurgence of apocalyptic as a historical and theological point of discussion is the publication of Johannes Weiß's *The Kingdom of God in the Preaching of Jesus* in 1892. While applauding the centrality of the concept of the "kingdom" in Ritschlian theology, Weiß's groundbreaking book exposed the chasm between the first century conception of the kingdom and the nineteenth century conception. His historical investigation led to a rediscovery of the thoroughgoing apocalyptic character of the gospel as attested in the New Testament. In particular, it foregrounded a theme that Schleiermacher (as noted above) could only perceive to be marginal to the New Testament: the conflict between God and Satan. In the mind of Jesus, Weiß insisted, the work to be accomplished consisted in "a struggle against Satan." Johannes Weiß, *Jesus' Proclamation of the Kingdom of God*, trans. R. H. Hiers and D. L. Holland (Philadelphia, PA: Fortress Press, 1971), 102.

28. In a 1915 sermon on Luke 16, Barth declares that when Jesus looked at the world "with the eyes of the love of God," he saw "the *powers and forces* [Mächte und Gewalten] that entered between God and men. They cover the face of God. They make their hearts alien to the divine home from which they are derived. They block their consciences in strangely narrow prisons, in which they can no longer be aroused and are only able to cry out." Karl Barth, *Predigten 1915*, ed. Heinrich Schmidt, *Gesamtausgabe*, I.27 (Zürich: TVZ, 1996), 260. Displaying none of Schleiermacher's reluctance in connecting the immoral

formative period in their theological development, "There was much talk at that time in Safenwil of the principalities, powers, and authorities which are 'made a spectacle of' by Christ."[29] Those New Testament themes and tropes that struck large swathes of modern theology as incidental at best and theologically and ethically irresponsible at worst, namely the apocalyptically charged conception of salvation as Christ's triumph over powers and principalities that hold human beings in bondage, were themes and tropes integral to Barth's proclamation and theological labour.[30]

activity of the world to demonic activity, Barth, in another sermon from the same year, claims that the Great War has been "brought about" by "forces" (*Gewalten*). In the context, we see that he is not simply talking about political or moral forces but "the forces of evil" (*die Mächte des Bösen*) even "the devil." Barth, *Predigten 1915*, 308. We see this connection between human sin and the power of Satan again in a 1916 sermon, where Barth states that "whoever commits sin is of the devil, to him the devil is his God and Father. Whoever does sin is also doing injustice, i.e. service of the devil." Putting the matter in the starkest terms possible, he contends that "You are either in one war camp or in the other. You either have to say yes with God or no with the devil!" Karl Barth, *Predigten 1916*, ed. Anton Drewes, *Gesamtausgabe*, I.29 (Zürich: TVZ, 1998), 280–1. Jumping forward to 1923, Barth remains committed to this "apocalyptic" mode of thought. He states:

> The devil is a liar from the beginning. He is a very serious reality here below, in the world of spirits and of the spirit which surrounds us—in the air we breathe, even if the atmosphere is very Christian, very ideal. He, who denies that the devil is here, is a fool—today more so than ever. The devil is the prince of this world. (Karl Barth, *Predigten 1921–35*, ed. Holger Finze, *Gesamtausgabe*, I.31 [Zürich: TVZ, 1998], 57

These references serve to indicate that Barth's summary description of "the revelation that Jesus brought" in a 1916 sermon—the revelation of "the living God, who triumphs over all devils and idols"—is no aberration but a description that takes us to the heart of his understanding of the gospel. Barth, *Predigten 1916*, 87.

29. Eduard Thurneysen, "Introduction," in *Revolutionary Theology in the Making: Barth-Thurneysen Correspondence, 1914–1925*, ed. and trans. James D. Smart (London: Epworth Press, 1964), 15.

30. The conception of salvation as a three-agent drama is deemed central to the apostle Paul's theology in early twentieth-century works by William Wrede, Johannes Weiß, and Albert Schweitzer. See William Wrede, *Paul*, trans. Edward Lummis (London: Philip Green, 1907); Johannes Weiß, "Die Bedeutung des Paulus für den modernen Christen," in *Zeitschrift für die Neutestamentliche Wissenschaft und die Kunde des Urchristentums*, ed. D. Erwin Preuschen (Giessen: Alfred Töpelmann, 1920), 127–42; Albert Schweitzer, *The Mysticism of Paul the Apostle*, 2nd ed., trans. William Montgomery (London: Adam & Charles Black, 1953). These scholars were doubtful, however, that such a "mythological" conception of salvation could be taken up by modern Christians. Later scholars attentive to the apocalyptic contents of Paul's have been far less anxious about that concern. See in particular J. Christiaan Beker, *Paul the Apostle: The Triumph of God in Life and Thought* (Edinburgh: T&T Clark, 1980); *Paul's Apocalyptic Gospel: The Coming Triumph of God*

As I hope to demonstrate in the present volume, *Church Dogmatics*—particularly in the wake of Barth's pivotal doctrine of election in *CD* II/2—continues along this trajectory, providing the kind of "systematic" rigour beyond the scope of the earlier material. Seeking to grapple with the reality of Satan on the basis of divine revelation, Barth constructs a complex and daring "report" (*Bericht*) of the third agent, one that is not confined to "God and Nothingness" in §50 but that is also baked into the doctrines of election, creation, and reconciliation.[31] Of course, revelation no more delivers a complete and indisputable doctrine of Satan than it does of Christology or pneumatology or soteriology. But the event of revelation compels fragmentary thoughts on the will and work and nature of God's opponent, thoughts that—contrary to Schleiermacher—do not leave the doctrine of salvation untouched.

The Argument

The argument of this book is that, in the wake of his pivotal doctrine of election in *CD* II/2, Barth pursues a doctrine of salvation that offers sustained and nuanced attention to God's saving event in Christ as a three-agent event. What has happened in the Christ-event, he claims, is that "the lordship of Satan was broken" in the cosmos.[32] One of the aims of the following chapters is to demonstrate that this is not an incidental claim but one that takes us to the very heart of Barth's soteriology.

If there is a single theological formulation indicating that the argument of this book may not be immediately derailed and that Wingren's judgment needs reappraisal—the judgment that Barth's theology lacks a devil—it is Barth's enigmatic and unsettling observation in *CD* IV/1 that in the event of Christ's crucifixion, "The will of God was done as the will of Satan was done."[33] Here, in

---

(Philadelphia, PA: Fortress Press, 1992); J. Louis Martyn, *Galatians: A New Translation with Introduction and Commentary* (New Haven, CT: Yale University Press, 1997); "The Apocalyptic Gospel in Galatians," *Interpretation* 54, no. 3 (2000): 246-66; Martinus C. de Boer, *The Defeat of Death: Apocalyptic Eschatology in 1 Corinthians 15 and Romans 5* (Sheffield: Sheffield Academic Press, 1988); "Paul, Theologian of God's Apocalypse," *Interpretation* 56, no. 1 (2002): 21-33; Beverly Roberts Gaventa, "The Cosmic Power of Sin in Paul's Letter to the Romans: Toward a Widescreen Edition," *Interpretation* 58, no. 3 (2004): 229-40; "Interpreting the Death of Jesus Apocalyptically: Reconsidering Romans 8:32," in *Jesus and Paul Reconnected: Fresh Pathways into an Old Debate*, ed. Todd D. Still (Grand Rapids, MI: Eerdmans, 2007), 125-45; "Neither Height nor Depth: Discerning the Cosmology of Romans," *Scottish Journal of Theology* 64, no. 3 (2011): 265-78.

31. I use the word "report" under the advisement of Barth in *CD* III/3, 295, where he contends that theology can only aim to be a "report" of the history of God's dealings with God's creatures.

32. *CD* II/2, 333.

33. *CD* IV/1, 268.

the most mature form of his doctrine of salvation, he speaks not only of God and the devil in the same breath; he speaks also of an identity of God's will and work and word and Satan's will and work and word. It is part of the burden of this book to uncover the theological underpinnings of such a striking claim and to explore its consequences. In so doing, I hope to shed light on some of the less frequently explored corners of Barth's massive theological project—corners occupied by enigmatic concepts such as the "left hand" of God and God's alien work (*opus alienum*)—and to propose constructive solutions to certain problems that emerge when these corners are illuminated. Issues pertaining to the doctrine of election, the doctrine of the atonement, and the doctrine of the resurrection will receive fresh attention as I unfold Barth's grasp of God's saving act in Christ as an act intended to "destroy the works of the devil."

Forensic Apocalyptic and Cosmological Apocalyptic

At first blush this argument may not seem the most paradigm-shifting—though it may be such to those convinced of Barth's "general lack of interest in soteriology."[34] But to present Barth's doctrine of salvation as a three-agent drama goes clearly against the grain of much current scholarly opinion. One may readily admit that the doctrine of salvation can be developed as an account of God's triumph over His enemies. For many, however, it seems doubtful that Barth would contribute a great deal to that account. While appreciating the particularities and nuances of his soteriology, scholars have tended to place it firmly within the tradition of forensicism, broadly construed[35]—a placing that effectively banishes the third agent from the scene.[36]

---

34. Alister E. McGrath, *Iustitia Dei: A History of the Christian Doctrine of Justification*, 3rd ed. (Cambridge: Cambridge University Press, 2005), 400.

35. Rudolf Bultmann describes a "forensic" act as "the act of a Judge in court," with the word forensic derived from the word "forum" (law-court). Rudolf Bultmann, *Theology of the New Testament: Volume I*, trans. Kendrick Grobel (New York: Charles Scribner's Sons, 1951), 172, 272. Following Bultmann's understanding of a forensic act, I take a forensic soteriology to be one that is particularly attached to God's role as Lawgiver and to the idea that salvation must satisfy certain legal requirements.

36. Broadly forensic readings of Barth's soteriology include Robert D. Preus, "The Doctrine of Justification and Reconciliation in the Theology of Karl Barth," *Concordia Theological Monthly* 31, no. 4 (1960): 236–44; Bertold Klappert, *Die Auferweckung des Gekreuzigten: Der Ansatz der Christologie Karl Barths im Zusammenang mit der Christologie der Gegenwart* (Neukirchen-Vluyn: Neukirchener Verlag, 1981); Bruce L. McCormack, "For Us and Our Salvation: Incarnation and Atonement in the Reformed Tradition," *Greek Orthodox Theological Review* 43, nos. 1–4 (1998): 281–316; Günter Thomas, "Der für uns 'gerichtete Richter': Kritische Erwägungen zu Karl Barths Versöhnungslehre," *Zeitschrift für Dialektische Theologie* 18, no. 2 (2002): 211–25; Colin E. Gunton, *The Actuality of Atonement: A Study of Metaphor, Rationality and the Christian*

These forensic interpretations stand in contrast with the attention given over the last couple of decades to Barth's formative role in theology's "apocalyptic turn," a role suggestive of the fact that his soteriology is tethered to the gospel's word of deliverance from usurping powers and principalities inimical to God's purposes.[37] Yet at the same time, precisely these studies on the apocalyptic character of Barth's theology have for the most part either passed over the doctrine of salvation and the role of the third agent therein in favour of metatheological and epistemological concerns or—and ironically—doubled down on the forensic reading of his soteriology.[38]

Prominent among purveyors of this last tendency are Shannon Nicole Smythe and Bruce McCormack. Utilising Martinus de Boer's heuristic distinction between a "cosmological apocalyptic" pattern of Jewish eschatology and a "forensic apocalyptic" pattern, they have recently associated Barth with the forensic apocalyptic pattern. A brief outline of de Boer's influential distinction will unveil the significance of this association. According to de Boer's landmark essay, the defining feature of the cosmological apocalyptic pattern of Jewish eschatological thought is the presence and lordship of evil powers, powers ultimately responsible for the current perverse state of the cosmos. In this evil age, however, the cosmological pattern of apocalyptic discerns that this perverse state of the cosmos is not the will

---

Tradition (London: T&T Clark, 2003); David Lauber, *Barth on the Descent into Hell: God, Atonement and the Christian Life* (Burlington: Ashgate, 2004); W. Travis McMaken, "Election and the Pattern of Exchange in Karl Barth's Doctrine of the Atonement," *Journal of Reformed Theology* 3, no. 2 (2009): 202–18; Adam J. Johnson, *God's Being in Reconciliation: The Theological Basis of the Unity and Diversity of the Atonement in the Theology of Karl Barth* (London T&T Clark, 2012); Matthias Grebe, *Election, Atonement, and the Holy Spirit: Through and beyond Barth's Theological Interpretation of Scripture* (Cambridge: James Clarke, 2015).

37. On Barth's role in theology's apocalyptic turn, see, among others, Robert W. Jenson, "Apocalyptic and Messianism in Twentieth Century German Theology," in *Messianism, Apocalypse and Redemption in 20th Century German Thought*, ed. Wayne Cristaudo and Wendy Baker (Adelaide: ATF Press, 2006), 3–12; Nathan R. Kerr, *Christ, History and Apocalyptic: The Politics of Christian Mission* (Eugene, OR: Cascade, 2008); Davis, "The Challenge of Apocalyptic to Modern Theology."

38. There are at least two notable exceptions. Walter Lowe spies in Barth's theology "a return of the repressed; the entire vocabulary that theology tends to keep at arm's length—invasion, conflict, powers, triumph—the vocabulary of *Christus victor*, presses upon us." Walter Lowe, "Why We Need Apocalyptic," *Scottish Journal of Theology* 63, no. 1 (2010): 52. And Douglas Harink locates Barth's "Paulinism"—a Paulinism on display not only in his commentary on Romans but also in *Church Dogmatics*—in his conviction that "God's revelation in Jesus Christ is *God's apocalyptic triumph* over all the enslaving powers and gods of this world," a conviction that displays "a powerful grasp of the logic of Paul's gospel." Douglas Harink, *Paul among the Postliberals: Pauline Theology beyond Christendom and Modernity* (Grand Rapids, MI: Brazos Press, 2003), 47–8, 50.

of God and that it "will not be tolerated by Him for very long."[39] There will be a "last judgment" on these "suprahuman angelic powers," but this judgment will take the form of "a cosmic confrontation, a war."[40] God will triumph in this war, and the powers who rule the world will be banished, thus establishing the "new age." In this pattern of thinking, moreover, the righteous in the present are "those whom God has collectively elected to be His witnesses to His rightful claim on the world in the midst of the old age where evil cosmological rulers hold sway." The cosmological pattern thus "underscores the human need for God's help and action."[41]

By contrast, the defining feature of the forensic apocalyptic pattern of Jewish eschatological thought is its emphasis on the wilful disobedience of human beings before their Creator and Lawgiver. This disobedience brings about death, with Adam and Eve replacing the evil powers as the primary agents responsible for the human plight. In the final judgment, which takes place in a courtroom setting, the righteous will be revealed as "those who chose the Law" and the wicked as those who did not.[42] The forensic pattern thus "underscores human accountability to God for sin and its terrible consequences."[43]

What is it about Barth's doctrine of salvation, then, that keeps it in close company with forensic apocalyptic? According to Smythe and McCormack, it was not always so. Barth's 1922 commentary on Romans is reckoned to be a text heavily indebted to the cosmological apocalyptic pattern, to such an extent that it downplays the forensicism that is basic to Paul's thought.[44] Here, in McCormack's view, is where the problems begin. For if forensic apocalyptic is *not* considered basic to Paul, he contends, there can be no proper conception of the salvific reality achieved in the death of Jesus. What is required to speak of the temporal realisation of God's eschatological aims is "the understanding that *God* is the subject who not only acknowledges the way of Jesus in raising Him from the dead but who destroys the being of sin in the cross."[45] Yet such an understanding, according to McCormack, is funded by forensic apocalyptic, not cosmological. This, he argues, was the conclusion eventually reached by Barth, whose soteriology subsequent to the 1922 commentary changed to "a version of forensic apocalyptic."[46]

---

39. Martinus C. de Boer, "Paul and Jewish Apocalyptic Eschatology," in *Apocalyptic and the New Testament: Essays in Honour of J. Louis Martyn*, ed. Marion L. Soards and Joel Marcus (London: Bloomsbury, 2015), 175.

40. de Boer, "Paul and Jewish Apocalyptic Eschatology," 175.

41. de Boer, "Paul and Jewish Apocalyptic Eschatology," 181.

42. de Boer, "Paul and Jewish Apocalyptic Eschatology," 176.

43. de Boer, "Paul and Jewish Apocalyptic Eschatology," 181.

44. Bruce L. McCormack, "Longing for a New World: On Socialism, Eschatology and Apocalyptic in Barth's Early Dialectical Theology," in *Theologie im Umbruch der Moderne: Karl Barths frühe Dialektische Theologie*, ed. Harald Matern and Georg Pfleiderer (Zürich: TVZ, 2014), 146.

45. McCormack, "Longing for a New World," 148.

46. McCormack, "Longing for a New World," 148.

Highlighting Barth's immersion in the theology of the magisterial Reformers in the 1920s, Smythe argues that this is a key reason for the forensic shape of his later soteriology. Indeed, she submits that his soteriology "becomes more consistently forensic than that of the Reformation,"[47] with "forensic" intended as a shorthand that embraces the concepts of decision, declaration, sentence, verdict, judgment, acquittal, and pardon.

Barth's mature doctrine of election in *CD* II/2 is also considered pivotal by Smythe and McCormack. In Barth's hands, this doctrine is said to perform a similar function to Calvin's (forensic) idea of imputation.[48] And on account of the ontological import of the doctrine of election in Barth's thought, forensicism "is not simply a tool for thinking through the atoning work of Christ and justification; it is the frame of reference that is basic to the whole of his soteriology."[49] For McCormack, "forensic" is a synonym for "legal," and as such "it is a term that finds its home in the setting of a court trial."[50] In McCormack's view, then, the later Barth shares with forensic apocalyptic the view of salvation as, essentially, a courtroom drama.[51]

There are obvious points in favour of this "forensic apocalyptic" reading of Barth's soteriology, not least his explicit decision in *CD* IV/1 to develop the doctrine of the atonement within a juridical framework. I explore this decision in later chapters. But three weaknesses of this interpretation of Barth's soteriology can be identified here in anticipation of the more detailed arguments to come.

First, McCormack observes that, in the wake of *CD* II/2, the military metaphors so prominent in Barth's commentary on Romans "have been abandoned in favor of a judicial frame of reference for treating Christ's atoning work, justification, etc."[52] As will be shown in due course, this is simply not the case. Indeed, if we abandon the military metaphors, then Barth's soteriology becomes virtually unintelligible.

Second, McCormack and Smythe are certainly right in what they highlight as a key emphasis in Barth's mature soteriology: the destruction of the being of the sinner. But where they reference this destruction, one is led to believe that, for Barth, salvation is a two-agent event: an event between God and the sinner. In his

47. Shannon Nicole Smythe, *Forensic Apocalyptic Theology: Karl Barth and the Doctrine of Justification* (Minneapolis, MN: Fortress Press, 2016), 18–19.

48. Bruce L. McCormack, "Can We Still Speak of 'Justification by Faith'? An In-House Debate with Apocalyptic Readings of Paul," in *Galatians and Christian Theology: Justification, the Gospel, and Ethics in Paul's Letter*, ed. Mark W. Elliott et al. (Grand Rapids, MI: Baker Academic, 2014), 181.

49. Bruce L. McCormack, "*Justitia aliena*: Karl Barth in Conversation with the Evangelical Doctrine of Imputed Righteousness," in *Justification in Perspective: Historical Developments and Contemporary Challenges*, ed. Bruce L. McCormack (Grand Rapids, MI: Baker Academic, 2006), 192.

50. McCormack, "*Justitia aliena*," 170.

51. McCormack, "Can We Still Speak of 'Justification by Faith'?," 180.

52. McCormack, "Longing for a New World," 149.

essays on the later Barth's relationship to apocalyptic, for instance, McCormack omits reference to the cosmological force of *das Nichtige* from Barth's mature soteriology, as well as to the kingdom of Satan and the powers of death and destruction. Even Barth's notion of sin as a power under which human beings are held captive—a notion at least as "cosmological" as it is "forensic"—is underplayed. Within strong forensic readings of Barth's soteriology, his claim in *CD* III/3 that nothingness is what brought Christ to the cross, and what Christ defeated on the cross, is often cut off from the surrounding part-volumes and confined to Barth's reflections on the problem of evil, when in reality this claim comes to its most mature expression in his doctrine of reconciliation, having first germinated in his doctrine of election.[53]

Third, the (merited) attention paid by these readings to the destruction of the sinner on the cross is not complemented by attention to the raising to life of the new human in the resurrection. The soteriological importance of the resurrection becomes obscured when "destruction" is the definitive word on God's reconciling work. In some ways, this is a problem inherited from Barth himself—indeed, it is a problem inherited from large swathes of the theological tradition—and I will seek to address it in a later chapter. But when the resurrection is afforded a central place in the doctrine of atonement, "cosmological" language cannot help but invade the theological terrain.[54] Barth himself recognises as much in his dogmatic lectures from Göttingen in the 1920s. There he suggests that the orientation of theological thought to the resurrection of Christ funds the notion of "the work of Christ as the work of our *redemption* from Satan and death," thereby shifting the theologian's language from that of "law" and "ethics" to that of "war" and "power."[55]

Barth's suggestion is an intriguing one. It not only proposes a connection between soteriologies to which the resurrection is an afterthought and soteriologies to which the third agent is superfluous. It also proposes that the marginalisation of the resurrection directly leads to the absence of Satan from doctrines of salvation. Following Barth's argument that sin is only known in the light of grace, or, more generally, that the plight is only known in the event of its solution, his suggestion might be phrased as follows: the identification of the resurrection as the solution engenders a "cosmological apocalyptic" conception of the plight.[56] This insight will ultimately prove key to the argument of this book.

---

53. *CD* III/3, 305.

54. As Gerhard Forde observes, the most important dogmatic advance of the *Christus Victor* motif is "the manner in which the resurrection regains its proper place in atonement doctrine." Gerhard O. Forde, "The Work of Christ," in *Christian Dogmatics: Volume 2*, ed. Carl E. Braaten and Robert W. Jenson (Philadelphia, PA: Fortress Press, 1984), 40.

55. Karl Barth, *Unterricht in der christlichen Religion 3: Die Lehre von der Versöhnung/Erlösung 1925/26*, ed. Hinrich Stoevesandt, *Gesamtausgabe*, II.38 (Zürich: TVZ, 2002), 83–4.

56. On the apostle Paul's reversal of the common order of plight-solution (a reversal that Barth can be understood to have followed), see E. P. Sanders, *Paul and Palestinian Judaism: A Comparison of Patterns of Religion* (Philadelphia, PA: Fortress Press, 1977), 442–7.

A Protestant Soteriology?

Though forensic readings of Barth's soteriology continue to predominate, a growing number of scholars have noted what might be termed the "cosmological logic" at work in Barth's soteriology. Otto Weber thought Barth to have freed the doctrine of reconciliation from "the curious isolation" into which Protestant Orthodoxy had placed it by grasping the truth that reconciliation is "also liberation from the rule of satanic powers."[57] The *"triumphal"* motif has been identified by Paul Dafydd Jones as one which best reveals Barth's perspective on the atonement in the later volumes of *Church Dogmatics*,[58] while Fleming Rutledge understands Barth's talk of "spheres" and "powers"—talk that betrays a willingness to utilise "martial" language—to anticipate some of the major soteriological concerns of Pauline apocalyptic scholars.[59] In the light of Gustaf Aulén's analysis of the doctrine of the atonement, the presence of elements in Barth's soteriology commensurate with the so-called classical view of atonement have been detected. David Mueller, for example, highlights "Barth's predilection for military imagery to describe Christ's reconciling work" in his doctrine of reconciliation and posits that "the imagery of the classic '*Christus Victor*' (Christ, the Victor) atonement theory resounds with great force in Barth's description of the drama of reconciliation."[60]

It might be reckoned, however, that a three-agent account of atonement goes some way towards severing the doctrine of salvation from the Protestant tradition. Given that a forensic soteriology and a Protestant soteriology are virtually synonymous, this book's shift away from forensicism as the dominant soteriological idiom might appear to put Barth at some remove from Protestant theology. Bruce McCormack is particularly alert to the "temptation" for interpreters of Barth to deflate some of his most Protestant sensibilities and to enlist the Swiss theologian among the ranks of the so-called new orthodoxy: a Catholic-Orthodox movement

---

57. Otto Weber, *Foundations of Dogmatics: Volume 2*, trans. Darrell L. Guder (Grand Rapids, MI: Eerdmans, 1983), 225.

58. Paul Dafydd Jones, "Barth and Anselm: God, Christ and the Atonement," *International Journal of Systematic Theology* 12, no. 3 (2010): 277n35.

59. Fleming Rutledge, *The Crucifixion: Understanding the Death of Jesus Christ* (Grand Rapids, MI: Eerdmans, 2015), 512.

60. David L. Mueller, *Foundation of Karl Barth's Doctrine of Reconciliation: Jesus Christ Crucified and Risen* (Lewiston: Edwin Mellen Press, 1990), 331. See also George S. Hendry, *The Gospel of the Incarnation* (London: SCM Press, 1959), 124; Donald G. Bloesch, *Jesus Is Victor! Karl Barth's Doctrine of Salvation* (Nashville, TN: Abingdon Press, 1976), 43; Frank M. Hasel, "Karl Barth's *Church Dogmatics* on the Atonement: Some Translation Problems," *Andrews University Seminary Studies* 29, no. 3 (1991): 211; Bruce Demarest, *The Cross and Salvation: The Doctrine of Salvation* (Wheaton, IL: Crossway, 2006), 34; Matthias D. Wüthrich, *Gott und das Nichtige: Zur Rede vom Nichtigen ausgehend von Karl Barths KD § 50* (Zürich: TVZ, 2006), 168; Jeff McSwain, *Simul Sanctification: Barth's Hidden Vision for Human Transformation* (Eugene, OR: Pickwick, 2018), 208.

seeking to orientate contemporary theology to the thought forms of patristic and medieval theology.[61] Capitulation to this temptation is manifested in various ways. One of them—the most pertinent to the current study—consists in "the suppression of the judicial element" in Barth's doctrine of reconciliation.[62]

Does the present book give in to this temptation? Its heuristic association of Barth with "cosmological apocalyptic" could be read as a way of numbering him with those *Christus Victor* soteriologies of the patristic period and thus as a thinly veiled attempt at distancing Barth from his Protestant heritage. Barth's own critiques of the Protestant tradition, and his envious nod towards the holistic soteriology of the Eastern Church, indicate that he himself was not averse to such distancing every now and then. Two examples of such critiques from *Church Dogmatics* are particularly pertinent to the current study.

First, in his account of *das Nichtige* in *CD* III/3, Barth describes the miracles and acts of Jesus as "objective manifestations of His character as the Conqueror not only of sin but also of evil and death, as the Destroyer of the destroyer, as the Saviour in the most inclusive sense."[63] But, crucially, it is not only the miracles that are constitutive of Christ's militant action. The incarnation, cross, and resurrection are also events intelligible only within the context of a cosmic conflict, for in them "God exposed Himself to nothingness even as this *enemy* and *assailant* [Angreifer]" and did so only to fight it off (*zurückzuschlagen*).[64] An "unmistakable emphasis" in the New Testament witness to Christ is thus its witness to Him as the "total Saviour," the "total Victor," the one who directs His own power against the power of nothingness. To erase or overlook this witness is to "annul its testimony and silence the voice of Him to whom it testifies."[65] It is therefore a "serious matter" for the Western Church to have succeeded "in minimising and devaluing ... this New Testament emphasis."[66] Barth judges Protestant theology especially to have been "far too moralistic and spiritualistic" and therefore "blind to this aspect of the Gospel."[67]

Second, at the conclusion of his analysis of the miracles of Christ in *CD* IV/2, Barth observes a "dimension of the Gospel" that has, with a few exceptions, been overlooked by both the Reformers (Luther and Calvin are named) and scholastic

---

61. Bruce L. McCormack, "Karl Barth's Historicized Christology: Just How 'Chalcedonian' Is It?," in *Orthodox and Modern: Studies in the Theology of Karl Barth* (Grand Rapids, MI: Baker Academic, 2008), 230. Included in the "new orthodoxy" McCormack lists the evangelical Catholicism of Robert Jenson, Carl Braaten, George Lindbeck, and Reinhard Hütter, the communitarian ethics of Stanley Hauerwas, and the radical orthodoxy of John Milbank.

62. McCormack, "Karl Barth's Historicized Christology," 231.

63. *CD* III/3, 311.

64. *CD* III/3, 311.

65. *CD* III/3, 311.

66. *CD* III/3, 311.

67. *CD* III/3, 311.

and liberal Protestantism. The content of this dimension is the "mercifully powerful, unconditionally complete *liberation* from destruction, from *death*, from evil [*Bösen*] as the *power* of the evil one [*der* Gewalt *des Üblen*]."[68] Where Protestantism was orientated by the problem of repentance—and thus "one-sidedly anthropological"—it should have been orientated by the presupposition of repentance, namely, the powerful and presuppositionless in-breaking of the kingdom of God.

By Barth's own reckoning, then, must an elevation of the "three-agent" drama in *Church Dogmatics* place him at odds with a thoroughly Protestant soteriology? On the contrary, I contend that it can in fact be taken as a gesture towards a *more* Protestant soteriology. While the Reformers' doctrine of salvation has typically been described as an intensely forensic rendering of the doctrine, their attentiveness to God's conflict with Satan leaves an indelible mark on their understanding of the work of Christ. Luther, in his own way, can be seen to advance an ontologically daring perspective on salvation as God's triumph in Christ over sin, death, and the devil (as well as the law and the wrath of God).[69] As he comments on the second article of the Apostles' Creed in his Larger Catechism, "Let this be the summary of this article, that the little word Lord simply means the same as Redeemer, that is, he who has brought us back from the devil to God, from death to life, from sin to righteousness, and keeps us there."[70] A prominent place for the victory motif has also been observed within Calvin's doctrine of the atonement.[71]

---

68. *CD* IV/2, 233 rev.

69. Though it is not a judgment universally accepted in Lutheran circles (see, for example, Paul Althaus, *The Theology of Martin Luther*, trans. Robert C. Schultz [Philadelphia, PA: Fortress Press, 1966]), Gustaf Aulén finds in Luther's doctrine of the atonement the pinnacle of the *Christus Victor* motif. See Aulén, *Christus Victor*, 101–22. For further analysis of the presence of this motif in Luther's thought, see Uwe Rieske-Braun, *Duellum Mirabile: Studien zum Kampfmotiv in Martin Luthers Theologie* (Göttingen: Vandenhoeck & Ruprecht, 1999).

70. Martin Luther, "The Large Catechism," in *The Book of Concord: The Confessions of the Evangelical Lutheran Church*, ed. Robert Kolb and Timothy J. Wengert, trans. Charles P. Arand et al. (Minneapolis, MN: Fortress Press, 2000), 434.

71. Charles A. M. Hall, *With the Spirit's Sword: The Drama of Spiritual Warfare in the Theology of John Calvin* (Zürich: EVZ-Verlag, 1968). It has been noted that "One of [his] favorite themes of the atonement was Christ as victor, who conquers the foes of His people" (Robert A. Peterson, *Calvin's Doctrine of the Atonement* (Phillipsburg: P & R, 1983), 46). According to Thomas Parker, the victory motif is one of five ways in which Calvin expressed his view of the atonement. T. H. L. Parker, *The Oracles of God: An Introduction to the Preaching of John Calvin* (London: Lutterworth Press, 1947), 87–8. On Calvin's use of a multiplicity of atonement metaphors, including that of victory, see Darren O. Sumner, "Theory and Metaphor in Calvin's Doctrine of the Atonement," *Princeton Theological Review* 13, no. 2 (2007): 49–60.

Moreover, despite the critical remarks directed at Protestant theology mentioned above, Barth himself is not unaware Protestantism's deployment of military themes in its soteriology. Criticising the dismissal of the conception of Christ's work as a victory over Satan by "modern Lutherans" (Julius Kaftan and Otto Scheel are cited), he associates this conception with Martin Luther and, more recently, with the two Blumhardts. Crucially, Barth concludes that the emphasis on the work of Christ as a work of redemption from sin, death, and the devil is "not a relapse behind the Reformers" but a "corrective renewal of thoughts that are inalienable not only to the Eastern church, but to the whole Christian church."[72] The kind of three-agent view of salvation developed across *Church Dogmatics* thus owes a considerable debt to both Martin Luther and John Calvin and can be conceived to lie firmly within Protestant soteriology, or, even more narrowly, Reformed soteriology.[73]

Models of the Atonement

Talk of salvation as the defeat of the devil runs up against the fact that the Bible has other ways of talking about salvation. "The biblical text itself," it has been observed, "offers a striking kaleidoscope of metaphors," with each metaphor serving to articulate a particular facet of what is a many-sided event.[74] These metaphors are thus seen to possess non-competitive relations with one another, motivating accounts of the atonement that are "complementary rather than alternative or conflicting."[75] In accordance with this approach to the Bible's diverse witness to salvation, the conception of salvation as a three-agent drama can be appreciated as one that highlights an important aspect of the work of God in Christ. But, recognising that there are other equally valuable aspects of this work, the "victory" model is not considered to be the controlling or dominant model. It sits alongside the others in a way analogous to how the Gospel of Matthew sits alongside the Gospel of John or how the Book of Exodus sits alongside the Book of Jonah—as

---

72. See Barth, *Unterricht in der christlichen Religion 3*, 83–4.

73. For a recent exploration of Barth's debt to Luther and Calvin, see Kimlyn J. Bender, "The Reformers as Fathers of the Church: Luther and Calvin in the Thought of Karl Barth," *Scottish Journal of Theology* 72, no. 4 (2019): 414–31. On the "apocalyptic" character of Reformed soteriology, see Philip G. Ziegler, "The Adventitious Origins of the Calvinist Moral Subject," *Studies in Christian Ethics* 28, no. 2 (2015): 213–23; "'Bound Over to Satan's Tyranny': Sin and Satan in Contemporary Reformed Hamartiology," *Theology Today* 75, no. 1 (2018): 89–100.

74. Trevor Hart, *In Him Was Life: The Person and Work of Christ* (Waco, TX: Baylor University Press, 2019), 1. On the variety of atonement theories in the New Testament, see Joel B. Green, "Theologies of Atonement in the New Testament," in *T&T Clark Companion to Atonement*, ed. Adam J. Johnson (New York: T&T Clark, 2017), 115–34.

75. Hart, *In Him Was Life*, 4.

part of a canon of images, some of which may be more relevant or nourishing than others, but none of which can stake a claim to serve as a "canon within the canon."

It should be stated at the outset of this book, however, that a three-agent account of salvation sits rather awkwardly as one "metaphor" or "theory" of salvation among others. One could be forgiven, in fact, for suspecting it of threatening the non-competitive relations between the metaphors by seeking a dramatic triumph over all the others. Aulén even refused to think of *Christus Victor* as a "theory," preferring instead to think of it as a narrative "motif" or "theme." Fleming Rutledge, while striving to do justice to both the "apocalyptic" and "forensic" views of salvation, nevertheless asserts that "*the apocalyptic drama* is the non-negotiable context for the substitution model and all the others as well."[76] Philip Ziegler makes a similar argument for the capacity of a cosmological apocalyptic soteriology to absorb typically forensic—or "mediatorial"—concerns.[77]

What these theologians demonstrate is that the so-called military view of atonement is reluctant to be considered merely one image of salvation among others. In line with Trevor Hart's suggestion that some biblical metaphors "appear to be much nearer to the heart of the matter than others,"[78] their contention is that the notion of a three-agent conflict simply is the heart of the matter. There is not a myriad of reasons why the Son of God was revealed, with one of them being to destroy the works of the devil. Rather, this one reason absorbs all others and helps to make sense of them. The contention of "apocalyptic" theology, stated bluntly, is that all images of salvation, if they are to be faithful to the Christian gospel, cannot help but be images advanced against the backdrop of a three-agent drama of salvation.[79] When seen in this light, the triumph of the "redemption" metaphor or

---

76. Rutledge, *The Crucifixion*, 530. Others, naturally, have argued just the opposite. Thomas Schreiner, for instance, disputes that "the Christus Victor theme is fundamental and the main thing that God accomplished in Christ's death," claiming instead that the dominant plot in the story line of the Bible is "the need for forgiveness." Invoking the apostle Paul as his witness, Schreiner argues that "forgiveness of sins is fundamental, and hence cannot be dismissed merely as Western individualism." Thomas R. Schreiner, "Penal Substitution Response," in *The Nature of the Atonement: Four Views*, ed. James K. Beilby and Paul R. Eddy (Downers Grove: IVP, 2006), 50–1.

77. Philip G. Ziegler, *Militant Grace: The Apocalyptic Turn and the Future of Christian Theology* (Grand Rapids, MI: Baker Academic, 2018), 53–70. Ziegler's proposal, which leans on Ernst Käsemann's cosmological soteriology, is in part a response and alternative to Alan Spence's claim that, on the one hand, *Christus Victor* is incapable of doing justice to the "mediatorial" themes of guilt, forgiveness, reconciliation and, on the other, the elements from *Christus Victor* find a natural home within a mediatorial framework. Alan Spence, "A Unified Theory of the Atonement," *International Journal of Systematic Theology* 6, no. 4 (2004): 404–20.

78. Hart, *In Him Was Life*, 3.

79. Gustav Aulén makes this contention explicit in a follow-up article to his work *Christus Victor*. Of that earlier book he writes that its purpose was "to emphasize that the outlook of the Atonement as a drama, where the love of God in Christ fights and conquers

the "military view" of atonement need not be taken to herald the defeat of all other metaphors. However, if its claims are to be sustained, any three-agent soteriology will need to demonstrate that it can comprehend the concerns and themes of other soteriological accounts motivated from biblical sources.[80]

Returning to Barth, it is certainly not the case that forensic imagery is fundamentally foreign to his thought, present only on account of reluctant nods to traditional formulations. Language typically associated with forensicism—righteousness, sentence, verdict, judgment—abounds in *Church Dogmatics*. What I hope to expose is the way in which this language, and the corresponding model of the atonement, ultimately serves the articulation of the defeat of God's enemies that happens in the cross and resurrection of Christ. Recruited for such service, ostensibly forensic language cannot avoid taking on a meaning it will not possess in doctrines of the atonement where the third agent is absent or peripheral to the event under examination.

Scope and Chapter Summary

The restriction of this study to *Church Dogmatics*, it should now be clear, does not mean an escape from Barth's early apocalypticism; rather, in these pages, I deal with the (unanticipated) fruit of his revolutionary apocalyptic turn. An examination of Barth's soteriology is, for all intents and purposes, an examination of his theology.[81] Given its Christocentric perspective, *Church Dogmatics* amounts

---

the hostile powers, is a central and decisive perspective which never can be omitted and which indeed must stamp every really Christian doctrine of the Atonement." Gustaf Aulén, "Chaos and Cosmos: The Drama of the Atonement," *Interpretation* 4, no. 2 (1950): 156. See also Philip G. Ziegler, "'Bound Over to Satan's Tyranny': Sin and Satan in Contemporary Reformed Hamartiology," *Theology Today* 75, no. 1 (2018): 94: "Other soteriological motifs can and must then find their place and their meaning within this controlling vision of divine liberation and rescue from evil."

80. For example, a "cultic" account of the atonement can be developed as a three-agent soteriology insofar as Christ's sacrifice is understood to be an act directed against "the forces of death." For a recent study which urges any "cultic" presentation of the work of Christ to think in terms of a three-agent soteriology, see Matthew Thiessen, *Jesus and the Forces of Death: The Gospels' Portrayal of Ritual Impurity within First-Century Judaism* (Grand Rapids, MI: Baker Academic, 2020).

81. Otto Weber describes *Church Dogmatics* as "the most available example of a theology which revolves around the doctrine of reconciliation." Weber, *Foundations of Dogmatics* 2, 177. Similarly, Alasdair Heron argues that "Barth's handling of all the major dogmatic themes relates implicitly or explicitly to the nature of salvation." Alasdair I. C. Heron, "The Theme of Salvation in Karl Barth's Doctrine of Reconciliation," *Ex Auditu* 5 (1989): 109. More recently, Tom Greggs suggests that "Barth is above all else a theologian of the God of salvation." Tom Greggs, "Karl Barth," in *Christian Theologies of Salvation: A Comparative Introduction*, ed. Justin S. Holcomb (New York: New York University Press, 2017), 301.

to a monumental treatment of the doctrine of salvation, even when other doctrinal loci are on the table. Rather than endeavouring to comprehend the whole, I have decided to narrow my attention to three part-volumes in particular: the doctrine of election in *CD* II/2, the doctrine of nothingness in *CD* III/3, and the doctrine of reconciliation in *CD* IV/1. The book can be seen to progress from the earlier part-volume (*CD* II/2) to the later (*CD* IV/1), though this progression will not be rigidly maintained. If there is a portion of *Church Dogmatics* central to this study, it is Barth's discussion of cross and resurrection in §59.2 and §59.3, respectively, with the critical examination of these interrelated sections stretching across Chapters 3–5 of the present work.

A word or two should be said by way of explanation for the central position occupied by these two sections. First, following Barth, I take the doctrine of reconciliation to be at the centre of Christian knowledge. As sections particularly concerned with the saving event, §59.2 and §59.3 assume an unrivalled significance with respect not only to Barth's soteriology but his theology as a whole. Second, it is *these* sections which tend to foster, shape, and support forensic readings of Barth's soteriology. One could quite easily make a case for Barth's three-agent soteriology using §50 or §64 or §69. Nevertheless, without denying the obvious and important forensicism on display in §59, I want to trespass into what appears to be hostile territory and uncover the three-agent drama that lies within it—as well as show how "cheap" notions of this three-agent drama are subverted. The third and final reason for concentrating on these two sections is simply that they have proved endlessly disturbing and fascinating during my years of reading Barth. I do not claim to have conveyed fully that disturbance and fascination. But I hope at least to draw attention to elements in Barth's theology that do not fit neatly into received paradigms.

Chapters 2–5 of this work consider four interrelated aspects of Barth's soteriology: election, the cosmos and its judgment, cross, and resurrection. I begin, in Chapter 2, with the doctrine of election, arguing that it is in this doctrine as it is developed in *CD* II/2 (and utilised again in *CD* III/3) that Barth's conception of salvation as a three-agent conflict is formally worked out, thus giving his soteriology as a whole a decidedly cosmological dimension. Yet I also seek to show how Barth's understanding of Satan/nothingness within the context of his doctrine of election throws up certain problematics revolving around Barth's notion of the "left-handed" or "alien" work of God, the work by which Satan/nothingness receives its perverse existence—problematics that, as this chapter indicates, are potentially alleviated when the resurrection is given more soteriological weight.

Chapter 3 advances the argument of the book by considering Barth's twofold notion of judgment—judgment as rectification or deliverance (the positive, "biblical" form) and judgment as judgment unto death (the negative form)—as this appears in *CD* IV/1. It seeks to show the cosmological apocalyptic sensibilities that frame Barth's doctrine of the atonement, but also the logic behind the "negative" turn that this doctrine takes—a logic centred on humanity's captivity to Satan.

In Chapter 4, I offer a reading of Barth's *theologia crucis* in §59.2 that concentrates on his understanding of the cross as an event of destruction (*Vernichtung*) in which the will and work of God and Satan become indistinguishable. First, I elaborate on the theme of a catastrophic, apocalyptic judgment by reflecting on the link Barth makes between the darkness that covers the earth as the moment of Jesus's death approaches and the darkness that covers "the face of the deep" in Gen 1:2. Second, I examine the way in which typically "forensic" tropes like forgiveness and substitution are radically re-worked within this cosmological *theologia crucis*. Finally, I explore the nuances and implications of Barth's provocative pronouncement that in the event of the cross we are confronted with the unsettling reality of God's "covenant with death."

This fresh reading of Barth's *theologia crucis* provides a transition into the argument of Chapter 5. The question explored in this chapter concerns the place of the resurrection in Barth's three-agent account of salvation. A complete analysis of Barth's "theology of resurrection" is not pursued here.[82] Rather, I focus on those features of Barth's *theologia resurrectionis* that bring to a climax the soteriological concerns of the previous chapters: the defeat of Satan, the judgment of God, the "end of the world" in the cross, and the dialectic of the alien and proper work of God. Moving beyond Barth, though in close dialogue with some of the key claims in §59.3 and elsewhere, I argue that God's saving action is not only revealed in the resurrection, as he claims, but also accomplished. Put otherwise, the resurrection *saves*, not only as a revelatory act but as an act of deliverance, of rescue, of new creation.

The resurrection, then, is the definitive act of divine judgment in the positive, biblical sense of the term. It is an act of *Ur-teil*, of primal separation not only between creation and nothingness but between God and the nothingness with which He had made a covenant in the event of the cross—the nothingness whose final disappearance is decided in the resurrection as an act of pure grace, an act solely of the right hand of God that *ends* the work of His left.

---

82. For example, I bypass questions of historicity, embodiedness, and temporality, choosing to concentrate instead on what Gerrit Berkouwer has called the "soteriological significance" of this event. See G. C. Berkouwer, *The Work of Christ*, trans. Cornelius Lambregtse (Grand Rapids, MI: Eerdmans, 1965), 190.

Chapter 2

ELECTION AND THE DEFEAT OF SATAN

Jesus answered them, "Did I not choose you, the twelve? Yet one of you is a devil."

—John 6:70

No eternal covenant of wrath corresponds on the one side to the eternal covenant of grace on the other. Nor does an established or tolerated kingdom of Satan correspond in scope or duration, in dignity or authority, to the kingdom of Jesus Christ. On the contrary, just because God does not will always to chide with man, He has initiated the covenant of grace as the beginning of all His works and ways and to destroy the rule of Satan over mankind, thus opposing the kingdom of Jesus Christ to Satan in triumphant superiority.

—Karl Barth[1]

Introduction

There are a range of soteriologies within which the doctrine of election plays only a minor role, or no role at all. Karl Barth's soteriology is not one of them. While attempts to find in Barth's doctrine of election the heart of his dogmatic project are justifiable yet unsuccessful[2]—it is not unimportant that his doctrine of reconciliation opens with the assertion that it is at *this* point, and therefore not

---

1. *CD* II/2, 450.
2. *Pace* Hans Urs von Balthasar, *The Theology of Karl Barth*, trans. Edward T. Oakes (San Francisco, CA: Ignatius Press, 1992), 174, who calls the doctrine of election in *CD* II/2 the "heartbeat" of Barth's theology; and *pace* Arthur C. Cochrane, *The Existentialists and God: Being and the Being of God in the Thought of Søren Kierkegaard, Karl Jaspers, Martin Heidegger, Jean-Paul Sartre, Paul Tillich, Etienne Gilson, Karl Barth* (Philadelphia, PA: Westminster Press, 1956), 130, who describes the doctrine of election as "the basis of all other doctrines." More recently, Michael Horton has critiqued what he takes to be Barth's deployment of predestination as "the central dogma of his system." See Michael S. Horton, "Covenant, Election, and Incarnation: Evaluating Barth's Actualist Christology,"

in the doctrines of revelation, God, and creation that "the heart of the Church's dogmatics"[3] has been reached—there can be no doubting that in the doctrine of election, as it is expounded within the doctrine of God, Barth is making moves whose significance bears upon all that follows. It is thus fitting that the present work should begin here.

But there is a further and more substantial reason why an account of Barth's three-agent soteriology might take the doctrine of election as its point of departure. As noted in the previous chapter, Barth's doctrine of election in *CD* II/2 has recently been considered the motor behind his intensely *forensic* soteriology. What tends to be overlooked on such a reading, however, is that the doctrine of election in *CD* II/2 marks the introduction of the third agent as an object of dogmatic inquiry within *Church Dogmatics*.[4] A curious detail, worthy of more attention than it has thus far received in discussions of Barth's doctrine of election, is that Satan or the satanic is mentioned almost a hundred times in *CD* II/2—about half of the total number of references in the whole of *Church Dogmatics*.[5] Barth undoubtedly employs a range of ostensibly forensic concepts in *CD* II/2, such as

in *Karl Barth and American Evangelicalism*, ed. Bruce L. McCormack (Grand Rapids, MI: Eerdmans, 2011), 116.

3. *CD* IV/1, 3. As Smythe rightly remarks, grasping the centrality of the doctrine of the atonement in Barth's mature thought means entering into "the very heart of his theology." Shannon Nicole Smythe, "Karl Barth," in *T&T Clark Companion to Atonement*, ed. Adam J. Johnson (New York: T&T Clark, 2017), 237.

4. This is not to suggest that a third agent is entirely absent from the earlier part-volumes of *Church Dogmatics*. Scott Rodin has shown how Barth's account of the divine perfections in *CD* II/1 lays some of the groundwork for the "ontology" of the third agent that is to come. See R. Scott Rodin, *Evil and Theodicy in the Theology of Karl Barth* (New York: Peter Lang, 1997), 71–107. Furthermore, Barth's discussion of the power of God's Word "over against other powers" in *CD* I/2, 674–85 presents a highly "cosmological" account of God's revelation in Christ, one that in some ways anticipates the section "Jesus is Victor" in *CD* IV/3, 165–274. On the whole, however, the third agent remains at the very fringes of Barth's dogmatic interest and makes little impression on the material in these earlier part-volumes. For example, the most extensive doctrine of the atonement presented in *Church Dogmatics* prior to II/2—the doctrine of atonement found within the discussion of the divine righteousness in §30 (II/1, 397–406)—unfolds as a purely two-agent drama between God and sinful humanity.

5. There are about two hundred references to "Satan" and the "satanic" in the English translation of *Church Dogmatics*. Most of the remaining references are found in Barth's doctrine of reconciliation in volume four. When it comes to the doctrine of election, the attention of scholars has typically—and understandably—been drawn to the christological revision of the doctrine, and the consequences of this for issues concerning the doctrine of God (theological ontology), the doctrine of salvation (universalism), and theological ethics. None of these issues necessarily precludes attentiveness to what Barth says concerning Satan, yet that is largely what has transpired in practice.

the notion of double imputation. But these concepts ultimately serve to articulate Barth's account of salvation as the defeat of Satan. If the doctrine of election does indeed set the course for the rest of *Church Dogmatics*, it does so, I contend, as it opens up what Barth would later call the "military view" of atonement, not as it shuts this view down. And this in turn has significant import for Barth's doctrine of salvation.

This chapter will proceed in two parts. In the first part, I show that central to Barth's doctrine of election in *CD* II/2 is a fundamental concern for the triumph of God over the kingdom of Satan. Indeed, it will be established that with the introduction of the third agent in *CD* II/2, Barth's soteriology edges closer and closer to a military view of the doctrine as his theology matures. In the second part, I will critically examine the connection Barth draws between the activity of God and the "being" of Satan or nothingness. The pattern of election and rejection, or, more generally, of a proper work of God and an alien work of God, is vital to Barth's attempt to conceive an ontology of the third agent.[6] The aim of this second part is to tease out, with and against Barth, the tensive and eschatological character of the key dialectic of the divine *opus alienum-opus proprium* and, in doing so, to suggest that the three-agent soteriology sketched in this doctrine of election encourages an understanding of the resurrection as the decisive saving event.

2.1 Election and a Three-Agent Soteriology

In this first part, I outline the "logic" of the three-agent conflict as it emerges in Barth's doctrine of election in *CD* II/2, and as it is carried forward in *CD* III/3. I begin with a brief survey of Barth's doctrine of election prior to *CD* II/2 in order to indicate that *CD* II/2 represents something of an "apocalyptic turn" in Barth's developing doctrine of election. Thereafter, I outline the shape and content of the three-agent soteriology developed with respect to the doctrine of election in *CD* II/2. In a third section, I concentrate on the third agent who formally comes on the scene in *CD* II/2 (and appears again in a parallel section in *CD* III/3), seeking to display Barth's novel understanding of the reality of this agent.

The Doctrine of Election prior to CD II/2

The development of Barth's doctrine of election across his corpus is a much-discussed feature of his theology.[7] Overlooked in these discussions, however, is

---

6. As Wolf Krötke comments, "talk about nothingness has its place in Barth's theology in the relationship between God's Yes and No." Wolf Krötke, *Sin and Nothingness in the Theology of Karl Barth*, ed. and trans. Philip G. Ziegler and Christina-Maria Bammel (Princeton, NJ: Princeton Theological Seminary, 2005), 26.

7. See Bruce L. McCormack, *Karl Barth's Critically Realistic Dialectical Theology: Its Genesis and Development, 1909–1936* (New York: Oxford University Press, 1997); Matthias Gockel, *Barth and Schleiermacher on the Doctrine of Election: A Systematic-Theological*

Barth's move from a two-agent to a three-agent conception of election. In both the 1922 *Römerbrief* and the *Göttingen Dogmatics* of 1924–6—to take two of the most substantial pieces of pre-*CD* II/2 literature—Barth's doctrine of election is exclusively concerned with the God–human relationship. No other agent is in view. Election means election of the human being, and rejection means rejection of the human being, and the active subject in both cases is simply God. In both works, the doctrine of election is discussed only in relation to the *human being* as the object of either acceptance or rejection. So although Barth's is a determinedly *theocentric* doctrine of election in that its focus is on God as the *subject* of election and not on the psychology of election's human objects, it is clear in these earlier materials that the objects of election and rejection are simply human beings.[8]

This changes quite dramatically in *CD* II/2. In contrast to what comes before the publication of *CD* II/2 in 1942, this mature form of Barth's doctrine of election is bound up with his grasp of salvation as a three-agent conflict.[9] That is not to say that the God–human relationship is no longer central. Barth's doctrine of double predestination in *CD* II/2 states that God in Christ has elected Himself for fellowship with fallen humanity and thus for damnation and that He has elected humanity for fellowship with Himself and thus for salvation. In short, God has elected wrath for Himself and love for humanity.[10] The covenant of grace remains a covenant between two parties.[11] Yet this part-volume marks the formal introduction of a

Comparison (Oxford: Oxford University Press, 2006); Shao Kai Tseng, *Karl Barth's Infralapsarian Theology: Origins and Development, 1920–1953* (Downers Grove: IVP Academic, 2016).

8. The same is true of Barth's doctrine of election in the 1921–2 lectures on Ephesians. See Karl Barth, *The Epistle to the Ephesians*, trans. Ross Wright (Grand Rapids, MI: Baker Academic, 2017).

9. As Berkouwer helpfully observes, "it cannot be denied that the chaos appears on the horizon of Barth's theology at the point where he speaks of election." G. C. Berkouwer, *The Triumph of Grace in the Theology of Karl Barth*, trans. Harry R. Boer (London: Paternoster, 1956), 219. Thomas Altizer has also spied the centrality of the three-agent drama to Barth's doctrine of election and expresses the centrality in a logical formulation: if redemption simply is the annihilation of nothingness, then nothingness is "absolutely essential to redemption, and thus absolutely central to predestination." Thomas J. J. Altizer, *Godhead and the Nothing* (Albany: State University of New York Press, 2003), 61. While the logic by which Altizer expresses the relationship between election, redemption, and nothingness would need to be carefully teased out, he is right to propose that the presence of nothingness in the doctrine of election is reflexive of the presence of nothingness in the doctrine of reconciliation (redemption).

10. See *CD* II/2, 162: "Where man stands only to gain, God stands only to lose. And because the eternal divine predestination is identical with the election of Jesus Christ, its twofold content is that God wills to lose in order that man may gain. There is a sure and certain salvation for man, and a sure and certain risk [*Gefahr*] for God."

11. Intriguingly, however, Barth in *CD* IV/1 mentions God's making and confirming a "covenant [*Bund*] with death" in the context of his discussion of God's triumph as one

new object of rejection: Satan and the whole kingdom of darkness, later summed up by Barth as *das Nichtige*, nothingness.[12] As I demonstrate throughout this book, neither God as the electing covenant partner nor humanity as the elected covenant partner can be understood if the third agent—Satan in CD II/2, nothingness in CD III/3—is lost from view.[13]

Election and the Victory over Satan

When Barth pronounces in his doctrine of nothingness in CD III/3 that "The negative content and significance of God's saving decree and act in Jesus Christ are that [nothingness] should be finally routed and the creature liberated from it, as corresponds to God's sovereignty,"[14] he is making a pronouncement whose contours and contents harken back to the doctrine of election set forth in CD II/2. Consider the following description of the cosmic landscape at the heart of Barth's doctrine of election in CD II/2:

> Against the invasion [*Übergriff*] of the shadow-world of Satan [*Schattenwelt des Satans*] which is negated by Him and which exists only by the power of this negation, God must and will defend [*verteidigen*] the honour of His creation, the honour of man as created and ordained for Him, and His own honour. God cannot and will not acquiesce in the incursion [*Einbruch*] of this shadow-world upon the sphere of His positive willing, an incursion made with the fall of man. On the contrary, it must be His pleasure to see that Satan and all that has its source and origin in him are rejected.[15]

"concealed under that of His adversary, of nothingness, of that which supremely is not [*Allernichtigsten*]" (IV/1, 271 rev.). I return to this strange covenant in Chapter 4.

12. There is a brief anticipation of the revised doctrine of election of CD II/2 in Barth's Gifford Lectures delivered at the University of Aberdeen in 1937–8. Following on from his lecture on *Gottes Gnadenwahl* in Debrecen in 1936 (on which see McCormack, *Karl Barth's Critically Realistic Dialectical Theology*, 458–61), Barth's Gifford Lectures bind God's decree to "the existence of Jesus Christ." Karl Barth, *The Knowledge of God and the Service of God According to the Teaching of the Reformation: Recalling the Scottish Confession of 1560*, trans. J. L. M. Haire and Ian Henderson (London: Hodder & Stoughton, 1938), 78. Yet even these lectures, as in *Gottes Gnadenwahl*, no reference to a third agent is forthcoming.

13. I should clarify that it is not that this third agent sheds light on the covenant, but just the reverse: the covenant sheds light on the third agent. Barth's claim—and it is a more disconcerting claim than is often realised—is that Satan or nothingness is not known apart from God's self-revelation; rather, knowledge of God *includes* knowledge of Satan and nothingness. This point is reiterated forcefully in Krötke, *Sin and Nothingness in the Theology of Karl Barth*.

14. CD III/3, 302 rev.

15. CD II/2, 124 rev.

Of central importance within this landscape is "the shadow-world of Satan," understood by Barth as a hostile, invading force against which God must contend for the sake of His own honour and that of creation. Furthermore, human sin—"the fall of man"—is portrayed as a reality bound up with the invasion of Satan's kingdom into God's creation. The implication here is that human beings, precisely as creatures "powerless against the insinuations of the tempter and seducer,"[16] are seized upon as, in the words of Beverly Gaventa, Satan's "base of operations."[17]

God's election of Jesus Christ is with a view to this plight. As Barth avers, "He, the Elect, is appointed to check and defeat Satan on behalf of all those that are elected 'in Him.'"[18] In *CD* II/2, there is a clear deployment of a typically forensic trope in Barth's articulation of this defeat: the defeat happens as Christ, in the place of others, subjects Himself to the wrath of God. Yet this forensic trope is caught up in a broader cosmological soteriology, a soteriology expressed in Barth's use of "kingly" language. As Barth states, "all God's ways and works" move towards the erection of the kingdom of God as their consummation,[19] towards the establishment of God's lordship in the actual events that fulfil the divine decree.[20] Moreover, this kingdom, or, rather, the elected king of this kingdom, is understood to be a king not only in a moral or spiritual sense—a king "over men's hearts"—but also in a cosmological sense, that is to say, a king "over demons and sicknesses, over waves and storm, over death itself."[21] The ultimate purpose in the election of

---

16. *CD* II/2, 123.

17. The phrase is borrowed from Beverly Gaventa's rendering of Rom. 7:8, 11. See Gaventa, "The Cosmic Power of Sin," 234–5; "The Rhetoric of Violence and the God of Peace in Paul's Letter to the Romans," in *Paul, John, and Apocalyptic Eschatology: Studies in Honour of Martinus C. de Boer*, ed. Jan Krans et al. (Leiden: Brill, 2013), 64.

18. *CD* II/2, 123. Given Barth's description of the cosmic landscape, it comes as no surprise that he views the scene of Christ's temptations in the wilderness as an important moment in the defeat of Satan. I discuss Barth's treatment of the temptations in the next chapter.

19. *CD* II/2, 126.

20. *CD* II/2, 491. As Arthur Cochrane observes in the course of an exposition of Barth's doctrine of election, "Grace rules and the one elected acquires a lord." Cochrane, *The Existentialists and God*, 130. Cochrane makes this observation in relation to the place of human action or ethics within the covenant, but primarily and fundamentally the acquiring of a lord is, for Barth as for Luther, the acquiring of a saviour and redeemer, and only *then* is it the acquiring of one who commands.

21. *CD* II/2, 179. There is a critical edge to Barth's reference to Christ's lordship "over men's hearts" that should not go unremarked. Barth, it seems reasonable to infer, has his old teacher Adolf von Harnack in view with this reference. See Adolf von Harnack, *What Is Christianity? Lectures Delivered in the University of Berlin during the Winter-Term 1899–1900*, trans. Thomas B. Saunders (London: Williams and Norgate, 1902), 69:

> The kingdom of God comes by coming to the individual, by entering into his soul and laying hold of it. True, the kingdom of God is the rule of God; but it is the rule of the

Jesus, then, is His claiming and exercising of the lordship of God in the face of the satanic onslaught. Where, as Barth claims, human beings have given to "wrong" in all its cosmological depth the "nature and form" (*Wesen und Gestalt*) that by itself it could not have in God's creation,[22] Christ's establishment as king in his death and resurrection means that "the kingly rule of God Himself attains form and revelation [*Gestalt und Offenbarung*]."[23] Read in the light of this combination of claims from *CD* II/2 and *CD* IV/1, Barth's later description in *CD* IV/3 of Christ the Victor as the One "who robbed the devil of his right to [human beings] and death of its power over them" indicates that some notion of the devil's rights is significant to him.[24] In fact, it can be understood as a description quite in keeping with his doctrine of election and the trajectory of his soteriology thereafter.[25]

But how is the devil robbed of his "right"? And what does it even mean to speak of the devil's right within Barth's theology? Answers to these questions will be developed across the next three chapters. For the moment, however, I will outline two related concepts within Barth's doctrine of election that are particularly important in his development of a three-agent soteriology. These are the divine handing-over and the divine-human steadfastness.

The Divine Handing-Over Barth's lengthy treatment of the New Testament concept of *paradidōmi* (to hand over) in §35.4 of *CD* II/2—a subsection that deals with "The Determination of the Rejected"—is a key moment in the advancement of his three-agent soteriology.[26] At the heart of Barth's interpretation of this New

> holy God in the hearts of individuals; *it is God Himself in His power*. From this point of view everything that is dramatic in the external and historical sense has vanished; and gone, too, are all the external hopes for the future. Take whatever parable you will, the parable of the sower, of the pearl of great price, of the treasure buried in the field-the word of God, God Himself, is the kingdom. It is not a question of angels and devils, thrones and principalities, but of God and the soul, the soul and its God.

22. *CD* IV/1, 539.
23. *CD* II/2, 179.
24. Donald G. Bloesch, *Jesus Is Victor! Karl Barth's Doctrine of Salvation* (Nashville, TN: Abingdon Press, 1976), 44, states that "the devil has no rights over man" according to Barth.
25. *CD* IV/3, 390 rev.
26. On Barth's conception of *paradidōmi*, see Smythe, *Forensic Apocalyptic Theology*, 81–9; Shannon Nicole Smythe, "The Way of Divine and Human Handing-over: Pauline Apocalyptic, Centering Prayer, and Vulnerable Solidarity," *Theology Today* 75, no. 1 (2018): 77–88. For the argument that God's "handing over" of the Son is an action best understood within the context of a cosmic battle, see Beverly Roberts Gaventa, "God Handed Them Over," in *Our Mother Saint Paul* (Louisville, KY: Westminster John Knox Press, 2007), 113–23; "Interpreting the Death of Jesus Apocalyptically: Reconsidering Romans 8:32," in *Jesus and Paul Reconnected: Fresh Pathways into an Old Debate*, ed. Todd D. Still (Grand Rapids, MI: Eerdmans, 2007), 125–45.

Testament concept lies the cosmological struggle sketched above. What Barth calls the "technical meaning" of handing-over—"to be 'handed over' is to be delivered up in powerlessness [*Ohnmacht*] to strange and hostile overwhelming power [*Übermacht*]"[27]—is applied especially to what he considers to be the original and authentic handing-over: the handing over of God Himself in the eternal act of election. The handing-over of the Son is thus a handing-over to "evil powers" (*bösen Gewalten*) at whose hands the Son suffers and dies.[28] "The Son of God," Barth insists, "is left to Himself, indeed to the power of Satan."[29] More so than in any other instance of a handing-over to Satan (e.g. that referenced in 1 Cor. 5:5), it is in the handing-over of Jesus Christ "that there took place the true and proper handing-over of man in weakness to a strange and superior and hostile power [*Gewalt*]."[30] This is the true and proper handing-over because it is the handing-over of the Son of God.

Barth's apocalyptic treatment of the New Testament concept of *paradidōmi* is further bolstered by his understanding of the object who is determined to be handed over: the Son of God *enfleshed*. Indeed, the handing-over of the Son of God is truly a handing-over in the technical sense of that term precisely because the Son of God is determined to become flesh. Barth's logic runs as follows:

> If it is truly the will of the Father to send His eternal Son, and the will of the Son to obey His eternal Father in the execution of this mission; if it is truly the will of God to give Himself to man in such seriousness and completeness that He Himself becomes what man is—flesh, a bearer of human unworthiness and incapacity—then this means that it is the will of God to deliver Himself into the situation of powerlessness [*Ohnmacht*] against the powers to which man is subservient [*unterworfen*], giving Himself not merely to the constraint of the limitations of creaturely life, but to the curse of human guilt, to the depravity of the life of man as it is ruled and determined [*beherrschten und bestimmten*] by his sin, abandoning Himself to the utter opposite of His own divine form of existence [*Existenzweise*].[31]

In other words, that God wills the Son to be handed over is an unavoidable consequence of God's will for the Son to become what the human is—not only a creature but a creature under Satan's tyranny. What the above passage elucidates, furthermore, is that God's eternal decision to be for the human as the incarnate God is an utterly drastic event. For in assuming flesh, God does not assume something fitting to Himself, something analogous to His own existence. Barth

---

27. *CD* II/2, 490.
28. *CD* II/2, 494.
29. *CD* II/2, 494.
30. *CD* II/2, 494–5 rev.
31. *CD* II/2, 491 rev.

stresses the radical contrast between the divine life and the human life: God assumes the "exact opposite" (*genaue Gegenteil*) of what He is. His love for humanity is therefore a love for a humanity whose existence is "so contradictorily other" (*so konträr anders*) to His own.[32] "He Himself becomes what man is—flesh, a bearer of human unworthiness and incapacity [*Unwürdigkeit und Unfähigkeit*]."[33]

In *CD* II/2, Barth concentrates our attention on the realities of sin and slavery and on the apocalyptic situation in which the creature finds herself. The otherness of humanity, its being in the flesh, consists not only in its creatureliness but in the further fact that it is ruled by sin and enslaved by anti-God powers.[34] And it is precisely this enslaved human existence that Christ assumes when He hands Himself over for the sake of His love, allowing the "opposite" of the divine glory to "triumph" over Him.[35]

To those familiar with Barth's turn to "the humanity of God," particularly as this is expressed in *CD* IV/1, these claims in *CD* II/2 may give some pause. Do they not rest on Barth's (supposedly) older view of a God who is naturally distant and remote from human beings and thus stand in tension with his mature divine ontology? As Christophe Chalamet observes, however, a similar tension is exhibited in *CD* IV/1 itself in its treatment of "the journey of the Son into the far country." Chalamet asks,

> Is it really a "far journey"? Isn't Barth pre-supposing the "unbaptized" God of pure otherness and transcendence when using the adjective "far"? Isn't the world, since creation, despite its otherness to God as creation and not as emanation, also quite close to God? Was the world ever left to its own mechanisms and devices, as deists had it and as their modern day heirs have it?[36]

Christopher Holmes has also expressed worry regarding any distancing of God from humanity in relation to the doctrines of revelation and incarnation. If one takes it that Christ's flesh *hides* divinity, Holmes is concerned that one "assumes a view of God and humanity which, ultimately, short-changes the humanity of Jesus as that which is sanctified in the Spirit such that it becomes the very place of God's self-disclosure." In light of Barth's concept of the humanity of God, Holmes

---

32. *CD* II/2, 491/546.
33. *CD* II/2, 491.
34. For further discussion of "flesh," see Chapter 3.
35. *CD* II/2, 491. For an argument that Christ's assuming of sinful flesh (Rom. 8:3) is more a "cosmic" than an "ethical" claim, see Vincent P. Branick, "The Sinful Flesh of the Son of God (Rom 8:3): A Key Image of Pauline Theology," *Catholic Biblical Quarterly* 47, no. 2 (1985): 246–62.
36. Christophe Chalamet, "Divine Extravagance, or Barth's Challenges to Christian Theology in *Church Dogmatics* IV/1, §59.1 ('The Way of the Son of God into the Far Country')," *Zeitschrift für Dialektische Theologie* 32, no. 1 (2016): 103.

asks: "Can the humanity of Jesus be thought to be opposite God if God's being includes humanity within itself?"³⁷

Without withdrawing his own pointed questions, Chalamet punctuates them with two important caveats—caveats supportive of the claims made in *CD* II/2 mentioned above. First, he thinks it wise to remember "the abundance of evil, idolatry and injustice which so often characterizes our world and which make it a reality very foreign to, indeed in open rebellion against, God's original intention."³⁸ Barth's notion of "flesh," I contend, contains precisely these aspects of existence, thereby intensifying the scandal of God's humanity. Second, Chalamet insists upon the *newness* of God's act in His journey into foreign territory.³⁹ Whatever the humanity of God might mean, it cannot mean that the incarnation is a matter of nature taking its peaceful course.⁴⁰ For when Barth speaks of the humanity of God, he does not signify a metaphysical coordination of God and human beings or "the openness of the created order to the working of God."⁴¹ He signifies the catastrophic and offensive event in which God has united Himself with that which is "so contradictorily other" (*so konträr anders*).⁴² Furthermore, by concentrating on the determination of God to assume *flesh*, Barth ensures that the content of this otherness—the twofold otherness of the human to God and of God to the human—is graspable not with an a priori knowledge of the Creator/creature contrast but only in the event of revelation wherein Christ is revealed to be the "man of heaven" (1 Cor. 15:49), the "Son of God with power" (Rom. 1:4).

In sum, then, both with respect to the one to whom Christ is handed over (Satan) and the form of the one handed over (weak, enslaved flesh), Barth evinces

---

37. Christopher R. J. Holmes, "Disclosure without Reservation: Re-Evaluating Divine Hiddenness," *Neue Zeitschrift für Systematische Theologie und Religionsphilosophie* 48, no. 3 (2006): 375.

38. Chalamet, "Divine Extravagance," 103.

39. Chalamet, "Divine Extravagance," 103.

40. Barth's comments on Eph. 1 in his 1921–2 lectures illustrate well the kind of "military view" of the incarnation presented in *CD* II/2: "The message of the incarnation is not proclaimed as an idea in the common sense of the word, but the word from the peaceful kingdom enters the world as a battle cry, as a declaration of war." He continues: "Here One [God] wills to rule as a monarch, and all other claims that life makes on us are called into question by Him. Here, it is a matter of God's decisive war against idols." Karl Barth, *Erklärungen des Epheser- und des Jakobusbriefes, 1919–1929*, ed. Jörg-Michael Bohnet, *Gesamtausgabe*, II.46 (Zürich: TVZ, 2009), 53. One can find a similar depiction of the incarnation, replete with military imagery, in *CD* I/2, 59–64.

41. Hart, *In Him Was Life*, 42. For a clarification of the way in which a focus on Christ's flesh as the revelation of God does not collapse divinity into humanity but in fact *heightens* the distinction, see Paul T. Nimmo, "The Divine Wisdom and the Divine Economy," *Modern Theology* 34, no. 3 (2018): 409–10.

42. *CD* II/2, 491.

a thoroughly cosmological understanding of an event that lies at the core of God's being as the electing God.

Divine–Human Steadfastness A second soteriological concept, one which "constitutes the meaning and purpose of the election of Jesus," is also given a distinctly cosmological rendering.[43] This concept is the divine and human steadfastness (*Beharren*).[44] In a statement that encourages the kind of apocalyptic reading of Barth's doctrine of election presently hazarded, we are told that "the lordship of Satan was broken by the divine-human perseverance which took place in Jesus Christ as decreed at the beginning of all God's ways and works."[45] These divine ways and works, of which election is the beginning, are concerned with the "whole complex of problems which accompany and threaten creation"—the problems of the shadow-side of election[46]—and concerned with them in such a way "that those problems should be overcome and solved, the divine lordship over Satan actualised and the positive will of God as Creator vindicated and enthroned."[47] And to the crucial soteriological question of *how* those problems are solved, how the triumph of the electing God is achieved, Barth answers by appealing to a two-fold steadfastness.

Three remarks can be made at this point. First, it is crucial for Barth that "there is steadfastness on both sides," that is, on the divine side and on the human side— both actualised in Jesus Christ. It is crucial because only in virtue of this *two*-sided steadfastness is Satan "resisted, defied and defeated both by the God against whom he revolted and also by the man against whom he had triumphed."[48] A persistent criticism of three-agent soteriologies—one thinks in particular of Gustaf Aulén's *Christus Victor* motif—is that the humanity of Christ is effectively irrelevant to the accomplishment of God's triumph.[49] Barth's interest in a divine–*human* steadfastness goes some way to shielding him against such criticisms.

43. *CD* II/2, 126.
44. *Beharren* could also be rendered as "perseverance," "insistence," or perhaps "cleaving." In *CD* II/1, *Beharren* is spoken about as an attribute of God, synonymous with the divine constancy (496). There is a special concentration of this noun in II/2, with Barth linking it to the *theologia crucis* and, in particular, to the *theologia resurrectionis*.
45. *CD* II/2, 333.
46. It should be noted that the shadow-side of election is quite other than what Barth describes as the shadow-side of creation. On the shadow-side of creation, see *CD* III/1, 370–5. On the perils of confusing the shadow-side of creation with that of election, see *CD* III/3, 295–302.
47. *CD* II/2, 126.
48. *CD* II/2, 125. By including the need for human steadfastness within "the peculiar secret of the election of the man Jesus," Barth has laid the groundwork for the inclusion of theological ethics in his doctrine of God. He has also laid the groundwork for his particular interest in the temptation episodes in the wilderness and in Gethsemane, discussed in Chapters 3 and 4, respectively.
49. George Hendry, for example, criticises the apparent marginalisation of the humanity of Christ in the *Christus Victor* motif. Hendry, *The Gospel of the Incarnation*, 123. Leonard

Second, Barth identifies the word of human steadfastness with Christ's prayer in Gethsemane and the Word of divine steadfastness with the resurrection of the dead. A curious detail in *CD* II/2 is Barth's counterintuitive identification of Christ's prayer as the answer to the Word of the resurrection.[50] In *CD* IV/1, that identification is reversed: there it is the resurrection that constitutes God's (delayed) answer to Christ's prayer.[51] The later identification, I contend, is to be preferred, not only because it fits with the way the story runs in the Gospels but also because it avoids a possible and problematic identification of the Word of the resurrection with the "hard will of God," with God's "holy wrath."[52] Barth, in *CD* II/2, quite rightly thinks of Christ's prayer as a response to His encounter with God's "hard will." To claim, in the same paragraph, that this prayer is an answer to the Word of resurrection serves only to confuse.

Third, Barth's use of the language of "wager" and "hazard" and "risk" in his doctrine of election mitigates against the critique that his construal of this doctrine election turns the drama of salvation into a pseudo-drama, with history being the scripted display of a protological triumph.[53] If election is a wager that *consists in*

Hodgson goes even further, arguing that Aulén's *Christus Victor* motif results in "a docetic Christology." Leonard Hodgson, *The Doctrine of the Atonement* (New York: Scribner, 1951), 147. Eugene Fairweather, while acknowledging that Aulén is "right in seeing in the whole story the triumph of God over the powers of evil," is critical of his failure "to recognize that the very heart of this divine triumph is the conquest of sin by the perfect human obedience of the Word made flesh." Eugene R. Fairweather, "Incarnation and Atonement: An Anselmian Response to Aulén's *Christus Victor*," *Canadian Journal of Theology* 7, no. 3 (1961): 175. Fairweather's criticism is taken up more recently by Hans Boersma. Seeking a doctrine of the atonement centred on the concept of hospitality, Boersma finds Aulén's monergistic soteriology of "a divine fiat achieved on the cross without any input from the human side" to work against "the genuine acceptance and participation on the part of the guest." Hans Boersma, *Violence, Hospitality, and the Cross: Reappropriating the Atonement Tradition* (Grand Rapids, MI: Baker Academic, 2004), 185.

50. *CD* II/2, 126.
51. *CD* IV/1, 305.
52. *CD* II/2, 126.
53. For criticism of Barth's doctrine of election along this line, see Emil Brunner, *The Christian Doctrine of God: Dogmatics, Vol. 1*, trans. Olive Wyon (Philadelphia, PA: Westminster Press, 1949), 351: "Election means that everything has already taken place in the sphere of pre-existence"; Berkouwer, *The Triumph of Grace in the Theology of Karl Barth*, 257: "Barth's revised supralapsarianism blocks the way to ascribing *decisive* significance to history"; Oswald Bayer, "The Word of the Cross," trans. John R. Betz, *Lutheran Quarterly* 9, no. 1 (1995): 50: "Insofar as what happens in time corresponds to the eternal election, history stands—contrary to Barth's intention—in danger of again becoming metaphysics"; Gerhard O. Forde, "The Work of Christ," in *Christian Dogmatics: Volume 2*, ed. Carl E. Braaten and Robert W. Jenson (Philadelphia, PA: Fortress Press, 1984), 70–1: "Everything is anticipated and established in God's decision to elect, to be known as a God of grace. Creation, fall, and redemption are simply the spelling out in time of that decision."

faith, a very different understanding of the function of the doctrine of election in Barth's theology is opened up. Election, as Barth understands it, need not be taken to settle eternally the conflict that the very act of election initiates. Rather, election can be understood as God's decision to stake the fate of creation on the faith of the Son sent "in the likeness of sinful flesh" (Rom. 8:3). Only if Barth's understanding of the life and passion of Christ indicates a mere pseudo-struggle is his doctrine of election liable to the critique mentioned above. And as is demonstrated in Chapter 4, when I turn to Barth's account of Christ's prayer in Gethsemane, he thinks of this as anything but a pretence or sham.

Election and the Being of Satan

I have sketched above the three-agent account of salvation that is formally set in motion with the doctrine of election in *CD* II/2. What remains to be considered is the way in which Barth pursues a description of the third agent within the context of that doctrine.[54]

As Barth parses his core insight that Jesus Christ is the electing God and the elected human, he does so with a particular orientation to the cross: "Jesus was foreordained to suffer and to die."[55] It is in the course of explaining this foreordination to death that the concept of Satan emerges. The foreordination of Christ to suffer and die means that "a wrath is kindled, a sentence is pronounced, a punishment is carried out, a rejection takes place."[56] In other words, election, as election unto death, involves *judgment*. And Satan, according to Barth, is the prime object of this judgment. Satan is this object of eternal judgment as "the very sum and substance of the possibility which is not chosen by God," as "the very essence of the creature in its misunderstanding and misuse of its creation and destiny and in its desire to be as God, to be itself a god."[57] Satan and the whole kingdom of which he is the head are thus conceived by Barth as "the shadow which accompanies the light of the election of Jesus Christ," the shadow which in Barth's view "is necessary as the object of rejection."[58]

---

54. Certain works are especially helpful in getting to grips with Barth's complex account of the third agent. Among them are Wilfried Härle, *Sein und Gnade: Die Ontologie in Karl Barths Kirchlicher Dogmatik* (Berlin: Walter de Gruyter, 1975), 227–69; Rodin, *Evil and Theodicy in the Theology of Karl Barth*; Martin Hailer, "Karl Barths Nichtiges und Martin Luthers Deus absconditus," in *Die Unbegreiflichkeit des Reiches Gottes: Studien zur Theologie Karl Barths* (Neukirchen-Vluyn: Neukirchener Theologie, 2004), 34–91; Krötke, *Sin and Nothingness in the Theology of Karl Barth*; Wüthrich, *Gott und das Nichtige*.

55. *CD* II/2, 122.

56. *CD* II/2, 122 rev.

57. *CD* II/2, 122.

58. *CD* II/2, 122. As Bromiley correctly adjudges, Barth deals with nothingness/Satan not as "metaphysical evil" but as "that which lies under the divine non-willing and rejecting." Geoffrey W. Bromiley, *Introduction to the Theology of Karl Barth* (Edinburgh: T&T Clark, 1980), 144.

It is here that the strangeness of Satan's existence manifests itself. Barth does not think of "the shadow-world of Satan" as an object that exists independently and that is only subsequently rejected or negated by God. Rather, this shadow-world is an object or reality only on the basis of God's negating and rejecting it. As Barth states, it "exists only in virtue of this negation."[59] If God did not reject it, it would not be.

The strangeness of this rejected existence is further developed in *CD* III/3, with the concept of *das Nichtige* (nothingness) now effectively standing in for the concept of Satan in *CD* II/2.[60] There Barth ventures a statement crucial to his theology as a whole and to his doctrine of the third agent. "*God's activity* as grounded in His *election*," he writes, is the "*ontic* context in which nothingness is real."[61] Election is put forward here as having foundational significance. It is the "ground" of God's activity, such that all of God's acts are the acts of the electing God. In Barth's view, it follows from the grounding of God's activity in election that God's action is also "always a zealous, wrathful, and judging action."[62] We will have cause to question the "always" in due course. What Barth is pressing here, in the terminology of the divine perfections, is that God is always also the *holy* God. God's holiness means that "His being and activity always take place in a definite conflict, in a real negation, both defensive and aggressive."[63] Nothingness is on the other side of this conflict; it is that against which God "asserts Himself and exerts His positive will."[64]

---

59. *CD* II/2, 124.

60. Any technical distinction between Satan/demons and nothingness, of the kind discussed with respect to III/3 in Krötke, *Sin and Nothingness in the Theology of Karl Barth*, 52–4, is simply not in play in *CD* II/2. I will thus treat Satan and nothingness as virtually coterminous, with the awareness that Barth's language becomes more precise in *CD* III/3. But see also Wüthrich, *Gott und das Nichtige*, 174, where it is argued—against Krötke—that Satan can and should be thought of as a form of nothingness that "transcends or complements" its forms as sin, evil, and death as discussed in *CD* III/3.

61. *CD* III/3, 351. This rooting of the account of nothingness in the doctrine of election is not the same as its being "rooted in a theory of divine aseity," as Rose contends. Matthew Rose, *Ethics with Barth: God, Metaphysics and Morals* (Farnham: Ashgate, 2010), 181.

62. *CD* III/3, 351 rev.

63. *CD* III/3, 351 rev. When Matthew Rose, outlining Barth's concept of nothingness, states that "God is the Father of lights, and the light of his holiness does not require the shadow of nothingness" (Rose, *Ethics with Barth*, 179), there is a clear downplaying of what appears for Barth to be the essentially *militant* character of holiness. One of the most remarkable features of Barth's doctrine of the perfections of the divine loving in *CD* II/1 is the fact that they are elucidated only with respect to God's dealings with what is not God or, rather, with what is *against* God. These are not the perfections of an isolated "perfect being." Krötke is thus right to surmise from Barth's doctrine of God that "God's eternal being has already been touched by sin." Krötke, *Sin and Nothingness in the Theology of Karl Barth*, 5.

64. *CD* III/3, 351.

The allusion to divine holiness recalls Barth's treatment of the perfections of the divine loving in *CD* II/1.⁶⁵ In the course of outlining grace and holiness as perfections of the divine loving, Barth leaves us with an unsolved problem.⁶⁶ He speaks of grace and holiness as divine opposition to (creaturely) resistance. Yet in order to avoid the impression of an eternal dualism, he posits a form of grace unknown to us, a form in which it is not an overcoming or triumph.⁶⁷ Something similar is wrought in respect of holiness. Barth writes:

> In [God], of course, there is no sin which He has first to resist. But in Him there is more. There is the purity, indeed He is Himself the purity, which as such contradicts and will resist everything which is unlike itself, yet which does not evade this opposing factor, but, because it is the purity of the life of the Father, Son and Holy Spirit, eternally reacts against it, resisting and judging it in its encounter with it, but in so doing receiving and adopting it, and thus entering into the fellowship with it which redeems it.⁶⁸

The notion of holiness as an *eternal* resistance and judgment is left hanging in the air; it remains a sort of disposition or readiness of God, but one that has no object (at least in eternity) by which to become act. This can be explained by the two-agent framework that governs the discussion of the divine perfections in *CD* II/1 (and that also governs its doctrine of atonement).

The properly dogmatic introduction of the third agent in *CD* II/2 expands the theological conceptualities open to Barth. When he sets to writing *CD* III/3, he can now think of the holiness of God as almost "creating" its own object of resistance.⁶⁹

---

65. On this see Hailer, "Karl Barths Nichtiges und Martin Luthers Deus absconditus." Hailer quite rightly states that while Barth, in *CD* III/3, has picked up the thread from *CD* II/1, he has "sharpened the tone considerably" (75). Indeed, so much sharper does Hailer detect the tone to be in the later text that he submits that with Barth's "doctrine"—the quotation marks are important for Hailer—of nothingness there begins a "theological frontier-crossing into the neighbourhood of dualism" (*theologischer Grenzgang in Nachbarschaft zum Dualismus*).

66. On the problems inherent in this formulation, see the comments relating to grace as a divine perfection in Robert B. Price, *Letters of the Divine Word: The Perfections of God in Karl Barth's Church Dogmatics* (London: T&T Clark, 2012), 55–61.

67. *CD* II/1, 353–8.

68. *CD* II/1, 368.

69. Barth, it should be clarified, seeks at all turns to avoid thinking of nothingness as either divine or as a creature of God—"in a third way of its own nothingness 'is'" (*CD* III/3, 349). If he uses terminology that seems to belong properly to God or creatures (being, existence, reality), it bears remembering that all of these are bracketed within the absolute "No" of God and must be understood to be correspondingly qualified No. Krötke has drawn attention to the confusion attending Barth's attempt to speak of nothingness using categories "which describe creaturely existence within the sphere of creation." Krötke, *Sin and Nothingness in the Theology of Karl Barth*, 29.

And here, in turn, we see in what way election, as the act or event of God's holiness, is crucial to the knowledge of that object of resistance: "If the biblical conception of the God whose activity is grounded in election and is therefore always holy fades or disappears, there will also fade and disappear the knowledge of nothingness, for it will necessarily become unfounded/baseless [*gegenstandslos*]."[70] Barth's concern is to point out that if we do away with the electing God, then it is only a matter of time before we also do away with real knowledge of nothingness.[71] This is so because "Nothingness has no existence and cannot be known except as the object of God's activity insofar as the latter is always also a *holy* activity."[72]

Barth's description of Satan and the shadow-world in *CD* II/2 is echoed in his description of nothingness in *CD* III/3:

> Nothingness is that which God does *not* will. It lives only by the fact that it is that which God does *not* will. But it does live by this fact. For not only what God wills, but what He does not will, is *potent*, and therefore cannot be without real correspondence. What really corresponds to that which God does not will is nothingness.[73]

This gives to nothingness an inherently "problematic" being by virtue of its existence by the power of the left hand of God, by the power of God's *opus alienum* of wrath, jealousy, and judgment, a being entirely different to the being of God and the being of God's creatures.[74] But it does give nothingness a being nonetheless. As Barth explains, "because it is on the left hand of God, it really 'is' in this paradoxical manner."[75] The key claim, then, is that "As God is Lord on the left hand as well, He is the basis [*Grund*] and Lord of nothingness too."[76]

---

70. *CD* III/3, 351 rev.

71. The limits of the present work do not permit it, but it would be interesting to explore whether Barth's claim comports with the history of theology. Can the diminishment of apocalyptic be traced to theologians' unwillingness to engage with the doctrine of election, and can the "apocalyptic turn" be attributed, at least in part, to a retrieval of interest in the doctrine? The story of Barth's own relationship to apocalyptic themes can be told from numerous perspectives—the impact of New Testament scholarship at the turn of the twentieth century, the influence of the Blumhardts, the intellectual, political, and cultural situation of the time, and not least Barth's own grappling with the contents of the biblical text—but one further, promising perspective could be Barth's engagement with the doctrine of election.

72. *CD* III/3, 351 rev.

73. *CD* III/3, 352 rev.

74. The concept of God's left hand first appears in *Church Dogmatics* within the doctrine of God, where Barth circumscribes all human existence within the limits set by the divine Yes and the divine No. The Yes stands for God's right hand, the No, His left. See *CD* II/1, 557–8.

75. *CD* III/3, 351.

76. *CD* III/3, 351.

Four conclusions can be seen to follow from this account of Satan (*CD* II/2) supported by the subsequent doctrine of nothingness (*CD* III/3). First, nothingness "is not adventitious" (*nicht von ungefähr*), that is to say, it is not by chance or accident.[77] And so while it is an opponent of God in the strictest sense, it is not out with the lordship of God.[78] Human beings cannot master or comprehend it, but God can and does. Second, and related to the first, any kind of absolute or metaphysical dualism is ruled out. Nothingness "is not a second God, nor self-created. It has no power that is not given to it by God."[79] This is what makes Barth's notion of a cosmological conflict somewhat disorientating, for the opponent of God has its basis in God. Third, Barth can nevertheless be seen to open the door for a certain kind of dualism, what in *CD* III/1 he calls "a dualism which is dissoluble."[80] Barth, in a move that sets him apart from much of the theological tradition, endeavours to conceive of nothingness as an opponent of God "from the beginning" (Jn 8:44). Fourth, as a "reality" bound up with God's being and act as the electing God of the covenant, there can be no talk of covenant and covenant activity—either on the divine side or on the human side—without nothingness and chaos in view.[81] That the ruler of this world must be judged and defeated is central to Barth's description of God in Christ as the One who elects Himself the covenant partner of humanity. It follows from this that the covenant, and therefore the action of both the divine and human covenant partners, are unavoidably apocalyptic realities from the very beginning; that is to say, covenantal existence and activity are always already caught up in the three-agent drama. In its problematic being on the left hand of God, nothingness "is present from the very outset with God and His creature."

---

77. *CD* III/3, 351.

78. The oppositional character that *das Nichtige* possesses for Barth has occasionally eluded scholars. Jürgen Moltmann, for example, mistakenly thinks that Barth has dropped the "apocalyptic dimensions" of nothingness by replacing the notion of a "conflict" between light and darkness with the "platonic" notion of a "difference between *light and shadow*." Jürgen Moltmann, "Zwölf Bemerkungen zur Symbolik des Bösen," *Evangelische Theologie* 52 (1992): 5. Cf. Jürgen Moltmann, *God in Creation: An Ecological Doctrine of Creation*, trans. Margaret Kohl (London: SCM Press, 1985), 334n29. Also misguided is Paul Jersild's description of *das Nichtige* as a "neutral concept" in Barth's theology. See Paul Jersild, "Judgment of God in Albrecht Ritschl and Karl Barth," *Lutheran Quarterly* 14, no. 4 (1962): 336. Overlooked by Moltmann and Jersild is what John McDowell calls "the intolerability of *das Nichtige*" in John C. McDowell, "Much Ado about Nothing: Karl Barth's Being Unable to Do Nothing about Nothingness," *International Journal of Systematic Theology* 4, no. 3 (2002): 324.

79. *CD* III/3, 351 rev.

80. *CD* III/1, 384.

81. See N. T. Bakker, "Der Mensch vor und nach dem Nichts: Anthropologische Erkundungen im Niemandsland (über K. Barths Lehre vom Nichtigen)," *Zeitschrift für Dialektische Theologie* 2, no. 1 (1986): 118: "The origin of nothingness does not lie in God the Creator, nor in the human of creation, but in the covenant, in the alliance of these two."

Barth continues, "In this way it is involved from the very outset in the history of the relationship between God and His creature, and therefore from the very outset the biblical witness to this history takes its existence into account."[82] This in turn means that at issue in the history of the covenant, the history elected by God, is "the repulse [*Abwehr*] and final removal [*Vernichtung*]" of the threat that nothingness poses to the creature.

2.2. The Third Agent in Relation to God's Opus Alienum and Opus Proprium

Thus far I have endeavoured to trace the apocalyptic contours of Barth's doctrine of election as these emerge in *CD* II/2 and are echoed in *CD* III/3, giving an outline of how Barth's introduction of the third agent (Satan/nothingness) in his doctrine of election establishes his soteriology as a three-agent soteriology. Barth sees God's electing grace as initiating a cosmic struggle between God and Satan, between what God chooses and what God does not choose. The doctrine of election still concerns the electing God and the elected human. It still concerns the covenant. Broadly construed, fellowship and friendship between God and human beings are its aim. But the "covenantal ontology" developed in *CD* II/2, it should now be recognised, is one that does not dampen but rather amplifies a "military view" of the atonement.[83] How this amplification manifests itself in the doctrine of reconciliation in *CD* IV/1 will be of primary concern in the remaining chapters. Before proceeding to these chapters, however, there needs to be added to the largely descriptive account of Barth's three-agent doctrine of election in part 1 above a critical evaluation and some corrective manoeuvres.

The second part of this chapter proceeds in two steps. First, I consider four lines of critique regarding Barth's account of Satan/nothingness, focussing on problems largely internal to Barth's theology. And second, with a view to navigating a way through these problems, I interrogate the key dialectic of God's *opus alienum-opus proprium*, seeking to accent and develop the more tensive construal of the relationship between these two works that occasionally surfaces in Barth's thought.

Critiques of Barth's Account of Satan/Nothingness

There are at least four (intersecting) lines of critique regarding Barth's account of nothingness that bear upon matters of soteriology and merit careful investigation.

---

82. *CD* III/3, 352.

83. I borrow the term "covenantal ontology" from Bruce L. McCormack, "Grace and Being: The Role of God's Gracious Election in Karl Barth's Theological Ontology," in *The Cambridge Companion to Karl Barth*, ed. John Webster (New York: Cambridge University Press, 2000), 92–110.

Barth, we recall, conceives of Satan and nothingness not only as the object of wrath and rejection—as the object, that is, of God's *opus alienum*—but as that which "is" by virtue of this alien work. Nothingness "'is,'" he reasons, "in its connexion with the activity of God. It 'is' because and as and so long as God is against it."[84] It is the third agent's strange basis in God that leads Matthias Wüthrich to suggest that Barth's interrelating God and nothingness is "remarkable yet problematic."[85] It is remarkable because "Barth simply works on the assumption that in the story of Jesus Christ as witnessed by the Bible, this nothingness as such is simply 'there' and refuted by God. And because it is 'there', it also must (indirectly) originate from God's healing and powerful saving decree."[86] Just as Barth does not reason from the election of Jesus forward to the history of Jesus but from the history of Jesus back to election, neither does he reason from an original principle of evil forward to its historical manifestation but from its historical manifestation in the history of Christ back to the eternal divine decree.

Yet within this remarkable feature of Barth's thought, Wüthrich locates a particular problem. Conceiving of nothingness as a reality grounded in God "leads to a *tremendous, radicalized incrimination of God in the face of nothingness*."[87] It appears to be one thing to say that God *permits* nothingness but quite another to say that God is somehow its basis, its ground, and its reason for being, such that it has no being independent of God's activity.[88]

A second line of critique stems from the first: this incrimination of God appears to call for a notion that sits uncomfortably with Barth's doctrine of God, namely, the notion of "God against God."[89] An immediate problem with such a notion

---

84. *CD* III/3, 353.

85. Matthias D. Wüthrich, "Lament for Nought? An Inquiry into the Dismissal of Lament in Systematic Theology: On the Example of Karl Barth," in *Evoking Lament: A Theological Discussion*, ed. Eva Harasta and Brian Brock (London: T&T Clark, 2009), 67.

86. Wüthrich, "Lament for Nought?" 69.

87. Wüthrich, "Lament for Nought?" 67.

88. On God as the ground of nothingness, see the discussion in Härle, *Sein und Gnade*, 236–41.

89. Gerrit Berkouwer proposes that, for Barth, "The purpose of God's *proper* work is to make an end to His *alien* work" and indeed that "Barth goes so far as to speak of the victory of the opus proprium over the opus alienum." G. C. Berkouwer, *The Triumph of Grace in the Theology of Karl Barth*, trans. Harry R. Boer (London: Paternoster, 1956), 74, 243. Rodin suggests that in §50, Barth presents "an internal war of sorts between the two hands of God." Rodin, *Evil and Theodicy in the Theology of Karl Barth*, 187. Thomas, teasing out the implications of Barth's description of the "being" of nothingness, proposes that it is possible to conceive of the cross as an event that deals with "the conflict between the left and the right hand of God, between the *opus alienum* and the *opus proprium*," that is to say, as an event that "deals with this dark side of the working [*Schaffens*] of God." Günter Thomas, "Der für uns 'gerichtete Richter': Kritische Erwägungen zu Karl Barths Versöhnungslehre," *Zeitschrift für Dialektische Theologie* 18, no. 2 (2002): 218. Thomas argues that Barth's fundamentally legal or forensic understanding of the atonement leaves

can be voiced, namely, that it seems to refashion the cosmic conflict as one not only between God and nothingness or Satan but also between God and God.[90] Is it not counterintuitive, particularly when considering Barth's relentless pursuit of a doctrine of election that is wholly light and gospel, to make God's election and rejection the *problem* and in this way to attribute directly to God the responsibility (and blame) for the situation from which the cosmos needs saving? Barth certainly wants to affirm that God takes the responsibility *upon* Himself, but he never goes so far as to declare that God is *guilty* in some way, with the cross then understood as (also) God's own liberation from guilt.[91] As David Bentley Hart has argued, to make this theological gesture would be to confuse who requires forgiveness from whom.[92] Nevertheless, in the light of Barth's doctrine of nothingness—and, more

him in various theological and logical binds. I address some of Thomas's concerns in more detail in Chapter 5.

90. This is the problem that Jüngel has with Luther's *The Bondage of the Will*. According to Jüngel, "The hidden and the revealed God seem to stand in contradiction to each other, so that in the end it is not *evil against God* but rather *God* against God." Eberhard Jüngel, "The Revelation of the Hiddenness of God: A Contribution to the Protestant Understanding of the Hiddenness of Divine Action," in *Theological Essays II*, ed. John Webster, trans. Arnold Neufeldt-Fast and John Webster (Edinburgh: T&T Clark, 1995), 136. The root of this problem, for Jüngel, is the notion that God *in Himself* could be someone other than the *revealed* God.

91. McCormack, in an essay on the cry of dereliction, takes tentative steps towards this position. He writes:

"Accepting responsibility": Barth does not mean this in quite the sense that is needed, in my judgment. God, for Barth, "accepts" responsibility for the evil *we* have done. He takes it upon himself as something added to him that would not otherwise have been his. But it seems to me that this formulation is finally inadequate for addressing the case Saramago brings against the Christian God. Saramago is saying that the Christian God (should he exist) *is* guilty; that it was his eternal plan of redemption that made sin and evil necessary, that God should take responsibility not because he feels compassion for us but because he truly is responsible for all that has taken place. Confronted with Saramago's challenge, it seems to me, no other answer will do but death in God as a self-imposed act of public acknowledgment of the evil that was, in a very real sense, necessary to the accomplishment of the ends of God's love. Such an acknowledgment is, I would say, a moral obligation.

Bruce L. McCormack, "The Passion of God Himself: Barth on Jesus's Cry of Dereliction," in *Reading the Gospels with Karl Barth*, ed. Daniel L. Migliore (Grand Rapids, MI: Eerdmans, 2017), 167. McCormack's strikingly provocative conclusion is that "the love of God contains, in its very nature, the seeds of death, sin, and misery" (172).

92. David Bentley Hart, *The Beauty of the Infinite: The Aesthetics of Christian Truth* (Grand Rapids, MI: Eerdmans, 2003), 373–5. Hart's argument is against certain "tragic theologies" of the suffering God. He names Hans Urs von Balthasar and Eberhard Jüngel as proponents of such a tragic vision in one form or another, before engaging more extensively

to the point, in the light of the events of the cross and resurrection on which that doctrine aims to be based—it bears pondering whether the idea an intra-divine conflict, as a vital part of the three-agent conflict, can be entirely avoided.⁹³ As Gerhard Forde suggests, to avoid that idea in the name of an assured identity of the hidden God with the revealed God would perhaps be to risk an even more fatal outcome: the mixing of the *deus ipse* with the *deus revelatus* such that the terror of divine wrath is comprehended and thereby either neutralised or eternalised.⁹⁴

A third line of critique of Barth's account of the third agent concerns the impossibility of nothingness's termination. Given that God's (left-handed) activity is the ground of nothingness's strange being, how can Barth finally envisage and elucidate the *end* of nothingness? If nothingness lives by the activity of God's left hand, then more of this activity—more rejection, more wrath, more opposition— would seem only to perpetuate its existence, thereby eternalising the third agent.⁹⁵ It is for this reason questionable whether the triumph over nothingness can be

---

with the work of Donald MacKinnon and Nicholas Lash (380–94). For a similar critique of certain "sentimental" styles of this tragic theology, see Gerhard O. Forde, *On Being a Theologian of the Cross: Reflections on Luther's Heidelberg Disputation, 1518* (Grand Rapids, MI: Eerdmans, 1997), viii–ix. It should be noted, however, that Forde's critique proceeds from a markedly different set of premises than those of Hart. The problem, for Forde, is not so much the sense of the tragic that imbues this theology or the problematic surrendering of the ancient doctrine of divine impassibility (Forde himself is more than willing to surrender the latter), but the failure to remember and foreground the enmity between God and humanity. The God who suffers does not suffer with us or as One who identifies with us. Christ dies alone, forsaken even by God (ix). The suffering God does not come "to join us in our battle against some unknown enemy," but to kill and to make alive. The critiques offered by Hart and Forde, though founded on differing presuppositions and though followed by radically opposed alternatives, are not to be dismissed out of hand. If Hart and Forde have one thing in common, it is an insistence on the importance of the resurrection of Christ for Christian faith and Christian theology. This importance is explored in detail in Chapter 5.

93. According to Aulén, a distinct characteristic of Luther's *Christus Victor* account of salvation is his willingness to confront the troubling idea of an intra-divine conflict, a willingness based on his understanding of divine wrath as a tyrannical power from which the cosmos must be liberated. See Gustaf Aulén, *Christus Victor: An Historical Study of the Three Main Types of the Idea of Atonement*, trans. A. G. Hebert (London: SPCK, 1970), 111–16; *The Faith of the Christian Church*, 2nd ed., trans. Eric H. Wahlstrom (London: SCM Press, 1961), 202–4.

94. In Forde's view, Barth's theological attempt to banish the *deus ipse* in his doctrine of election only succeeds in blending the *deus ipse* with the *deus revelatus*. Forde, "The Work of Christ," 71.

95. Härle, *Sein und Gnade*, 263; Thomas, "Der für uns 'gerichtete Richter,'" 217n14; Martin Wendte, "Lamentation between Contradiction and Obedience: Hegel and Barth as Diametrically Opposed Brothers in the Spirit of Modernity," in *Evoking Lament: A Theological Discussion*, ed. Eva Harasta and Brian Brock (London: T&T Clark, 2009), 90n62.

achieved by rendering it the object of wrath—let alone a wrath that, on the cross, is actually *executed* by the forces of death and destruction (understood by Barth in *CD* III/3 to be forms of nothingness). The notion that that which is the ground of nothingness could also be that which overcomes it seems to be at best paradoxical and at worst a misidentification of how and when the reality of nothingness is overcome.[96]

A fourth line of critique concerns Barth's use of the concept of God's *opus alienum*. God's rejection of nothingness, His being "against it in jealousy, wrath and judgment,"[97] is associated by Barth with the alien work of God. But would it not be more correct to see in God's rejection of nothingness an instance of the proper work of God, the work of God's right hand?[98] It does not seem alien to God that He would utter a rejecting No to nothingness. Indeed, the very idea of there being an alien work of God stands in considerable tension with Barth's doctrine of God. Is this alien act an act that is constitutive of the very being of God?[99] Or does this alien act "not belong to the nature of God"?[100] If the former, it would seem misguided to describe it as "alien." And if the latter, the identity Barth posits between God's being and act appears to fall apart.

Barth's description of Satan or nothingness as an "instrument" or "servant" of God might be one way to make sense of such an alien work of God.[101] But this description seems only to lead to further complications. Crucial to Barth's understanding of nothingness is that it is a relentless opponent of God and His redeeming work. As Paul Ricoeur rightly states, Barth "sees in evil a reality that is not commensurate with the goodness of God and of creation." Nothingness, in short, is "hostile to God."[102] This should sharply qualify what it might mean to speak of nothingness as an "instrument" or "servant" of God. Indeed, nothingness's "essence" as that which *resists* God's loving purposes potentially problematises any sense in which it might be spoken of as an "instrument."[103] Seen from the other side, we might also propose that God's instrumentalising of

---

96. Wüthrich also notes this "paradox" in Barth's account of nothingness's defeat: "Just as God's wrath, judgment and non-willing were the ground of nothingness, God's wrath, judgment and non-willing over nothingness willfully destroy nothingness by nothingness." Wüthrich, *Gott und das Nichtige*, 167.

97. *CD* III/3, 353.

98. This point has been helpfully raised in a recent paper entitled "The First and Final 'No': The Finality of the Gospel and the Old Enemy" by Philip G. Ziegler at the 2019 Karl Barth Conference in Princeton, New Jersey.

99. For Barth's treatment of "the being of God in act," see II/1, 257–72.

100. Härle, *Sein und Gnade*, 241.

101. *CD* II/2, 92; III/3, 367; III/4, 367; IV/1, 254, 306–7, 399, 408.

102. Paul Ricoeur, "Evil, a Challenge to Philosophy and Theology," trans. David Pellauer, *Journal of the American Academy of Religion* 53, no. 4 (1985): 643.

103. In Georg Pfleiderer, "The Atonement," in *Trinitarian Soundings in Systematic Theology*, ed. Paul Louis Metzger (London: T&T Clark International, 2006), 132, Pfleiderer criticises the "classic" theory of atonement for its notion that "the good power defeats the

nothingness *problematises God*—which brings us back to our first line of critique. The description of nothingness as a servant of God puts a question mark beside the God whose servant it is.

Re-thinking the Opus Alienum-Opus Proprium Dialectic

In light of the above critiques, this section will develop a tensive and eschatological relation between the two elements of the *opus alienum-opus proprium* dialectic—a tensive and eschatological relation that tends to be underplayed by Barth.

The distinction between God's *opus alienum* and *opus proprium* makes its first appearance in the first part-volume. In his explanation of the oneness of the Word of God in the differentiating of its form (law) from its content (gospel), Barth associates God's *opus alienum* with "wrath and judgment"—a wrath and judgment which are the "hard shell" of God's *opus proprium*, namely, God's grace.[104] This apparent inseparability between wrath and love and between the *opus alienum* and the *opus proprium* re-surfaces much later, in *CD* IV/2, during a discussion of the emergence of the theme of divine love in the Old Testament, where Barth suggests that the wrath (*opus alienum*) of God is seen to be a "necessary form" of God's love (*opus proprium*).[105] These two instances of the dialectic conform to one typical pattern of Barth's dialectical thinking in *Church Dogmatics*: the negative or alien (wrath, rejection) conceals, contains, and serves the positive or proper (love, grace, election).

Barth's final explicit use of the *opus alienum-opus proprium* dialectic in *Church Dogmatics* surfaces in *CD* IV/3. There a more tensive relationship between the *opus alienum* and *opus proprium* can be glimpsed. The distinction between God's alien work and God's proper work names the distinction between what the sending of Jesus means in a hostile world that rejects Jesus—wrath, judgment, punishment— and what the sending of Jesus means "in itself"—love.[106] The alien character of wrath—"God did not send His Son into the world to condemn the world" (Jn 3:19)—is thereby intensified. The sending of Jesus only "becomes" punishing wrath in the conflict with darkness. "But," Barth insists, "it is not so in itself."[107]

---

evil force with its own weapons." Such a notion "would mean that God accepts the rules of evil, which are war and not peace, hate and not love," which would be a moral contradiction.

104. *CD* I/1, 179.
105. *CD* IV/2, 763.
106. *CD* IV/3, 237.
107. *CD* IV/3, 237. In his analysis of what he deems to be the various phases of Barth's dialectical theology, Jacob Taubes discerns in the *Kirchliche Dogmatik* a Johannine dialectic focussed on the incarnation and the reality of love. For Barth, according to Taubes, "Divine grace is ultimately not judgment but love." See Jacob Taubes, "Theodicy and Theology: A Philosophical Analysis of Karl Barth's Dialectical Theology," in *From Cult to Culture: Fragments Toward a Critique of Historical Reason*, ed. Charlotte Elisheva Fonrobert and Amir Engel (Stanford, CA: Stanford University Press, 2010), 192. It is Taubes's claim that grace is, for Barth, finally love and *not* judgment that pushes back against the idea of

Audible in this distinction between what the sending of Jesus *becomes* and what it is *in itself* is an echo of Barth's contention in *CD* II/2 that

> Originally and finally [the doctrine of predestination] is not dialectical but non-dialectical. It does not proclaim in the same breath both good and evil, both help and destruction, both life and death. It does, of course, throw a shadow. We cannot overlook or ignore this aspect of the matter. In itself, however, it is light and not darkness.[108]

Barth, as noted above, typically formulates what we might call a *teleological* relationship between God's *opus alienum* and *opus proprium*. His view is that the former serves or is ordered towards the latter, a view which, as noted above, entails an understanding of Satan or nothingness as God's "instruments" or "servants" towards a positive purpose. We need not surrender this view as such. But, in keeping with the critiques outlined above, we should be alert to the tension that it generates as well as to the possibility of a more discordant relationship between the two *opera*. If the idea of a "conflict" or "war" between the alien and proper work of God (or the left and right hands of God) is foreign to the broad strand of Barth's thought, it is not entirely foreign to his thought as a whole.

What is clear is that if the concept of "alien work" is to do any proper *theological* work, the alien work must have a genuinely *alien* character. The concept of God's alien work must therefore point to something beyond God's wrath against nothingness. It must point in some way to a strange and disorientating Yes that God says to nothingness, a Yes signalling God's appointment of nothingness—a nothingness, we must remember, that is "adverse to grace, and therefore without it"[109]—to do divine work. Barth's notion of the divine service rendered by nothingness suggested that he knows an alien work of this kind.

Taking the alien work seriously as *alien* work, the relationship between God's *opus alienum* and *opus proprium* is best construed as an *eschatological* relationship, a relationship everywhere marked by the desire of the proper work to put an end to the alien work. Using language borrowed from Barth's doctrine of election in *CD* II/2, we can speak of an eschatological division between God's "coming" (proper) work and God's "perishing" (alien) work.[110]

---

grace *in* judgment. The tensive character between grace and judgment (or love and wrath) that is spied by Taubes is what I am seeking to emphasise, without necessarily subscribing to his contention that Barth's Pauline dialectic is consumed by a Johannine dialectic.

108. *CD* II/2, 13. A similar distinction is perhaps observable in Barth's enigmatic distinction between the "alien" form and the "pure" form of Jesus Christ in §70. See *CD* IV/3, 383–408 passim.

109. *CD* III/3, 353.

110. See *CD* II/2, 172:

> we do not find a proportion but a disproportion between the positive will of God which purposes the life and blessedness of man and the permissive will of God which ordains

But here it may be necessary to go beyond Barth, and to see that the *opus alienum* and the *opus proprium*, or the activity of the left hand of God and the activity of the right, can be thought to name not so much a hidden and revealed "form" of the one divine action of grace[111] but two unbalanced actions that correspond to two ages, the perishing and the coming; or, perhaps better, two actions that define or constitute these two ages.[112]

Put more concretely, the *opus alienum* can be associated with the cross and the *opus proprium* with the resurrection. One further instance of the *opus alienum-opus proprium* dialectic in *Church Dogmatics* bears mentioning in this regard. These concepts appear together again in a critique of Calvin's penitential teaching in *CD* IV/2. There Barth suggests that *vivificatio* ought to be associated with God's *opus proprium* and *mortificatio* with God's *opus alienum*.[113] Understanding the *opus alienum-opus prorprium* along this line undoubtedly shifts considerable soteriological weight to the resurrection. But if the resurrection really is, as Barth states in *CD* IV/1, the archetypal manifestation of divine grace,[114] it is surely to this event, more so than any other, that God's electing grace is finally directed: it is in this event that the "steadfastness" of God is actualised and the eternal will

---

him to seduction by Satan and guilt before God. In this disproportion the first element is always predominant, the second subordinate. The first is an authoritative Yes, the second a No which is determined only by the Yes, thus losing its authority from the very outset. The first is the coming form of the divine work, the second the perishing.

111. It can often appear that, for Barth, everything God does is just "grace" or "love" by another name. Robert Jenson has challenged this feature in Barth's thought. Though holding on to Barth's view of a purposive relationship between two seemingly contradictory acts of God, Jenson insists that God's condemnation serves God's grace "not … by becoming itself grace, but in the mode of suffering and overcoming." Robert W. Jenson, *Alpha and Omega: A Study in the Theology of Karl Barth* (New York: Thomas Nelson & Sons, 1963), 160.

112. That there is a relationship between the two works ought not to be denied. As Jüngel rightly cautions, the *opus alienum* and the *opus proprium* of God "are not to be understood as two unrelated activities of God running parallel to each other. In that case, the right hand of God would in fact not know what the left does." Jüngel, "The Revelation of the Hiddenness of God," 133. In the same essay, Jüngel correctly spies the importance of eschatology for this relationship (he speaks of the "eschatological effectiveness" of Good Friday on p. 140). Bertold Klappert discusses the "teleological dynamic" that is displayed in the cross, namely, the fact that God's No "serves" God's Yes. Klappert, *Die Auferweckung des Gekreuzigten*, 245–6. It is my proposal that "eschatological" is a more helpful descriptor than "teleological." The latter is not inappropriate, but it tends to minimise the rupture that is involved and instead suggests the outworking of a smooth process.

113. *CD* IV/2, 579. See also Karl Barth, *Ethics*, ed. Dietrich Braun, trans. Geoffrey W. Bromiley (New York: Seabury Press, 1981), 284, where Barth identifies the proper work of God with the "work of life and salvation."

114. *CD* IV/1, 304–5.

of God is finally accomplished. Barth makes this point in *CD* III/1, borrowing terminology that pervades his doctrine of election. He writes:

> It is quite clear that in the determination of His Son to be the Bearer of creaturely existence and its contradictions God did not in the same way will and accomplish His humiliation and death on the one side and His exaltation and resurrection on the other. He pronounced the Yes and No with differing emphases.[115]

Cross and resurrection are here expressed as elements in what Michael Beintker has called a "supplementary dialectic," that is, a dialectic in which one element in the dialectical pair is predominant.[116] As we will see in Chapter 5, Barth struggles to maintain the predominance of the resurrection in his mature doctrine of reconciliation; indeed, he can be taken to more or less abandon it. But we need not follow him down that path.

How, then, might the landscape of Barth's soteriology change if the resurrection is given priority as the event of God's proper work, the event in which the "divine lordship over Satan" is actualised "and the positive will of God as Creator vindicated and enthroned"?[117] Based on the above analysis, the conclusion to which we are drawn is that it is not God's *opus alienum*—that is to say, it is not the cross—that itself ends nothingness. Stated positively—in an argument to be fleshed out in Chapter 5—it is God's *opus proprium* in the resurrection that achieves God's eschatological victory over the forces of sin, death and the devil, forces that remain in power so long as Christ has not been raised from the dead and so long as we remain buried with Him.

To conceive of the relationship between the alien and proper work in this way puts considerable pressure on Barth's doctrine of God. We have not simply left Barth behind, however. As he himself writes, "It is God's *opus proprium*, the work of His right hand—and this hand alone—which renders pointless [*gegenstandslos*] and therefore superfluous [*überflüssig*] His *opus alienum*, the work of His left."[118] In other words, it is not that the *opus alienum* transitions into the *opus proprium* in a sequence but that the *opus proprium* eschatologically banishes the *opus alienum*.[119] Barth's understanding of divine action is not as "epochless" as critics

---

115. *CD* III/1, 383 rev. Cf. Barth's commentary on Romans, where he writes of the duality of election and rejection that "it involves no equilibrium [*Gleichgewicht*], but that it is the eternal overcoming of judgment by grace, hatred by love, death by life." *RII*, 347.

116. Michael Beintker, *Die Dialektik in der "dialektischen Theologie" Karl Barths: Studien zur Entwicklung der Barthschen Theologie und zur Vorgeschichte der "Kirchlichen Dogmatik"* (München: Chr. Kaiser Verlag, 1987), 38–40.

117. *CD* II/2, 126.

118. *CD* III/3, 361 rev.

119. I am here leaning on a metaphor employed by Barth to explain eschatological transformation: "it is not winter that brings spring, but spring that banishes winter." *CD* IV/2, 839.

have suggested.[120] Though we go beyond Barth in describing wrath as God's alien Yes to the destructive work of nothingness, we are still in a position to follow him in his assertion that God's *opus proprium* is "the limit of [the] No," of His wrath, as opposed to being simply the revelation of wrath as a form of grace.

Ricouer suggests that Barth's "coordination without conciliation between God's left and right hands" perhaps reopens the way to speculations "on the demonic aspect of the deity."[121] One further use of the concept of God's *opus alienum* might, at a stretch, be taken to support this suggestion. In a discussion of God's covenant relationship with Israel in I/2, God's alien work is identified with "the strict lordship of the hidden God," that is, with God's work of "punishment."[122] Barth then proceeds to venture the striking claim that Israel's sin can occasionally be understood as "the human side of God's hiddenness."[123] In other words, God's hiddenness in God's alien work and Israel's sin "correspond and mutually condition [*entsprechen und bedingen*] each other."[124] Can Barth's doctrine of nothingness be read as a further development of this claim, such that nothingness is understood to be the "cosmological" side of God's hiddenness? His notion of God's hiddenness under Satan's lordship in §59.2, discussed in Chapter 4, suggests that it can.

Barth would undoubtedly recoil at the idea of a demonic aspect of the deity. Yet wrestling with a kind of demonic aspect of the deity may ultimately be unavoidable for any theology making an appeal to the concept of the alien work of God—not for the sake of explaining evil or comfortably integrating it into a dogmatic system, but precisely for the sake of resisting any desire for integration.[125]

I noted earlier that the notion of the atonement as an event that cleanses divine guilt can be ruled out of bounds. Nevertheless, when Barth addresses the question

---

120. See Paul Althaus, *Gebot und Gesetz: Zum Theme "Getetz und Evangelium"* (Berlin: Evangelische Verlagsanstalt, 1953), 27.

121. Ricoeur, "Evil, a Challenge to Philosophy and Theology," 644.

122. *CD* I/2, 90.

123. *CD* I/2, 90.

124. *CD* I/2, 90.

125. Ricoeur, "Evil, a Challenge to Philosophy and Theology," 644, remarks that "Barth both so encouraged and so refused" those speculations concerning the demonic aspect of the deity. Given the linkage Barth draws between the reality of nothingness and the *holiness* of God, it is worth mentioning the characterisation of holiness in Paul Tillich, *Dynamics of Faith* (New York: Harper Torchbooks, 1958), 15. Holiness, Tillich argues, is a reality marked by a "divine-demonic" ambiguity. Barth, one might justifiably claim, is at some remove such a description of "the holy." Nevertheless, Barth's positive reception of the following words from Johannes Wichelhaus's *Die Lehre der heiligen Schrift* ought not to be overlooked: "The holiness of God is terrible to man. In His holiness God has for man the appearance of a Moloch, a Saturn, a consuming fire." Wichelhaus, Barth claims, "was certainly right" when he wrote these words. II/1, 365 (The citation for the Wichelhaus volume is given by Barth as *Die Lehre der hl. Schrift³*, 1892, p. 343.)

of *why* God acts to save us, his answer gestures towards the kind of consideration I have been rehearsing above:

> Because the sin of the disobedient is also their need, and even while it affronts Him it also moves Him to pity. Because He knows quite well the basis of Satan's existence and the might and force with which sinners were overthrown and fell in the negative power of His own counsel and will. Because in the powerlessness of sinners against Satan He sees their guilt, but in their guilt He sees also their powerlessness. Because He knows quite well that those who had no strength to resist Satan are even less able to bear and suffer the rejection which those who hear Satan and obey him merit together with him. Because from all eternity He knows 'whereof we are made' (Ps. 103:14). That is why He intervened on our behalf in His Son.[126]

The "intervention," to be sure, is for us and for our salvation. But Barth, as much as any theologian before or since, has grasped that the creature's salvation and God's own glory are not two things but one.[127] Particularly interesting in the above passage is the idea that God intervenes because "He knows quite well the basis of Satan's existence and the might and force with which sinners were overthrown and fell in the negative power of His own counsel and will." It is Satan's "basis" in the shadow of God's election, I contend, which makes the doctrine of election a critical moment in Barth's articulation of the three-agent drama of salvation. Yet it is also Satan's "basis" in the shadow of God's election, which means that election, as the *beginning* of God's ways and works, cannot be the eternal resolution of the three-agent conflict. It is a beginning that foreshadows the end, yet the end is not merely a return to the beginning.

Conclusion

The intention of this chapter has been twofold. First, I have sought to chart the "apocalyptic turn" in Barth's doctrine of election in *CD* II/2. The third agent had up to this point in *Church Dogmatics* been a marginal figure. In the wake of *CD* II/2, this marginalisation no longer obtains. In election, God has risked a history with humanity marked by conflict with this third agent, a conflict not decided metaphysically but in the events of cross and resurrection as events of divine and human faith(fulness).

---

126. *CD* II/2, 124. In the light of this passage, at least, it is not clear that, in Krötke's words, "the thought of an *ontological* human 'susceptibility' to nothingness is ruled out." Krötke, *Sin and Nothingness in the Theology of Karl Barth*, 72.

127. Cf. *CD* III/3, 159; IV/1, 214; IV/3, 228; *TCL*, 30. The intrinsic connection between the creature's salvation and God's glory is perhaps the defining feature of Anselm's *Cur Deus Homo*.

Second, I have highlighted certain problematic features that attend Barth's conception of Satan/nothingness. Yet the critiques of Barth's account of nothingness advanced here are not so much critiques launched against Barth's theology from the outside as they are critiques internal to *Church Dogmatics*. Barth's descriptions of Satan and of nothingness in *CD* II/2 and *CD* III/3, respectively, throw a question mark over some of his own theological positions and encourage the reader to travel along new avenues signposted but not fully explored by Barth.

Without seeking to resolve all the conceptual difficulties in Barth's account of nothingness, this work correspondingly proceeds both with and against Barth towards a new conception of God's triumph over Satan. The effect of a more tensive and eschatological grasp the *opus alienum-opus proprium* dialectic introduced above is threefold. First, space is given for an alien work of God that is genuinely alien and not always already neutralised by a positive association with the proper work of God. Second, this space opens a pathway for thinking towards a very particular conception of "God against God" that is conceivable within the terms of Barth's theology. And third, the concentration on the resurrection as the event of divine victory takes us beyond the notion of a good salvation directly or indirectly accomplished by evil "instruments," of a "*felix culpa* theory of evil,"[128] and gestures towards an elucidation of the *ending* of the reality of nothingness—even in its form as supposedly useful instrument. The account of the third agent in *CD* II/2 and *CD* III/3, I claim, makes these developments "with and against Barth" tenable in the pursuit of articulating and developing his soteriology. It is the burden of the remaining chapters to demonstrate as much.

---

128. Wendte, "Lamentation between Contradiction and Obedience," 90n62.

Chapter 3

THE JUDGMENT OF SATAN'S WORLD

For God did not send the Son into the world to judge the world, but that the world might be saved through Him.

—John 3:17[1]

Now is the judgment of this world; now the ruler of this world will be driven out.

—John 12:31

There are only two possibilities when a human being confronts Jesus: the human being must either die or kill Jesus.

—Dietrich Bonhoeffer[2]

Introduction

The task of the next three chapters is to elaborate Barth's claims in *CD* II/2 that "the lordship of Satan was broken by the divine-human perseverance which took place in Jesus Christ"[3] and that God's reconciling act involves His "intervening for man ... against the rule of Satan in the world of men."[4] This endeavour appears to hit a stumbling block in *CD* IV/1, however. At the close of the exposition of the death of Christ in §59.2 ("The Judge Judged in Our Place"), Barth reflects on the path just taken. As the title of the section suggests, and as Barth makes explicit, this path is located within the "*juridical* sphere."[5] Barth recognises the existence of other habitable spheres available to the theologian. One of those mentioned by

---

1. Translation from the NASB.
2. From "Lectures in Christology," in Dietrich Bonhoeffer, *Berlin: 1932–1933*, ed. Larry L. Rasmussen, trans. Isabel Best and David Higgins, *Dietrich Bonhoeffer Works* 12 (Minneapolis, MN: Fortress Press, 2009), 307.
3. *CD* II/2, 333.
4. *CD* II/2, 501.
5. *CD* IV/1, 274.

him is the "military" sphere, to which he connects texts such as Mk. 3:27, Col. 1:13, and Eph. 6:11–12, and with which he associates the Eastern Church, as well as Martin Luther.[6] For Barth, the so-called military view of the work of Jesus Christ concentrates on the character of this work as "a victorious overcoming of the devil and death which took place on our behalf."[7] But Barth states that by presenting his analysis of the death of Christ within a juridical (or forensic) framework, he has deliberately chosen not to present the death of Christ primarily in accordance with the military view. Such a statement appears to deliver a hammer-blow to the kind of three-agent soteriology I seek to unfold in this book.

But this would be a conclusion too hastily drawn. It is the aim of the present chapter to indicate as much. The argument to be advanced is that the three-agent soteriology formally initiated in *CD* II/2 (and reiterated and developed in *CD* III/3) is further articulated in *CD* IV/1. To that end, two distinct conceptions of divine judgment, the place of the third agent with respect to these judgments and the attendant conception of the cosmic plight addressed by these judgments, will be explored. These two concepts of judgment are a judgment in its proper form as God's rescue of a beleaguered cosmos and a judgment in its alien form as God's destruction of an unfaithful cosmos. Navigating the logic behind Barth's shift between the two forms is key to grasping the dynamics of the three-agent soteriology he pursues. The chapter will close with an examination of Barth's reading of the temptation narrative in Lk. 4:1–13 and parallels, a reading that exemplifies the three-agent character of his soteriology hitherto discussed and lays some of the groundwork for the *theologia crucis* that is to come.

3.1. Judgment as Rescue and Rectification

"The coming into the world of the Son of God," Barth insists, "includes within itself the appearance and work of the Judge of the world and of every man."[8] This emphasis on Christ's identity as the Judge could appear to bind Barth to a theology whose governing framework is a legal relationship (*Rechtsverhältnis*) between God and the human being, with any notion of a third agent at best marginalised. Indeed, it might be claimed that the *covenantal* framework given to Barth's doctrine of reconciliation[9]—or even to his theology as a whole[10]—leads him quite

---

6. The other spheres mentioned are the financial and the cultic, the latter of which is sketched in *CD* IV/1, 274–83.

7. *CD* IV/1, 274.

8. *CD* IV/1, 216–17.

9. The introductory paragraph to Barth's doctrine of reconciliation in *CD* IV/1 contains sections entitled "The Covenant as the Presupposition of Reconciliation" (§57.2, 22–66) and "The Fulfilment of the Broken Covenant" (§57.2, 67–78).

10. J. L. Scott, for example, describes the covenant as a "dominating concept" in Barth's theology. See J. L. Scott, "The Covenant in the Theology of Karl Barth," *Scottish Journal*

3. The Judgment of Satan's World

naturally to an understanding of the relationship between God and human beings as fundamentally a *legal* one. In one of his early sermons, Barth does declare just such a grasp of that relationship. Preaching on Amos 3:1-2 in 1913, he states that "The relationship of God to His own is a legal relationship" (*Das Verhältnis Gottes zu den Seinigen ist ein Rechtsverhältnis*).[11] Barth's continual recourse to the language and reality of "covenant" throughout *Church Dogmatics* might seem only to entrench this early conviction.

The priority Barth gives to the gospel over against the law paints the concepts of judgment and the covenant in an altogether different light, however.[12] In *CD* IV/2,

---

of Theology 17, no. 2 (1964): 185. Eberhard Busch, similarly, views "covenant" as a "basic concept" (*Grundbegriff*) in Barth's dogmatics in Eberhard Busch, "Der theologische Ort der Christologie: Karl Barths Versöhnungslehre im Rahmen des Bundes," *Zeitschrift für Dialektische Theologie* 18, no. 2 (2002): 121-37. And in an essay tracing Barth's interactions with federal theology, Rinse Reeling Brouwer comments on his sense of surprise at the fact that the category of "covenant" became "such an important concept" in *Church Dogmatics*, a surprise generated by Barth's early preference for "kingdom" over against "covenant." See Rinse H. Reeling Brouwer, "Karl Barth's Encounter with the Federal Theology of Johannes Cocceius: Prejudices, Criticisms, Outcomes and Open Questions," *ZDT Supplement Series* 4 (2010): 162. For an elaboration of this essay, see Rinse H. Reeling Brouwer, *Karl Barth and Post-Reformation Orthodoxy* (Farnham: Ashgate, 2015), 107-48.

11. A sermon on April 27, in Karl Barth, *Predigten 1913*, ed. Nelly Barth and Gerhard Sauter, *Gesamtausgabe*, I.8 (Zürich: TVZ, 1976), 193. On Barth's 1913 sermons, and the themes they share with his dialectical theology—including the theme of judgment—see McCormack, *Karl Barth's Critically Realistic Dialectical Theology*, 92-104. Judgment, according to McCormack, is a theme that brought the young Karl Barth into considerable tension with his theological teachers. McCormack traces the roots of this tension to the influence of Albrecht Ritschl on Protestant theology at the turn of the twentieth century. Ritschl, in McCormack's view, is a theologian for whom "every legal or judicial interpretation of the relation between God and the sinner was to be set aside." McCormack, *Karl Barth's Critically Realistic Dialectical Theology*, 93. It should be clarified that when I later argue that Barth goes on to reconceive in different terms this *Rechtsverhältnis* between God and humanity, I am not intending to claim that Barth returns to a Ritschlian neglect of divine judgment or wrath. As Barth himself states, "The critics of the term 'wrath of God' and especially A. Ritschl … were quite wrong when they said that 'wrath' is not a quality or activity or attitude which can be explained in the light of God's being, or brought into harmony with His love and grace" *CD* IV/1, 490.

12. Does Barth really give priority to the gospel *over against* the law? Four instances of such priority from *Church Dogmatics* are worth highlighting. First, in §18, Barth reflects on the eschatological reality of a "fellowship which is ultimately and finally freed [*befreiten*] from the Law [*Gesetz*]," a reality which he speculates is enjoyed by the angels now and which lies ahead of human beings "in the *coming* world of eternal life" (*CD* I/2, 438). From an eschatological perspective, then, the life of the children of God is in a certain sense *lawless*. A similar vision of eschatological life is also advanced in §71, where Barth discusses the liberation of the Christian. This liberation means, among other things, that the Christian

Barth criticises as false any depiction of the covenant as "a purely legal relationship [*Rechtsverhältnis*], and the will and action of God recognisable within this legal relationship only as the jealous assertion and validation of the claim to Israel's reverence and obedience which resulted from His election."[13] Without denying that the covenant includes a legal aspect, Barth insists that God's covenant with His people is not fundamentally a matter of law but of *liberation*.[14] "Behind the whole form of the covenant as Law and holiness [*Rechts- und Heiligkeitsgestalt des Bundes*]," he argues, "there always stands the great context of the *act of liberation* (and the corresponding acts that followed) which was constitutive for the existence of Israel and quite unforgettable to it."[15] We strike here what I contend to be the nerve centre of Barth's soteriology, wherein it can be perceived that any

> "no longer has to live under the Law [*unter dem Gesetz*], but may now live under the Gospel [*unter dem Evangelium*]" (IV/3, 670). Implied here is a tension between life "under the Law" and life "under the Gospel." It is *not the same thing* to be under the latter as it is the former. This tension also bubbles to the surface, third, in §53. During his treatment of the Sabbath, Barth remarks that the history of the human under the command of God
>
> > really begins with the Gospel and not with the Law [*mit dem Evangelium und nicht mit dem Gesetz*], with an accorded celebration and not a required task, with a prepared rejoicing and not with care and toil, with a freedom given to him and not an imposed obligation, with a rest and not with an activity, in brief, with Sunday and not with a working day which could lead to Sunday only after a succession of gloomy working days. (*CD* III/4, 52)
>
> With the gospel *and not with* the law—the contrast is starkly drawn. Finally, in Barth's ethics of creation, this contrast decisively shapes Barth's understanding of the relation of parent to child. "In the end-time which begins with the first parousia of Jesus Christ," Barth instructs, "the task of parents is not primarily and decisively to attest the *Law* [*Gesetz*] to their children, but primarily and decisively the *Gospel* [*Evangelium*]" (*CD* III/4, 282 rev.). Practically speaking, this primacy of the gospel over against the law entails that "in the relation of human fathers to their children severity and discipline, commands, judgment and punishment can have only a secondary place, and no longer assume the primary role which is apparently allotted to them in the Book of Proverbs" (282).

13. *CD* IV/2, 762.

14. For an argument that Barth's theology, in its assumption that grace and merit are mutually exclusive categories, thereby "suffers from a potentially unhealthy antipathy towards the role of law," see John Halsey Wood, "Merit in the Midst of Grace: The Covenant with Adam Reconsidered in View of the Two Powers of God," *International Journal of Systematic Theology* 10, no. 2 (2008): 133–48. Wood seeks, in effect, to bring together the "covenantal nomism" of the New Perspective on Paul with the federal notion of a "covenant of works," and through the lens of the scholastic notion of the two powers of God (*potentia absoluta* and *potentia ordinata*) he finds in this Adamic covenant not the "legalism" detected by Barth but the dynamic of grace, obedience, merit, and reward.

15. *CD* IV/2, 762 rev.

forensicism is contained within a soteriology fundamentally "cosmological" in character.[16] Expressed otherwise, and in keeping with the findings of the second chapter, covenant is for Barth first a cosmological and then a forensic description of the God–human relationship.[17]

This prioritising of God's great act of rescue is also an overlooked feature of "The Judge Judged in Our Place," in *Church Dogmatics* IV/1. In this section, the concept of judgment is introduced not in relation to the law as such but in relation to the reason for Christ's coming: our salvation.[18] Salvation is the "positive" answer to the Anselmian question of *cur deus homo?* It is, in fact, the only answer. When Barth introduces the concept of judgment, he introduces it only in connection with this positive answer, and he therefore advances a conception of judgment and of the divine judge that is fundamentally *positive*.[19] Put otherwise, the concepts of judgment and of Christ as the Judge are, from the very beginning, concepts that are soteriological—or, better yet, evangelical (in the sense of "having to do with the gospel").

---

16. As this happens, the meaning of the forensic language begins to shift quite radically. This shift can be seen in Barth's later comment on the righteousness of God:

> His righteousness revealed in the gospel (Rom. 1:17) is not the empty distributive justice of a world judge scrutinizing, assessing, rewarding, and punishing people from a distance. Rather, it consists of his own work in the establishment of his divine right and therefore in assisting, protecting, and helping the right of mankind against all his near and distant enemies, and primarily against the nearest of them all, namely, himself. (*TCL*, 17)

17. Only with an important qualification could we accept the claim of Trevor Hart that the God–human relation is, for Barth, "an ethical one captured helpfully in the central scriptural metaphor of covenant." Trevor Hart, "Revelation," in *The Cambridge Companion to Karl Barth*, ed. John Webster (New York: Cambridge University Press, 2000), 54. The "ethical" relation between God and the human, as Barth understands it, is profoundly shaped by the motif of God's eschatological triumph over sin, death, and the devil and the corresponding ontological implications of this triumph for human existence. If this motif is sidelined, "ethical" becomes a misleading description.

18. Barth applies a somewhat technical meaning to salvation as he begins his doctrine of reconciliation. "Salvation," he writes, "is fulfilment, the supreme, sufficient, definitive and indestructible fulfilment of being. Salvation is the perfect being which is not proper to created being as such but is still future." *CD* IV/1, 8. Salvation, for this reason, is for Barth a wholly eschatological concept; indeed, he describes it as the "eschaton" of created being.

19. Though Neil MacDonald helpfully draws attention to Barth's depiction of Jesus as the eschatological Judge in §59.2—and thus connects Barth with the historical work of Weiss and Schweitzer—the fundamentally positive meaning that judgment holds for Barth is largely absent from MacDonald's analysis. See Neil B. MacDonald, *Karl Barth and the Strange New World within the Bible: Barth, Wittgenstein, and the Metadilemmas of the Enlightenment* (Carlisle: Paternoster, 2000), 234–55.

The positive sense of judgment in §59.2, moreover, is quite in keeping with a military view of salvation, the view of salvation as an act of divine rescue. The Judge, Barth presses us to remember, "is not simply or even primarily the One who pardons some (perhaps a few or perhaps none at all!) and condemns the rest (perhaps many and perhaps all!)."[20] This stringently forensic characterisation of the Judge—the Judge as the One who, in the court of law, pronounces a verdict of pardon or condemnation—is not immediately dismissed. But it is a characterisation that is of secondary importance. "Basically and decisively," Barth asserts, the Judge is "the One whose concern is for order and peace, who must defend the right and fight off the wrong, so that His existence and coming and work is not in itself and as such a matter for fear, but something which indicates a favour, the existence of One who brings salvation."[21]

The divine Judge, as depicted by Barth in this basic, decisive, and ultimately *positive* sense, has the characteristics and functions of one who delivers people from a dire situation, thereby rectifying a cosmos thrown into chaos. Barth's comment on the Old Testament judges bears this out. These judges are "described as men awakened by God and their main office is to be helpers and saviours in the recurrent oppression of the people at the hand of neighbouring tribes. It was only in addition to this activity in 'foreign affairs' that they engaged in judging in the narrower sense of the term."[22] Barth also highlights the "forgotten" fact that in the New Testament, "the coming of the Judge means basically the coming of the Helper and Deliverer [*Helfers und Erretters*]."[23] This biblical view of the divine Judge and divine judgment thus requires a wider semantic range than that provided by a strictly forensic or juridical context.[24]

20. *CD* IV/1, 217.

21. *CD* IV/1, 217. David Mueller correctly writes: "Opposing both a venerable theological tradition of late medieval theology and the history of its art—which portrays Christ as the just Judge who metes out punishment or reward—Barth reclaims the biblical tradition which associates God's righteous judgments with his salvific activity." Mueller, *Foundation of Karl Barth's Doctrine of Reconciliation*, 309. This is a long-standing conviction of Barth's. Introducing his early correspondence with Barth, Eduard Thurneysen indicates the importance of this view of judgment to their theology, stating that God's "judging is, as we liked at that time to say, using a phrase of Blumhardt's, a 'setting to rights.' God's judgment is a gracious judgment, a saving event." Thurneysen, "Introduction," 15.

22. *CD* IV/1, 217.

23. *CD* IV/1, 217 rev.

24. As Robert Bagnato calls to our attention in "Karl Barth's Personalizing of 'Juridical Redemption,'" 52n18, this view of the divine Judge as the Deliverer or Rectifier is anticipated in *Dogmatics in Outline* (a set of lectures on the Apostles' Creed delivered in Bonn in 1946). Lecturing amidst "the semi-ruins of the once stately Kurfürsten Schloss" (Eberhard Busch, *Karl Barth: His Life from Letters and Autobiographical Texts*, trans. John Bowden [London: SCM Press, 1976], 334) on the theme of the eschatological judgment of "the quick and the dead," Barth anticipates the view of the judge and judgment articulated in *CD* IV/1: "In the Biblical world of thought the judge is not primarily the one who rewards

As Barth turns to the fourth aspect of Christ's being and act "for us" in §59.2—the great positive fact that in all of this Christ has done what is "right" or "just"—the positive form of judgment as rectification is again at the forefront of his thought. The Judge, fundamentally, is the one who rectifies and rescues. When we have to do with the justice or righteousness of God, we have to do with "the omnipotence of God creating order, which is '*now*' ... *revealed* and *effective* as a turning from this present evil aeon (Gal. 1:4) to the new one of a world reconciled with God in Him, this One."[25] At the outset of §59.2, as well as at its conclusion, then, Barth creates space for a more "cosmological" soteriology precisely where he initially seemed to forgo it.

Sin as Oppressing Power

If Christ the Judge is fundamentally Christ the deliverer, from what, then, does the cosmos need to be delivered? The focus of §59.2 is on sin. This might suggest that Barth's doctrine of the atonement is "ethical" in the way recommended by Ritschl. There is a paradoxical sense in which it is, and I will return to that in the next part of the chapter. But Barth's view of judgment in its most fundamental or proper form is inseparable from a "cosmological" understanding of our plight, that is to say, from an understanding of the human creature as a creature under assault. It remains to be demonstrated that the three-agent character of the doctrine of salvation remains in force even when sin is in view, as it is in §59.2.

As a first step in this demonstration, §59.2 must be set in its wider context. Sin, we are told in *CD* III/3, is a form of nothingness. Without erasing the responsibility of the creature, Barth recognises Scripture's description of sin as the creature's "surrender to the alien power of an adversary."[26] As he argues elsewhere, sin is itself

---

some and punishes the others; he is the man who creates order and restores what has been destroyed." See Karl Barth, *Dogmatics in Outline*, trans. G. T. Thomson (London: SCM Press, 1966), 135. For a recent portrayal of the final, eschatological judgment as a "judgment for life's sake," see Ziegler, *Militant Grace*, 97–110.

25. *CD* IV/1, 256. Barth insists on the identification of God's act of righteousness and God's act of love. We should be clear: righteousness, for Barth, is *not* the "negative" aspect of the divine love nor is it the negative counterpart to divine love; it is a supremely positive perfection of the divine love. It is, in fact, identical with the divine love.

26. *CD* III/3, 310. As Highfield writes, "When the human being sins, it not only willingly cooperates with nothingness, but it also falls prey to it." Ron Highfield, *Barth and Rahner in Dialogue: Toward an Ecumenical Understanding of Sin and Evil* (New York: Peter Lang, 1989), 66. For Rudolf Bultmann, individual responsibility and determination by an outside force constitute a contradictory pair in the New Testament witness. He writes: "Criticism is especially called for ... by a peculiar contradiction that runs throughout the New Testament: on the one hand, human beings are cosmically determined, and, on the other hand, they are summoned to decision; on the one hand, sin is fate, and, on the other hand, it is guilt." Rudolf Bultmann, "New Testament and Mythology: The Problem of Demythologizing the New Testament Proclamation (1941)," in *New Testament and Mythology and Other Basic*

a usurping force, and with its "usurped authority and power" it has become, if *not de iure* then *de facto*, "my owner and lord."[27] Sin, so understood, is not fundamentally the "impossible possibility" of the *act* of the creature as it rejects the grace of God nor is it fundamentally a relational concept, though it is undeniably these also.[28] More fundamentally still, sin is a usurping and enslaving *power*.[29] As declared by Barth in his *Shorter Commentary on Romans*, "Sin and obedience are ... not in the first place our actions, but powers which have dominion over us."[30] The cosmos

Writings, ed. and trans. Schubert M. Ogden (Philadelphia, PA: Fortress Press, 1984), 11. The idea of an opposition between responsibility and enslavement is not unique to Bultmann. If we recall Martinus de Boer's distinction between forensic apocalyptic and cosmological apocalyptic outlined in our introduction, a considerable aspect of this distinction is whether the emphasis is placed on agency and responsibility (forensic apocalyptic) or on enslavement (cosmological apocalyptic). Lou Martyn, for instance, similarly opposes "personal guilt" and "corporate enslavement," with Paul's theology showing interest in the latter and not the former. Martyn, *Galatians*, 101. The target of Martyn's critique, it must be said, is not "responsibility" or "guilt" as such, but "the picture of the human being as a lonely and basically autonomous figure." J. Louis Martyn, "Afterword: The Human Moral Drama," in *Apocalyptic Paul: Cosmos and Anthropos in Romans 5–8*, ed. Beverly Roberts Gaventa (Waco, TX: Baylor University Press, 2013), 162. Indeed, in this later treatment of the matter, Martyn does not strictly oppose sin as power and sin as act but locates them in a relationship in which the former, for Paul, is *primary* and the latter *secondary*. This ordered relationship notwithstanding, however, he continues to perceive a "tension" between the two that is "real and complex" (163). As an aid to explaining it, he pictures the sinner as a prisoner who has become complicit with the jailer. This picture, I think, is one that is in essence shared by Barth, though as will be observed below, Barth is even more specific: the prisoner is complicit with the jailer by putting to death the One who has come to liberate.

27. *CD* IV/1, 587. Barth states this in his exegesis of Romans 7–8 in his doctrine of justification.

28. On sin as the impossible act of the human creature, see John Webster, *Barth* (London: Continuum, 2000), 102; *Barth's Ethics of Reconciliation* (Cambridge: Cambridge University Press, 1995), 94–5; Matthew Rose, *Ethics with Barth: God, Metaphysics and Morals* (Farnham: Ashgate, 2010), 187–95. On sin as a relational concept, see Matt Jenson, *The Gravity of Sin: Augustine, Luther and Barth on* homo incurvatus in se (London: T&T Clark, 2007).

29. Wolf Krötke, in an outline of Barth's concept of sin, speaks of sin as possessing an "annihilating force" by which human beings are powerfully seized. See Wolf Krötke, "Sin," in *The Westminster Handbook to Karl Barth*, ed. Richard E. Burnett (Louisville, KY: Westminster John Knox Press, 2013), 202.

30. Karl Barth, *A Shorter Commentary on Romans*, ed. Maico Michielin, trans. D. H. van Daalen (Aldershot: Ashgate, 2007), 44. This insight regarding the status of sin as a subduing power can be found in various commentaries on Paul's letter to the Romans, for example, Johann P. Lange, *The Epistle of Paul to the Romans*, trans. John F. Hurst (New York: Charles Scribner's Sons, 1869); Frédéric Godet, *Commentary on St. Paul's Epistle to the Romans*, trans. A. Cusin, vol. 1 (Edinburgh: T&T Clark, 1881); Anders Nygren, *Commentary on*

dwells "under the dominion of sin,"[31] with the sinner understood by Barth as one who is "in bondage" to it.[32] The work of Christ thus involves nothing less than "a transformation [*Veränderung*] from the dominion of sin to the dominion of righteousness."[33] When Barth refers to sin as a "power that has been overthrown," the implication is that sin is a power that *needed* to be overthrown, that it is a power that had illegitimately seized control.[34] If sin is understood in this light, Christ the Judge of sin is, fundamentally, sin's overthrower, the One who rescues the cosmos from sin's seizure of power.

This cosmological understanding of sin is accompanied by a somewhat peculiar and unsettling, even "nihilistic," set of anthropological claims.[35] Barth states in *CD* II/2 that "Man in himself and as such, confronted with Satan and his kingdom, has in his creaturely freedom no power to reject that which in His divine freedom God rejects."[36] As a description of the sinful human, this could be understood as a fairly conventional articulation of a particularly Protestant sensibility. But Barth intends this as a description of the human as a good, unfallen creature. He writes: "The very fact that man was not God but a creature … had meant already a certain jeopardising of the honour of God as whose instrument man had been created."[37]

Romans, trans. C. Rasmussen (Philadelphia, PA: Fortress Press, 1949); Ernst Käsemann, *Commentary on Romans*, trans. Geoffrey W. Bromiley (Grand Rapids, MI: Eerdmans, 1980); James D. G. Dunn, *Romans 1-8* (Dallas: Word Books, 1988); Joseph A. Fitzmyer, *Romans: A New Translation with Introduction and Commentary* (New York: Doubleday, 1993); Douglas J. Moo, *Epistle to the Romans* (Grand Rapids, MI: Eerdmans, 1996); Robert Jewett, *Romans: A Commentary*, ed. Eldon Jay Epp (Minneapolis, MN: Fortress Press, 2006).

31. *CD* IV/1, 144.
32. *CD* III/2, 36.
33. *CD* II/1, 456 rev.
34. *CD* II/1, 456. Donald Bloesch argues that Barth "goes beyond" the classical view by denying the idea of the devil having "rights over man," a denial which rules out the notion of a transaction with the devil. Bloesch, *Jesus Is Victor!*, 44. But does Barth entirely lack the notion of Satan as one who has "rights" over the human creature? Barth's description in *CD* IV/3 of Christ the Victor as the One "who robbed the devil of his right to [human beings] and death of its power over them" suggests that the classical idea of the devil's rights is not entirely foreign to him. *CD* IV/3, 390 rev.
35. In Maarten Wisse's essay on Augustine and Barth referenced above, he mentions certain "nihilistic" elements in Barth's theology, elements not shared by the Radical Orthodox appropriations of Barth's theology of grace (Wisse, "Was Augustine a Barthian?," 61). Though Wisse does not identify any of these nihilistic elements, I think Barth's view of the human creature as presently outlined is a reasonable candidate for inclusion in this category.
36. *CD* II/2, 122 rev.
37. *CD* II/2, 163. See II/1, 503 for a similar claim:

> [I]t is a mark of created being as distinct from divine that in it conflict with God and therefore mortal conflict with itself is not ruled out, but is a definite possibility even if

This is so because the human stands on the "frontier of that which is impossible, of that which is excluded, of that which is contradictory to the will of God."[38] And the human stands there as one possessing "no power to resist Satan," in "culpable powerlessness" (and, as will be examined below, in powerless culpability).[39]

A similar depiction of the human creature's perilous situation is further developed in the doctrine of creation that follows the doctrine of election, where Barth describes the human as "not nothing but something, yet something on the brink of nothing, secure, yet in jeopardy."[40] As Rosemary Radford Ruether remarks with respect to Barth's theological anthropology, "Creaturely existence by itself is utterly vulnerable to chaos."[41] Ruether is in fact left with the suspicion that, on Barth's terms, "the first creation was a bit of a bad job, or at least only a very provisional conquest of chaos."[42] Yet Barth, in *CD* IV/2, expressly refrains from equating creaturely vulnerability with "an innate potentiality for evil" in human nature. Instead he insists that, "unlike God, man is indeed exposed to the assault of chaos by reason of his creatureliness." The human being so understood therefore confronts "the nothingness which is intrinsically alien to him ... with a certain frailty [*Anfälligkeit*]."[43]

This "frailty" is captured by a Pauline term that is key to Barth's doctrine of atonement in *CD* IV/1: flesh. In §59, for example, the claim is advanced that Christ came into the world "in order to overcome sin where it has its dominion, in the flesh."[44] The fundaments of a Pauline apocalyptic soteriology are contained within

> it is only the impossible possibility, the possibility of self-annulment and therefore its own destruction. Without this possibility of defection or of evil, creation would not be distinct from God and therefore not really His creation. The fact that the creature can fall away from God and perish does not imply any imperfection on the part of creation or the Creator. What it does mean positively is that it is something created and is therefore dependent on preserving grace, just as it owes its very existence simply to the grace of its Creator. A creature freed from the possibility of falling away would not really be living as a creature. It could only be a second God—and as no second God exists, it could only be God Himself.

38. *CD* II/2, 163.
39. *CD* II/2, 124 rev.
40. *CD* III/3, 296 rev.
41. Rosemary Radford Ruether, "The Left Hand of God in the Theology of Karl Barth: Karl Barth as a Mythopoeic Theologian," *Journal of Religious Thought* 25, no. 1 (1968): 18.
42. Ruether, "The Left Hand of God in the Theology of Karl Barth," 20.
43. *CD* IV/2, 398 rev.
44. *CD* IV/1, 198. Barth earlier defines flesh as follows: "'Flesh' in the language of the New (and earlier the Old) Testament means man standing under the divine verdict and judgment, man who is a sinner and whose existence therefore must perish before God, whose existence has already become nothing, and hastens to nothingness and is a victim to death" *CD* IV/1, 165.

this claim.[45] Looking at *CD* III/3, it can be determined that the term "flesh," as employed by Barth, does not refer merely to the sinful affections or lusts of the human being that stand as postlapsarian anthropological constants. To be *flesh*, according to Barth, is to be "a creature in mortal peril, a creature threatened and actually corrupted, a creature which in face and in spite of its goodness, and in disruption and destruction of its imparted goodness, was subject not to an internal but to an external *attack* [*Anfechtung*] which it could neither contain nor counter."[46] The term "flesh," in other words, denotes the creature's destructive relationship to the third agent.

Returning to §59.2, we are now primed to see how the dogmatic material surrounding this section seeps its way into it. Evident in this section is a persistent effort to think of sin and salvation from sin in ways that exceed a narrow, two-agent forensicism.[47] Barth's rhetoric throughout gestures towards an "apocalyptic" grasp of sin as power.[48] Arguing for the significance of what it means to say that Christ takes on *flesh*, he remarks that Christ "had to battle with that which assaulted Him as one man with others, which for the first time brought all its power to bear against Him as the Son of God in the flesh."[49] Implied here is the notion of sin— that with which Christ had to battle—as a threatening and tempting power. Later in §59.2, that implication becomes explicit. Sin, Barth stresses,

> is also the source, which has to be blocked in the atonement, of the *destruction* which threatens man, which already engulfs him and drags him down. *Its* wages is death (Rom. 6:23). *It* is the sting of death (1 Cor. 15:56). By *it* death came into the world (Rom. 5:12). And the concept of death in the New Testament means not

---

45. See, for example, Wrede, *Paul*, 99.

46. *CD* III/3, 303.

47. Wüthrich is thus exactly right to state that "in Barth the death of Jesus Christ cannot simply be broken down to its relation to human sin and guilt." Wüthrich, *Gott und das Nichtige*, 165n83.

48. Günter Thomas, "Der für uns 'gerichtete Richter': Kritische Erwägungen zu Karl Barths Versöhnungslehre," *Zeitschrift für Dialektische Theologie* 18, no. 2 (2002): 211–25, questions the narrowness of Barth's forensic model for understanding the atonement. Thomas understands Barth's doctrine of reconciliation in §59.2 to be articulated using the model of a "legal system" (219). Specifically, Thomas argues that in §59.2, Barth's is a doctrine of reconciliation which presumes a "two-figure relation" (220). The third agent, which Thomas claims to be crucial to the biblical depiction of judgment as an act in which the "judge helps and restores the oppressed, the victim of sin," is missing from Barth's account (220). Thomas is partially right, insofar as Barth's doctrine of the atonement does shift away from this restorative view of judgment. I turn to examine this shift in the latter part of this chapter. But as I demonstrate here in this second part of the chapter, §59.2 in no way surrenders the view of salvation as a three-agent drama, nor does this section lack an awareness that judgment is fundamentally an act of divine rescue and rectification.

49. *CD* IV/1, 216 rev.

only the dying of man but the destruction which qualifies or rather disqualifies it, eternal death, death as the invincibly threatening force of dissolution.[50]

Sin and death are hereby presented as forces in league with one another. And sin, crucially, is understood not only as a breach of law but also as the source of cosmic destruction, a corrupting power under which humanity suffers—indeed, as a corrupting power under which *God* suffers. As Barth explains,

> We are not dealing merely with any suffering, but with the suffering of God and this man in face of the destruction which threatens all creation and every individual, thus compromising God as the Creator. We are dealing with the painful confrontation of God and this man not merely with any evil, not merely with death, but with eternal death, with the power of nothingness. Therefore we are not dealing merely with any sin, or with many sins, which might wound God again and again, and only especially perhaps at this point, and the consequences of which this man had only to suffer in part and freely willed to do so. We are dealing with sin itself and as such.[51]

The event of the passion of Christ, we can observe, is persistently described by Barth with recourse to military imagery. This event is a contest, a confrontation, a struggle between the power of God and the power of nothingness in its form as sin. And it is a contest being fought over the destiny of the cosmos, whose enthrallment to sin means that it is "rushing headlong into nothing [*Nichts*], into eternal death."[52] These convictions place Barth at some remove from doctrines of the atonement funded by a more ethical account of sin.

3.2. Judgment as the End of the World

The first part of this chapter has outlined the "positive" account of judgment that frames the soteriology of §59.2: the account of Christ the Judge as the One who comes to rescue the cosmos from the chaos that jeopardises it. When it comes to the matter of what the cross means and does, however, Barth is wary of simply developing this positive account of judgment. This wariness merits further scrutiny.

Without surrendering the primary and positive conception of judgment as a cosmic rectification and rescue, the claim of Barth's doctrine of reconciliation is that this rescue does not occur without a *Weltende*, an end of the world, an apocalypse. "It is not by the giving of medicine, or by an operation," Barth suggests, "but by the killing of the patient that help is brought."[53] The task at hand is to catch

50. *CD* IV/1, 253.
51. *CD* IV/1, 247.
52. *CD* IV/1, 213 rev.
53. *CD* IV/1, 296.

sight of the logic underpinning Barth's shift of focus to this "negative" form of God's judgment in §59.2. To do so I will consider the description of the cosmos as Satan's cosmos in §59.2, finding in this description a thread that runs through *Church Dogmatics*.

Satan is a figure regularly neglected by interpreters of Barth's doctrine of the atonement in §59.2. Yet for Barth, I argue, the coming of the cosmic deliverer reveals the cosmos to be Satan's cosmos.[54] As the Fourth Evangelist puts it, "this is the judgment, that the light has come into the world, and people loved darkness rather than light because their deeds were evil" (Jn 3:19). But what does it mean for the cosmos to be Satan's cosmos? First, I demonstrate that this is not a metaphysical description of the cosmos but a practical, and, ultimately, christological-eschatological one. The coming of the Messiah reveals the world to be under the power of the third agent, since the world rejects its divine rescuer. Second, I suggest that this absurd rejection, and God's strange willingness to be the God of wrath that sinful humanity desires Him to be, is what ultimately accounts for Barth's shift to negative, death-dealing judgment.

The Cosmos as Servant of Satan

One of the most decisive yet enigmatic elements of Barth's exegesis of the temptations in the wilderness in §59.2 is the description of Satan as the one "to whom the world belongs."[55] Much that Barth says concerning the doctrine of salvation is illuminated when this description is borne in mind, yet it is a description susceptible to misinterpretation at every turn. It is for this reason worth lingering over. What does Barth intend to signify with this striking claim? And what is at stake in making it? Material from elsewhere in *Church Dogmatics* will prove instructive at this point.

The notion of the cosmos as the kingdom of Satan receives its first explicit and sustained development in *Church Dogmatics* during Barth's discussion of Judas's "handing-over" or "delivery" of Jesus in *CD* II/2.[56] This is a notion anticipated earlier in the same part-volume. The elected covenant partner is the human being who did not live by the Word of God but "gave a hearing to Satan" and never more so than when this covenant partner "drove the Messiah of God to the cross."[57] Turning specifically to Judas as the "head" of sinful humanity, Barth states that precisely as the Messiah of God is driven to the cross, the dreadful reality is "confirmed that the world of men into which God sent His Son is the kingdom of

---

54. Fleming Rutledge correctly comments that implicit in Barth's notion of the "far country" or "foreign sphere" to which Christ comes—which, it should be noted, is part of the "journey" motif that governs Barth's Christology in volume IV—"is the notion of a competing realm, ruled by a 'foreign' Enemy." Rutledge, *The Crucifixion*, 510.

55. *CD* IV/1, 262.

56. *CD* II/2, 480–506.

57. *CD* II/2, 164.

Satan: the kingdom of misused creaturely freedom; the kingdom of enmity to the will and resistance to the work of its Creator."[58]

In the figure of Judas, Barth discerns the telos of Adam's original and fatal desire to be like God. Nothingness secures and exercises power over the creature, according to Barth, precisely as it entices the creature to be the judge of good and evil and thus to be the judge of nothingness, to effect the separation between the divine willing and the non-willing that God alone has effected and can effect. Barth's notions of sin as a "satanic desire" and of the cosmos as Satan's cosmos are at once less disconcerting and more disconcerting than they first appear. They are less disconcerting in that they do not necessarily point to some obviously monstrous, grotesque, sadistic impulse that governs the ways and works of human beings—though they by no means exclude such things. They are more disconcerting by virtue of what they do principally signify: ethics, the desire for the knowledge of good and evil.[59] Our satanic desire is not our attempt to be as bad as Satan but to be like God. Barth's theological ethics in *CD* II/2, his notion of human activity in the face of nothingness in *CD* III/3, and his doctrine of sin in *CD* IV/1 are all united on this point.[60] In this satanic desire for the knowledge of good and evil, Barth detects "an outward air of the most serious responsibility, the most stringent sense of duty, the most militant virtue." The human being who wills to be the judge of good and evil "wants to stand at God's side in defence of the cosmos great and small against the invasion of chaos and disorder and wrong—himself a cherub with drawn sword at the gate of paradise, or at the very least a watchman on the walls of Jerusalem."[61]

A critical question might be raised at this juncture: is this defence not the fulfilment of the vocation given to human beings as those who stand on the frontier of nothingness? Barth is emphatic that it is not. On the contrary, "it is a really shattering fact that he is mistaken in all this, that he ought not to do it at any cost, because he lets hell loose by doing it."[62] Barth explains why and how this is the case as follows:

> Because he is not the man to cut this figure, and if he thinks that he is, then he is well on the way to creating the very opposite of all that he intends to create in his godless goodness—unleashing chaos and disorder and wrong. Because he already gives place to them by this very fact. It is an unleashing of evil when the man to whom it does *not* belong to distinguish evil from good and good from

---

58. *CD* II/2, 501.

59. Barth expresses some surprise that more offence is not taken in the church at the fact that in Gen. 3 "the desire of man for a knowledge of good and evil is represented as an evil desire, indeed the one evil desire which is so characteristic and fatal for the whole race" *CD* IV/1, 449.

60. *CD* II/2, 594–99; III/3, 355–6; IV/1, 446–53.

61. *CD* IV/1, 450.

62. *CD* IV/1, 450.

evil, who is *not* asked to do so, who *cannot*, who is prevented and forbidden, still wants to be the man who can and pretends that he is this strong man. The truth is that when man thinks that he can hold the front against the devil in his own strength and by his own invention and intention, the devil has already gained his point. And he looks triumphantly over his shoulder from behind, for man has now become a great fighter in his cause."[63]

Our attempts to ward off chaos only betray us as the servants of chaos. We have usurped the position and role that belong to God. This role, it should be stressed, is not that of an "Architect, Guarantor and Executor" of a system of good and evil.[64] Barth, when he thinks of God as the Judge, does not think of God as the One who establishes and maintains a "moral world order" wherein piety is rewarded and transgression is punished,[65] but rather—as discussed in the first part of this chapter—God's being as the saviour, the rescuer, the true defender of the cosmos against its enemies.

The satanic desire intensifies as history proceeds. Where the original Adam simply wanted to co-exist with God, Judas, as the climactic representative of this Adamic desire, "has now raised his hand against God Himself, as did Cain against his brother Abel, to rid himself of Him, and therefore to be quite uncontested [*unangefochten*] in his divine humanity."[66] Judas is the Adam who "has now gone on to an open assault upon God."[67] According to Barth, it is Judas's attempt to be without God in the handing-over of Christ that has not only "confirmed" (*bestätigt*) but "brought to reality" (*wahrgemacht*) the "lordship of the devil."[68] Put otherwise, the devil is never more the lord of the world than when God sent His only Son into the world.

---

63. *CD* IV/1, 450–1.
64. *CD* IV/3, 459.
65. *CD* IV/3, 458.
66. *CD* II/2, 501 rev. This telling of the journey from Adam to Judas finds a rough correspondence in Barth's distinct but related discussions of sin in *CD* IV/1 and *CD* IV/2. Adam can be understood to represent the pride of humanity, which consists in the attempt to be like God (§60.2), while Judas can be understood to represent the sloth of humanity, which consists in the attempt to be without God (§65.2). On sloth as the (futile) attempt to be without God, see *CD* IV/2, 405, 410. As Paul Nimmo comments, sloth is expressed in an unbelief which culminates "in our rejection of Jesus Christ." Paul T. Nimmo, *Barth: A Guide for the Perplexed* (London: T&T Clark, 2017), 135. For an insightful interpretation of Barth's account of sloth which views it as a sin that, by virtue of its inculcating of individualism, empowers mammon, see David Haddorff, *Christian Ethics as Witness: Barth's Ethics for a World at Risk* (Eugene, OR: Cascade, 2011), 395–400. For an employment of Barth's account of sloth as a helpful bridge between the Augustinian-Lutheran notion of *homo incurvatus in se* and contemporary feminist hamartiologies, see Jenson, *The Gravity of Sin*, 168–87.
67. *CD* II/2, 501.
68. *CD* II/2, 482.

Judas's attempt, moreover, is successful in its own way, to the point where Barth can call the event of the cross a "triumph of hell."[69] The act of Judas, who stands as a representative of all humanity,[70] witnesses to what Barth calls "the lordship of Satan in the world of humans."[71] Barth, for this reason, can in *CD* II/2 describe Judas's act of handing-over Jesus as "a dark parallel to the very different presupposition about which the devil can boast in Lk. 4:6—that all the authority and glory of this world are delivered to him and to whom he wills to give them." "It is not for nothing," Barth claims, "that in Lk. 22:3, Jn 6:70, 13:2, 27, [Judas'] act is described as that of one possessed by Satan."[72] Instead of being a witness to the lordship of Christ, then, it appears that Judas is a witness to the lordship of Satan, a lordship to which Christ is handed over by the very cosmos He came to save. In doing what he did, Judas thus "completed the reaction of these other men to the man who was the Son of God."[73] Judas's action, in other words, is of eschatological significance. The crucifixion of Jesus, as an act of "self-preservation and self-defence" against the invading kingdom of God, is the "last word" of the "old aeon."[74]

Two remarks might be ventured here. First, for Barth, the question of the ownership of the cosmos is a practical question, best asked in another form: to whom do its human inhabitants give a hearing, or, alternatively, whose will is done on earth? And this question receives its answer in the figure of Judas, who stands for Barth as the climax of the world-history named Adam.[75] Second, the question of the ownership of the cosmos is a christological-eschatological question, the answer to which only comes to its fullest light with the coming of the Messiah. Christ, who comes to His own, unveils the world as Satan's world precisely as His coming forces the world to choose whom it will serve.

Yet the choice is in truth hardly any choice at all. Returning to §59.2, Barth asserts that those to whom Christ has come are under the power of Satan, for Satan is "the motor which drives them, the driver who without their knowing it determines and directs their activity."[76] Human being are not sovereign ethical agents who possess the power to keep or transgress the law; they are "instruments

---

69. *CD* II/2, 496.

70. Troublingly, though in line with his broader understanding of Israel, Barth can think of Judas, the handmaiden of Satan, as the presence of Israel within the apostolic community (the church). "As the representative of Israel within the apostolic group, within the Church, Judas is indeed the 'son of perdition,' the man into whom the Satan has entered, himself a devil." *CD* II/2, 471. Yet Barth also thinks of Judas as the "head" (*Spitze*) of both Jews and Gentiles, of the whole human world in its hostility to God. *CD* II/2, 501.

71. *CD* II/2, 501 rev.

72. *CD* II/2, 482 rev.

73. *CD* II/2, 501.

74. *CD* I/2, 62.

75. *CD* IV/1, 508: "it is the name of Adam the transgressor which God gives to world-history as a whole."

76. *CD* IV/1, 266.

of the power of temptation and the tempter," existing and acting "in the service of the will and dominion of Satan," and thus "ruled by him."[77]

When Barth states in §59.2 that the world belongs to Satan, the force of this claim rests on an apocalyptic-eschatological question concerning whose word is heard and heeded. The world belongs to Satan, in Barth's view, as it is Satan's "sphere of power" or "power base" (*Machtbereich*), and it is Satan's sphere of power insofar as the human lives by a word other than the Word of God, insofar as "it is [Satan's] will which is not only perceptible but everywhere done."[78]

The Exchange

We are now approaching the reason for Barth's shift to judgment in its death-dealing form in §59.2. The obverse of Satan's effective ownership of the cosmos is that the true Judge who has come to set the world to rights has in fact become "a stranger within it."[79] As Barth would have it, the Son has truly entered "the far country." On the basis of his brief survey of the Gospels in §59.2, Barth concludes that Christ "was not welcomed and accepted in the world and by the world in which He appeared in this superiority and in which He was the reflection of the fatherly heart of God and the self-representation of His kingdom. On the contrary, He was rejected and destroyed."[80]

It is precisely as Christ comes into the world as its deliverer that the sin of the world is truly actualised. Jn. 15:24 makes this point: "If I had not done among them the works that no one else did, they would not have sin. But now they have seen and hated both me and my Father." In the light of this text, Barth claims that "it is only in confrontation with [Christ] that there is any real sin."[81] He Himself *is* the good news of the love of God for the world, yet in His light human beings are revealed to be "blind and deaf and lame, driven and controlled by all kinds of demons, even dead."[82] As Barth writes,

> The Lord has been among them. And in the course, and as the result of His being among them, in fulfilment of His proclamation and work, and as its consequence, the Lord has shown Himself their Judge, the One for whom not one of them was a match, on whom they were all broken to pieces, in face of whom they all showed themselves once more and this time finally to be sinful and lost Israel, sinful and lost humanity and—we have to see and say it—an inadequate and also a sinful and lost band of disciples.[83]

---

77. *CD* IV/1, 266.
78. *CD* IV/1, 266 rev.
79. *CD* IV/1, 224.
80. *CD* IV/1, 249.
81. *CD* IV/1, 218.
82. *CD* IV/1, 225.
83. *CD* IV/1, 225.

The cosmos is for this reason "shattered" on the One who has come to rectify it. Barth, it should be noted, is aware of "one or two strands" in the Gospels "which point in another direction." But "the main strand," he contends, only confirms the diagnosis of the human situation in Romans 1–3.[84]

---

84. *CD* IV/1, 225. It is for this reason that Günter Thomas is partially right in observing that Barth, in §59.2, does not narrate the atonement from the side of the victim as such (though as Thomas correctly points out, the perspective of the victim is prominent in *CD* IV/2, particularly in "The Royal Man," 154–264). Barth is determined to portray Christ as one who stands quite alone as He journeys to the cross. The solidarity Christ shows with the cosmos—which is for Barth an important aspect of both His divinity and humanity—is not reciprocated. Humanity is not with Him or alongside Him or in solidarity with Him *as He saves*. He saves without us, and while we are against Him. Victims and perpetrators, sufferers and sinners, are indistinguishably piled into one great *massa perditionis*, with Christ then coming to stand in their place as the judged. Is this a defensible position? Accounts of the atonement emerging from liberationist and feminist perspectives have called it into question. Cynthia Crysdale, for example, in a work aiming to "retrieve" the cross, notes that the predominant focus on betrayal and the forgiveness of sins in typical theologies of redemption has proved alienating to the disempowered, and even harmful. Cynthia S. W. Crysdale, *Embracing Travail: Retrieving the Cross Today* (New York: Continuum, 2001), xiii. She seeks to develop a theology of the cross for those who identify with the Crucified, for the "wounded victims of the world" who "discover themselves not primarily as crucifiers of a sinless one but as victims who have been slain" (8). These scholars have drawn attention to the fact that Christ did not die merely betrayed and alone, but also in the company of his mother and other female disciples (Mark 15:40–1; John 19:25–27). Elisabeth Schüssler Fiorenza makes this observation in Elisabeth Schüssler Fiorenza, *In Memory of Her: A Feminist Theological Reconstruction of Christian Origins* (New York: Crossroad, 1994), 319–21. Crysdale, expanding on a similar observation, suggests that the women who accompany Jesus to His end, and even beyond it, do not experience the cross as a discovery of their own betrayal and guilt but as a revelation of their powerlessness, a powerlessness that is then challenged by the resurrection. Crysdale, *Embracing Travail*, 11–13. Are these followers, faithful to the end, to be numbered among the unrighteous, among those who are shattered in the presence of the Lord? A defence Barth proffers for a similarly sweeping judgment is found in Karl Barth, *Ethics*, ed. Dietrich Braun, trans. Geoffrey W. Bromiley (New York: The Seabury Press, 1981), 97, and is instructive on this score. There he states that "in every moment of action, we find that we are those who do not love [God] in return," and repeats the pronouncement of the Heidelberg Catechism that we are "prone by nature to hate God and neighbor." Anticipating an objection to such a universal pronouncement, Barth warns that one cannot escape this judgment "by pointing to the attitude and acts of individuals whose unselfishness, dedication, and readiness for sacrifice seem to rule out the assumption that they do not really love God and their neighbor but actually hate them." The reason for the impossibility of this escape relates to the *particularity*, even individuality, of the universal judgment. This is not a judgment with which we confront others but a judgment with which we ourselves are confronted. The question of whether we love God and

The enmity of the cosmos, as examined above, is not placated by the actual coming of the God of love, of the God who rescues and liberates with acts of healing and pardon. It is only increased, and its dire consequences exacerbated, to the point where the cosmos, in thrall to the word of Satan, breaks out in "open assault" on God. In line with Barth's distinctive grasp of the relationship between grace and sin, we are compelled to say not only that where sin abounds grace abounds all the more (Rom. 5:20) but also that where grace abounds *sin* abounds all the more. This appears to leave us in a certain bind: if humanity's "problem" is that it is an enemy of the love of God, can the "solution" to this problem be a further outpouring of this love more or less in keeping with what has come before? Would not such an outpouring, in and of itself, inevitably redound to the further entrenchment of humanity in its enmity, perpetuating a vicious cycle of grace and hatred of grace?

Two features of Barth's thought can be seen to help remove us from this bind. First, there is its eschatological character. The coming of Christ—grace incarnate—raises the stakes. Humanity has uttered many words against the grace of God in its Adamic history. But now, as noted previously, it utters the "last word" of the old age. In rejecting Christ, the Word of God full of grace and truth, the cosmos has done the worst it can do. Its iniquity, we might put it, has reached its full measure (Gen. 15:16). Second, Barth posits a strange working of God that makes use of the last word of the old age. Indeed, as we will discover in the next chapter, God's word becomes identical with this word. And precisely as it becomes identical with this word does the focus shift from judgment as rescue to judgment as death.

There remains the issue of the transition from judgment unto life to judgment unto death in §59.2. From the human side, the transition occurs because the world has exchanged the truth for the lie, the gracious God for the wrathful God, the Word of God for the word of Satan. As Barth states in *CD* II/2, "it was not [God] but we ourselves in our culpable weakness who delivered us up to Satan and to the divine wrath and rejection."[85] There is, however, a divine aspect to this: God accedes to this exchange. Going beyond Barth, one might even say: God has elected this exchange. This is the "risk" God took in becoming the God of a cosmos under satanic rule. God thus gives to Satan's world what it wants: the law of sin and death. Grace is exchanged for "non-grace," and God, the "friend" of humanity, "must be the enemy of the one who acts as though He were an enemy."[86] As Barth puts it in his doctrine of justification in *CD* IV/1, the sinner "does not have a gracious God

---

neighbour is a question "which we must put and answer, not for others or with reference to others, but strictly with reference to ourselves." The wager Barth makes—on the basis of the scriptural testimony, no doubt, but perhaps also in recognition of the experience of Christians through the ages—is that true saints do not seek to evade this judgment but accept it as a judgment that applies most especially to themselves.

85. *CD* II/2, 124.
86. *CD* IV/1, 483.

but a wrathful God. That is how he wants Him and that is how he has Him."[87] In other words, God in His death-dealing wrath is God *as the sinner wills God to be*, while the gracious God acquiesces to humanity's desire to be rid of Him.[88]

Barth claims that "It cost God dear enough ... to send His Son as the Saviour of the world."[89] It might perhaps be ventured that one of the "costs" of the atonement to God is that, as one aspect of the history of reconciliation, He "wills" to be to humanity the God He does not will to be—the Judge (in the negative sense) and not the Redeemer, the Destroyer and not the Life-giver. To venture such a statement seems to contradict Barth's claim in *CD* II/2, that "When we say God we say Creator, Reconciler and Redeemer, not the opposite. We say the same and not the opposite even when we say Judge, even when we speak of the holiness and wrath of God."[90] Certainly, Barth expresses stark opposition to the idea of a "cost" to God that involves God "entering into conflict with Himself."[91] But as observed in the latter part of Chapter 2, there is a strand of Barth's thought that is attentive to certain "tensions" in the workings of God, a strand wherein divine judgment and divine wrath may be seen to take on a form "opposed" to creation and reconciliation. I explore this in more detail in the chapters that follow.

3.3. Temptation and Obedience

The remainder of this chapter will explore an exegetical section of *CD* IV/1 which supports the argument of the present chapter from a more explicitly christological standpoint, which returns our discussion to a theme prominent in Chapter 2 (the perseverance or steadfastness of Christ), and which sets the trajectory for Chapter 4. Though often overlooked in treatments of Barth's doctrine of the atonement, his reading of the wilderness temptation narratives at the end of §59.2 captures the "apocalyptic" significance of what is at stake throughout this section by drawing explicit attention to the three-agent character of salvation.

The notion of an external attack upon human beings, already articulated in §50, is found in §59 under the language of *Anfechtung* (tribulation/affliction) and *Versuchung* (temptation). In assuming flesh, Christ assumes a human existence that is vulnerable to the forces of nothingness and the wiles of Satan.[92] As Barth

---

87. *CD* IV/1, 539. One can perhaps detect here a faint echo of Martin Luther's understanding of the relationship between faith and God. As Luther declared in a 1534 sermon, "As you believe in [God], so you have Him." Martin Luther, *Predigten 1533/34*, Luthers Werke: Kritische Gesamtausgabe [Schriften] 37 (Weimar: H. Böhlau, 1910), 562.

88. See *CD* I/2, 63: "God does not refuse Himself to this man that rebels against Him, but adopts the hiddenness prepared for him because of this rebellion."

89. *CD* IV/1, 216.

90. *CD* II/2, 171.

91. *CD* IV/1, 188.

92. Dietrich Bonhoeffer is especially alert to the vulnerability of Christ. He contends that Christ's temptation was in fact "harder" than Adam's. While Adam "carried nothing in

explains the matter, "in giving Himself up to this alien life [*die Fremde*] in His Son God did not evade the *source* [Ursprung] of man's fall and destruction, but exposed Himself to and resisted the temptation which man suffers and in which he becomes a sinner and the enemy of God."[93] In what follows I consider Barth's apocalyptic reading of the temptation narrative, before turning to his understanding of what is at stake in Christ's decision for obedience—or, using the language of *CD* II/2, his steadfastness—in the wilderness, namely, whether Christ's journey will end with or avoid the cross.

Temptation as Apocalyptic Warfare

It is against an apocalyptic backdrop that the temptation of Christ in both the wilderness and the garden are understood by Barth. The "existence of Jesus in temptability" (*Existenz Jesu in der Versuchlichkeit*) is an existence in a "fight" or "struggle" (*Kampf*).[94] In keeping with what we have observed thus far, this battle is not interpreted by Barth in a moralistic sense, as if the true struggle takes place within the human, as a struggle between the good impulses and the bad impulses.[95] Barth presents this as a cosmological struggle, a struggle between the power of God and the power of Satan, and thus a struggle that concerns the overthrow of Satan.[96] I deal with the temptation and obedience relating to events in Gethsemane

---

himself which could have given the tempter a claim and power over him," Christ, by contrast, "bore in himself the whole burden of the flesh, under the curse, under condemnation." Dietrich Bonhoeffer, *Creation and Temptation* (London: SCM Press, 1966), 103.

93. *CD* IV/1, 215 rev. As will be examined below, this construal serves to frame the question of obedience cosmologically. For Barth, we should also note, the question of temptation and assault relates not only to Christ's humanity but also to Christ's divinity. Our assumption, Barth claims, may be that God is "undisturbed [*unberührt*] in contrast to all tribulation [*Anfechtung*]," but this assumption is "shown to be quite untenable, and corrupt and pagan" by God's being and act in Jesus Christ. *CD* IV/1, 186 rev.

94. *CD* IV/1, 259, my translation.

95. This moralistic interpretation is not a distinctly Enlightenment sensibility. See, for example, John Calvin, *Institutes* I.XIV.19, where he criticises those "who babble of devils as nothing else than evil emotions or perturbations which come upon us from our flesh." John Calvin, *Institutes of the Christian Religion: Volume One*, ed. John T. McNeill, trans. Ford Lewis Battles (Louisville, KY: Westminster John Knox Press, 2006), 178.

96. Recalling de Boer's description of "forensic apocalyptic," we note that central to this pattern of thought is the notion of sin as "willful rejection of the Creator God" that is punishable by death and the idea that the gift of the law is God's remedy for this situation, with a person's posture towards the law determining their ultimate destiny (Martinus C. de Boer, "Paul and Apocalyptic Eschatology," in *Continuum History of Apocalypticism*, ed. John J. Collins, Bernard McGinn, and Stephen J. Stein [New York: Continuum, 2003], 359). In other words, the concept of obedience seems to appear most at home within a legal or forensic framework. Yet it bears remembering that de Boer's depiction of cosmological apocalyptic does not exclude the themes of obedience and disobedience per se. What separates the two

in the next chapter. But in order to understand this "second form" of the conflict between Christ and Satan,[97] Barth suggests that one should begin with its "first form": the temptations in the wilderness.[98]

At stake in the temptations of Christ in the wilderness, according to Barth, is the obedience of the Son of God. One of Barth's decisive moves in his exegesis of Luke 4:1–13 (and parallels) is to locate the centre of gravity of this episode not in its significance for spiritual edification but in its apocalyptic significance.[99] The

---

apocalyptic "tracks," according to de Boer's analysis, is not the matter of obedience as such but what we might call the "source" or "cause" of disobedience. In the forensic track, the cause is a misuse of the creature's free will; in the cosmological track, the cause is the dominion of evil powers who "lead astray" the cosmos into idolatry (de Boer, "Paul and Apocalyptic Eschatology," 358). What is important to note, then, is that in the cosmological track, just as in the forensic, there can be talk of human "acknowledgement of and submission to the Creator," of an *obedience* that bears witness to "the fact that these evil cosmological powers are doomed to pass away" (358-9). Barth's turn to obedience in *CD* IV/1, then, may be riper for a cosmological interpretation than initial appearances suggest. Indeed, de Boer himself has sought to wrestle talk of Christ's obedience away from a purely forensic frame of reference, doing so through engagement with Romans 5:12-21. In *The Defeat of Death*, for instance, he argues for a definite "cosmological" reading of this pivotal passage (Martinus C. de Boer, *The Defeat of Death: Apocalyptic Eschatology in 1 Corinthians 15 and Romans 5* [Sheffield: Sheffield Academic Press, 1988], 141–80). Paul's decisive contribution to the "Adam tradition" of Jewish apocalyptic, he argues, is the characterisation of sin and death as "cosmological intruders into the human cosmos" (161). The motif of "personal accountability or culpability," while not eradicated, is re-contextualised within a cosmological frame of reference (161). Lou Martyn has also done much to demonstrate that Christ's obedience can be framed cosmologically. In his commentary on Galatians, he makes an instructive reference to Rom. 5:19 in the context of one of the frequent discussions of "the faith of Christ." "The faith of Christ" or "Christ's faith," he contends, is a phrase used by Paul to refer to "Christ's trustful obedience to God in the giving up of his own life for us." Martyn then cites Rom. 5:19 as a parallel reference to Christ's faith. There, Christ's obedience "names the act by which Adamic Sin has been vanquished" (Martyn, *Galatians*, 361). Similarly, in a later essay on Galatians, Martyn remarks (in reference to Gal. 2:15-16a) that "what is known about God's way of making things right is that a person is rectified not by observing the Law, but rather by *the faith of Christ*, that is to say, his faithful deed of dying on the cross in our behalf" (J. Louis Martyn, "The Apocalyptic Gospel in Galatians," *Interpretation* 54, no. 3 (2000): 250).

97. On the wilderness and Gethsemane as two different forms of the one conflict with Satan, see *CD* IV/1, 265.

98. *CD* IV/1, 260.

99. Cf. Joel B. Green, *The Gospel of Luke* (Grand Rapids, MI: Eerdmans, 1997), 192: "4:1-13 presents a clash of cosmic proportions. This account thus exhibits the basic antithesis between the divine and the diabolic that will continue throughout Luke-Acts." See also Susan R. Garrett, *The Demise of the Devil: Magic and the Demonic in Luke's Writings* (Minneapolis, MN: Fortress, 1989), particularly 37–60, for an account of "the struggle

question of obedience, as part two of this chapter demonstrated, is an *apocalyptic* question; it is the question of whether one gives a hearing to God or to Satan. In opposition to pious or psychological readings of the temptations of Christ, Barth dismisses the notion that the wilderness stands for a place of solitude, a place ideal for quiet contemplation and prayer.[100] He instead leans on what he calls the "more ancient view" of the wilderness, the view that sees it as a place having "a close affinity with the underworld, a place which belonged in a particular sense to demons."[101] Jesus, Barth insists, was led by the Spirit into the desert to "encounter" the underworld and its demons and not to engage in a spiritual retreat or a "vision quest."[102]

What Barth says regarding the framework of the temptation narrative thus comports with the overarching dimensions of his soteriology already examined both in the earlier parts of this chapter and in the previous one. The temptations stand for Barth as a snapshot of the context of the whole life and work of Christ, who is "never at a safe distance from the kingdom of darkness," but who instead lives "along its frontier," only to finally dwell "within" it in His death. This is the very content of His solidarity with us who dwell in the present evil age. As Barth repeatedly insists, Christ does not assume a generic human nature, but *flesh*, and thus our "condition" (*Zustand*) as those under assault, as those *susceptible* to assault. Christ enters into the human and cosmic plight detailed above to such an extent that He exposes Himself (*sich auszusetzen*) to external threat.[103] He is not "immune" (*gefeit*) to the temptations posed by the kingdom of darkness; He is flesh and blood as we are and for this reason "capable" of being tempted.[104] But Barth also notes an important distinction between Christ and the rest of humanity. The rest of humanity is on the defensive against temptation and against the kingdom of darkness, warned not to seek it out. Christ, by contrast, is on the offensive. He suffers temptation, but He suffers it "with open eyes."[105]

If Barth can be said to reject a pious or psychological reading of the wilderness temptations, he can also be said to reject a legal or forensic reading. To say that

---

for authority" between God and Satan as a major theme in Luke-Acts. For a work that downplays the importance of Satan in Luke's Gospel, see Hans Conzelmann, *The Theology of St. Luke*, trans. Geoffrey Buswell (London: Faber and Faber, 1960).

100. One of these psychological readings can be found in H. K. Luce, *The Gospel According to S. Luke*, Cambridge Greek Testament for Schools and Colleges (Cambridge: Cambridge University Press, 1933), 116.

101. *CD* IV/1, 260.

102. See Marcus J. Borg, *Jesus: Uncovering the Life, Teachings, and Relevance of a Religious Revolutionary* (New York: HarperOne, 2006), 122, where Jesus' activity in the wilderness is described as a "practice" which can be placed "in a category called by anthropologists and historians of religion a 'vision quest' or 'wilderness ordeal.'"

103. *CD* IV/1, 260.

104. *CD* IV/1, 260.

105. *CD* IV/1, 261.

Christ's obedience is in question is not simply to say that Christ's observance or non-observance of the law is in question. Barth suggests that none of the temptations constitute "a temptation to what we might call a breaking or failure to keep the Law on the moral or judicial plane"—a suggestion that might explain the absence from Barth's exegesis of any reference to Jesus either as a Moses figure or, more generally, as one who recapitulates Israel's 40 years in the wilderness.[106] His treatment of Christ as the obedient human in §59.2 employs the language of "second Adam" and "first Adam"; his exegesis of the temptation narratives implicitly follows this pattern.[107]

The battle, then, is not between law observance and law-breaking in any moralistic sense.[108] To be sure, matters of decision and obedience are central to

---

106. *CD* IV/1, 261. The absence of any reference to Israel can be seen to sit in a certain degree of tension with Barth's earlier emphasis in *CD* IV/1 that Christ does not assume flesh in general but "Jewish flesh" (166). This absence also sits in tension with numerous commentaries. Joel. B. Green, for example, states that the "formative interpretive context" for the temptation narrative is "the testing of Israel in the wilderness" (Green, *The Gospel of Luke*, 192). Johnson, similarly, asserts that "the motif of testing recalls above all the wandering of Israel in the wilderness of Sinai for forty years" (Luke Timothy Johnson, *The Gospel of Luke* (Collegeville, PA: Liturgical Press, 1991), 76). Margaret Davies comments that "The baptism and testing of Jesus picture him as God's son in the metaphorical sense that Israel was God's son" (Margaret Davies, *Matthew*, 2nd ed. [Sheffield: Sheffield Phoenix Press, 2009], 44). Contending against this line of interpretation, at least in respect of Luke's Gospel, is Jerome Neyrey, who argues that "Moses and Exodus are not the correct background for understanding Jesus's temptations" (Jerome Neyrey, *The Passion According to Luke: A Redaction Study of Luke's Soteriology* [New York: Paulist Press, 1985], 173). According to Neyrey, the mention of Satan in the temptation narrative and the reference to Adam in Lk. 3:38 indicate a "Genesis background" to the temptations (173). An Adamic reading of the temptations can be traced back at least as far to Justin Martyr, who writes in chapter 103 of his *Dialogue with Trypho* that "since the devil had deceived Adam, he fancied that he could in some way harm him also" (Justin Martyr, *Dialogue with Trypho*, ed. Michael Slusser, trans. Thomas B. Falls [Washington, DC: Catholic University of America Press, 2003], 157). Petr Pokorný, "The Temptation Stories and Their Intention," *New Testament Studies* 20, no. 2 (1974): 121 argues that Mark's temptation narrative "alludes to a Jewish Adam-apocalypse and expresses the authenticity of Jesus' authority through a comparison with Adam, his antitype, who lost his struggle with Satan." For an Adamic reading of the temptations, see also Frederic Louis Godet, *A Commentary on the Gospel of St. Luke*, trans. E. W. Shalders and M. D. Cusin (New York: I. K. Funk, 1881), 133–4.

107. *CD* IV/1, 254, 257, 258, 263.

108. Barth's conception of obedience and righteousness can here be contrasted with that of Stephen Westerholm as outlined in "Righteousness, Cosmic and Microcosmic," in *Apocalyptic Paul: Cosmos and Anthropos in Romans 5-8*, ed. Beverly Roberts Gaventa (Waco, TX: Baylor University Press, 2013), 21–38. Key for Westerholm is that "the language of 'right' and 'righteousness' is simple moral vocabulary" (29). To be humanly righteous is to live "in harmony with the order of the cosmos" (28), an order which he claims is divinely

Barth's soteriology, as well as to his grasp of what is at stake in the temptation of Christ. But this decision and obedience occur in a flesh that is under external attack and in a cosmos that is lorded over by foreign powers. There is for this reason nothing self-evident about Christ's obedience. He is so other to us precisely because, as One who assumes the human condition, He "broke the common rule" of all human decisions.[109] We may have reason to doubt that this obedient decision *alone* is sufficient for "breaking the lordship of Satan in the world of men." But as highlighted in Chapter 2, the "persistence" (*Beharren*) of Christ remains an indispensable aspect of God's defeat of Satan. And so while the language of "decision" is understood by some to be a (Bultmannian) term that distracts from the cosmological character of the Christian gospel[110] and by others to be a term whose pervasiveness across *Church Dogmatics* signals Barth's intensification of forensicism,[111] it can instead be seen on the reading presented here to complement—one might even say *existentialise*[112]—Barth's cosmological soteriology.

The Decision for the Cross

Barth's apocalyptic framing of the temptation narrative is carried forward by his interest in the figure of the devil, who features prominently in the Matthean and Lukan accounts. Barth comments that the devil, as portrayed in Matthew and Luke, is not "obviously godless, or dangerous or even stupid."[113] While the devil is

established and articulated in the law given to Israel (29). Though he acknowledges a need to move from solution to plight (33), and though he, like Barth, thinks of Christ's obedience or righteousness as His journey to the cross (35), it is this general-ethical understanding of righteousness and obedience that governs Westerholm's thought, as well as a theological anthropology centred on "the moral nature of human beings" (34). For Barth, by contrast, the language of "right" and "righteousness" is primarily of cosmological significance.

109. *CD* IV/1, 260.

110. According to de Boer, Bultmann's claim that Paul has demythologised Jewish apocalyptic by emphasising "individual responsibility and 'decision'" represents a deapocalypticising of Paul's anthropology and soteriology. See Martinus C. de Boer, "Paul's Mythologizing Program in Romans 5–8," in *Apocalyptic Paul: Cosmos and Anthropos in Romans 5-8*, ed. Beverly Roberts Gaventa (Waco, TX: Baylor University Press, 2013), 4. Lou Martyn's critical appraisal of the concept of "decision" centres on what he considers the false view of the gospel as the offer of a new possibility that calls for decision. On this, see Martyn, "The Apocalyptic Gospel in Galatians," 251.

111. It is the elemental role that the concept of "decision" plays in Barth's mature theology that leads McCormack and Smythe to conclude that a distinctly *forensic* apocalyptic increasingly becomes the driving force behind his doctrine of justification in particular and his doctrine of salvation in general.

112. On Barth's existentialising of apocalyptic, see Smythe, "The Way of Divine and Human Handing-Over."

113. *CD* IV/1, 261.

certainly a representative of the kingdom of darkness with which Christ has to do battle, a personification of the non-willing of God,[114] Barth is alert to the fact that the adversarial nature of the devil is subtly drawn by the Evangelists.[115]

Christ is tempted by Satan in a singular way, by a "temptation with which He alone could be assailed."[116] For if Christ were to yield to Satan's cunning assault, Barth argues, "He would have done something far worse than any breaking or failure to keep the Law. He would have done that which is the essence of all evil."[117] This is a striking claim. The breaking of the law, Barth suggests, is one thing, but the succumbing of Christ to Satan's subtle attack would be quite another.

How is this escalation to be explained? Or, asked otherwise, on what basis does Barth think that Christ's disobedience, much more so than a failure to keep the law, would constitute "the essence of all evil"? Barth's thinking is here governed by a soteriological concern.[118] The essence of all evil is, fundamentally, the act that frustrates and nullifies the salvation of the cosmos. Specifically, the temptations constitute a battle between Christ and Satan concerning a way: a way that has the cross as its end and a way that does not. In Barth's reading, all three temptations have as their essential content the idea that Jesus ought to avoid the former way in favour of the latter. Failure to travel in the direction whose end and goal is the cross is considered by Barth to be the essence of all evil because "without [Christ's] obedience the enmity of the world against God would have persisted, without His repentance the destruction [*Vernichtung*] of the cosmos could not have been arrested, and man would inevitably have perished."[119]

114. See Chapter 2.

115. Barth thinks of Satan's temptation as an "insinuation" (*Einflüsterung*) as much as anything else, a term that betrays the subtlety of the act.

116. *CD* IV/1, 261. The singularity and gravity of what is at stake here is well expressed by Frederic Godet. While Godet understands the temptations in Adamic terms, he observes that

> This trial is not … a repetition of that of Adam, the father of the old humanity; it is the special trial of the Head of the new humanity. And it is not simply a question here, as in our conflicts, whether a given individual shall form part of the kingdom of God; it is the very existence of this kingdom that is at stake. Its future sovereign, sent to found it, struggles in close combat with the sovereign of the hostile realm. (Godet, *A Commentary on the Gospel of St. Luke*, 1:134)

117. *CD* IV/1, 261 rev.

118. Barth's soteriological approach can be contrasted to Colin Gunton's creational understanding of the temptations, wherein they are viewed as being "concerned in some way with the misuse of human power in relation to the created order." Gunton, *Actuality of Atonement*, 58.

119. *CD* IV/1, 261 rev. There is, however, some ambiguity here, which is addressed in Chapters 4 and 5. In being tempted away from the cross, Christ, it is claimed, is being tempted away from the willing of God and towards the non-willing of God, away from God and toward Satan, away from cosmic redemption and toward cosmic dissolution. But

This cosmological dimension is particularly evident in Barth's reflections on the second temptation of Christ (according to the Lukan order): the temptation to worship Satan in return for lordship over the kingdoms of the world. At stake in Satan's insinuation here is whether Christ will avoid engaging in radical conflict with the cosmos ruled by Satan by letting everything "remain as it had been."[120] In heeding Satan's suggestion, Jesus would have "determined to drop the question of the overcoming and removing of evil, to accept the undeniable fact of the overlordship of evil in the world, and to do good, even the best, on this indisputable presupposition, on the ground and in the sphere of this overlordship."[121] He would have loved the world—Barth imagines Christ fashioning a "world-kingdom" together with Satan on the basis of a "Christian-humanitarian viewpoint"[122]— while allowing everything to remain as it was.

Jesus, however, resists what Barth calls this more "realistic" and "practical" form of love, realistic and practical in the sense that the world loved in this way would remain under Satan's subtle tyranny precisely in that it would be a world loved without the shattering event of the cross, or perhaps a world within which the cross is transformed into a symbol or "worldview."[123] This would be a love that is not a seizure of power, a removal of that "indisputable presupposition" on the basis of which the rest of humanity lives and acts, but a "cheap" love that acts in open or tacit acknowledgement of Satan's seizure of power.[124]

In sum, the triumph over Satan in the wilderness reveals the goal of Christ's saving action to be a breaking of the lordship of Satan, a liberating of the cosmos from the powers of sin, death, and the devil. The saving significance of Christ's obedience in the face of external temptation is by no means unambiguous, however. The temptations, we have seen, are read by Barth as temptations for Jesus to avoid the cross as the end of His way. But there is a reverse side to this conception of the temptations: they are temptations that seem to minimise the plight of the cosmos and thus temptations that seem to suggest that the cosmos can be rectified not by way of its death and resurrection, by way of a true *Weltende* and new creation, but by less radical means—by way of restoration and healing with Satan's consent.

The subtlety of Satan's temptations now reveals itself. Satan, in the wilderness, is not trying to goad Christ away from His solidarity with humanity as such. He is attempting to goad Christ away from a solidarity that shatters. The promise of

---

is the cross for Barth not also an event willed by Satan? Is it not also an event of cosmic *destruction*?

120. *CD* IV/1, 262.
121. *CD* IV/1, 262.
122. *CD* IV/1, 262 rev.
123. *CD* IV/1, 262. For further critique of the cross as symbol, see *CD* IV/3, 441–4.
124. Luke Timothy Johnson notes that each of the temptations "involves a seizure of palpable power: the theurgic ability to change the elements of creation, the political and military control of humans, the capacity to force God's protection." Johnson, *Gospel of Luke*, 76.

the amelioration and improvement of the world, of a solidarity of a humanitarian kind, is what is held out to Christ. Barth does not seek to explain why Satan would wish for world-amelioration rather than world-destruction. He does not answer the question of whether Satan "knows" that Christ's obedience unto death would in fact also be a victory for Satan in one sense—albeit a pyrrhic victory. He does not speculate regarding any plan or design Satan might have for the world. We need only remember that, according to Barth, nothingness has many forms and that it manifests its power in the world never so triumphantly as in the expression of human morality and religion—which, according to Barth in *CD* IV/1, is the content of Satan's third temptation.[125]

Christ's decision for the cross, then, is a decision that takes Him on the path towards *the* event of eschatological judgment in its alien form. The rescue of the cosmos from the clutches of Satan takes the negative path of cosmic death and destruction. Christ has decided to hear humanity's "last word," a word that redounds to its own destruction. Picking up the thread from the second part of this chapter, for Christ to avoid the *Weltende*, to steer clear of judgment in its most catastrophic form, would mean only that the dynamic of grace and hatred of grace—the dynamic of the old aeon—is perpetuated. But to execute the *Weltende*—is this not already to have ceded final power to Satan? Recalling one of the lines of critique relating to Barth's account of nothingness in Chapter 2, it would seem that, in the execution of a *Weltende*, wrath and the whole activity of God's left hand would not be ended, but that the left hand of God would finally be the ruling hand.[126] I return to this discussion in the remaining chapters.

Conclusion

In this chapter, I have illumined Barth's doctrine of atonement in §59.2 by drawing on to the three-agent soteriology on display in the material that surrounds this section of *Church Dogmatics*, showing how this surrounding material presses in upon "The Judge Judged in Our Place." A section seemingly resistant to a three-agent account of salvation can in this light be seen to develop and deepen the understanding of salvation as Satan's defeat expressed in *CD* II/2. For all its juridical terminology, the nuances of this key section in *CD* IV/1 are best grasped when its "cosmological" features are made primary to its logic. This applies especially to the central concept of this section: judgment. When viewed in its fundamental, biblical, and positive form, judgment is not primarily indexed to the law or to

---

125. *CD* IV/1, 263–4. See also the discussion of religion as the manifestation of the "resisting element" in the human in *CD* IV/3, 258–60.

126. Günter Thomas has posed a similar dilemma: "If nothingness, in the process of creation, receives its 'being' on the basis of the negation of rejection, then how can a divine rejection ever be thought of in which nothingness is not '*created*,' but really *abolished*, so that it no longer 'is'?" Thomas, "Der für uns 'gerichtete Richter,'" 217n14.

God's identity as Lawgiver but to God's gracious lordship of His people over against His (and their) opponents. Indeed, the law (however one might want to interpret that term) plays a relatively minimal role in the doctrine of atonement advanced in §59.2—a sign, at the very least, that Barth's is a juridical account of atonement of a different order. The language of battle—language that evokes the three-agent character of the salvation event—is largely responsible for that difference.

Everywhere in §59 Barth presupposes that two of the agents (God and Satan/nothingness) are warring over humanity. But humanity is not merely an innocent victim of an external attack. The cosmos carries forward Satan's rule, never more so than when it sets itself up as the judge between good and evil, as the defender of the world against the incursion of chaos. Wittingly or otherwise, however, the cosmos has in actual fact established itself as the defender of the world against the incursion of God's kingdom. Its "last word," its eschatological act of self-preservation, is to send its own deliverer to His death. God, in turn, acquiesces to this act. The world wills for the rule of non-grace, and God gives to the world what it wants. Judgment becomes a matter of the end of the world, a matter of destruction and death. This death-dealing form of judgment in the event of Christ's Passion, and Satan's role in it, is the focus of the next chapter.

Chapter 4

GOD'S COVENANT WITH DEATH

In the cross of Christ God is really and finally to become hidden from the world, from this aeon. And thereby judgment will be passed upon this aeon.
—Karl Barth[1]

Man himself is "in his sins." What help to him is their forgiveness if he himself is not helped? He himself needs renewal.
—Karl Barth[2]

Introduction

In a lecture on Psalm 117, Martin Luther ventures a characteristically provocative claim: "God cannot be God unless He first becomes a devil."[3] Considerable material content is packed into these few words. Together they appear to announce the good if unsettling news that "God for us" is not a static reality but an achievement, or, to use a term much favoured in twentieth-century theology, a story (Barth himself might simply say: a history). Put in "apocalyptic" terms, the theological claim underpinning Luther's announcement might be phrased thusly: God for us names an eschatological victory. That is the good news. The unsettling news is that this is a victory won only in the aftermath of God becoming a devil. The "history" of God for us, according to Luther, is chequered.

Though Luther and Barth might at first glance appear poles apart in their understanding of God's "history," I submit that Barth's *theologia crucis* in §59.2 and his *theologia resurrectionis* in §59.3 unfold a claim strikingly similar to Luther's, particularly when viewed within the context of *Church Dogmatics* as a whole. Whether Barth would wish to express himself in Luther's provocative terms is doubtful. But a close examination of these two sections of *Church Dogmatics*

---

1. *CD* I/2, 86.
2. *CD* IV/1, 407.
3. Martin Luther, "Psalm 117," in *Selected Psalms III*, ed. Jaroslav Pelikan, trans. Edward Sittler, Luther's Works 14 (Saint Louis: Concordia Publishing House, 1958), 31.

accentuates their resonance with the work of a theologian whose influence on *CD* IV/1 is grossly underappreciated.[4] It is part of the burden of the next two chapters to indicate as much.

We have seen Barth describe the crucifixion of Jesus as the "last word" of the old age. It is the cosmos's final act of self-preservation against the invasion of divine grace in the person of Jesus. What the rulers of this age did not understand, however, is that with the crucifixion of Jesus an apocalypse was about to break out on the world, in at least two senses of that term: a revelation of the cosmos as Satan's cosmos and a catastrophic destruction of that cosmos. What the cosmos intended as an act of self-preservation, God intended as an "end of the world" (*Weltende*). It is to the crucifixion of Christ as world-ending event (cf. Gal. 6:14) that I turn in this chapter.

The first part of the chapter will introduce the theme of a catastrophic, apocalyptic judgment by reflecting on the link Barth makes in *CD* III/1 between the darkness that covers "the face of the deep" in Gen. 1:2 and the darkness that covers the earth as the moment of Jesus's death approaches. The doctrine of atonement in *CD* IV/1, I contend, should be read as a development of that insight. In the second part of the chapter, I will look more closely at the effect of the cross as an event of annihilation (*Vernichtung*), finding in Barth's apocalyptic construal of the cross's meaning a subversion of typical forensic tropes such as forgiveness and substitution.

The third part of the chapter shifts the focus from Barth's account of what the cross does to and for the human to the dynamic between God, Christ, and Satan. In §59.2, Barth tells the story of the obedience or faith of Christ as an *apocalyptic* story by concentrating on two moments of temptation: in the wilderness and in Gethsemane. In the latter half of the previous chapter, I concentrated on the former moment. It is the chief task of the concluding part of this chapter to focus on the latter moment, while also considering the wider resonance of its themes in Barth's theology. Here I reflect on Barth's arresting claim that God has made "a covenant with death" (*einen Bund mit dem Tode*) and is "about to keep it."[5] After exploring the possible biblical provenance of this claim, I argue that the notion of

---

4. Rinse Reeling Brouwer is one of the few who have observed a significant resemblance between the contents of *CD* IV/1 and the theology of Martin Luther. Rinse H. Reeling Brouwer, "The Royal Man: Some Hermeneutical, Dogmatic, Biblical Theological, and Contextual Remarks," *Zeitschrift für Dialektische Theologie* 33, no. 1 (2017): 106.

5. *CD* IV/1, 271 rev. The English translation renders this as a "tryst with death." Following Alexander Massmann, *Citizenship in Heaven and on Earth: Karl Barth's Ethics* (Minneapolis, MN: Fortress Press, 2015), 354, I speak instead of a "covenant." I do so to amplify the radical (and biblical) nature of Barth's language at this point. Given the importance of "covenant" to Barth's soteriology as a whole, the notion of death as a covenant partner of God adds a further layer of complexity to Barth's three-agent soteriology. As will become clear in what follows, the "death" with which God makes a covenant is to be understood not biologically but apocalyptically; it is death understood as what Krötke calls "a form of nothingness." Krötke, *Sin and Nothingness in the Theology of Karl Barth*, 47.

God's covenant with death, a covenant "kept" in the event of cosmic annihilation that occurs in Christ's crucifixion, injects into Barth's three-agent soteriology a terrifying concealment of the first and primary agent (God), such that—to borrow Luther's turn of phrase—one does "not know whether God is the devil or the devil is God."[6] Without banishing Satan from the scene, without thinking of Christ's passion as anything less than a divine confrontation with the powers of sin, death, and the devil, Barth insists that "In this world Satan can have only the power which is *given* and *allowed* [gegeben *und* gelassen] him as he is powerfully upheld [gehalten] by the left hand of God."[7] In this third part, therefore, I will investigate what for Barth is the true terror with which Christ is confronted as he journeys to the cross: that Satan's lordship rests on the lordship of God's left hand.[8]

4.1. The Darkness of All Darkness

Barth's understanding of the crucifixion of Jesus as a catastrophic event of eschatological judgment is not a theological imposition. Such an understanding is weaved into the Passion story itself. "When it was noon," we are told, "darkness came over the whole land until three in the afternoon" (Mk 15:33; Mt. 27:45). Narratively, the onset of an unexplained darkness signals that "something world-shaking—literally—is about to happen."[9] The descent of darkness is one of several "signs of the tremendous event taking place."[10] More specifically, creation's dark turn can be said to reflect "an apocalyptic darkness pointing to judgment."[11] Commentators have heard in the evangelists' description of the darkness of Calvary an echo of various Old Testament texts, in particular Exodus 10 and Amos 8, in which a dark day of terrifying judgment is

---

6. Martin Luther, *WA TR* 5, 600.

7. *CD* IV/1, 267.

8. In her analysis of Jn. 12:20-36, Judith Kovacs spies a dynamic in John's Gospel that can be seen to be reflected in Barth's *theologia crucis*: the notion of a cosmic conflict with Satan underlies John's view of the death of Christ, yet "Satan is not the most important actor in the drama." Kovacs writes, "In the end, Jesus' death comes about only because it is the will of the Father (cf. 19:11; see also 3:14, 16; 8:28), which is willingly accepted by the Son (cf. 12:27-28; 10:18)." Judith L. Kovacs, "'Now Shall the Ruler of This World Be Driven Out': Jesus' Death as Cosmic Battle in John 12:20-36," *Journal of Biblical Literature* 114, no. 2 (1995): 230.

9. Ulrich Luz, *Matthew 21-28*, ed. Helmut Koester, trans. James E. Crouch (Minneapolis, MN: Augsburg Fortress, 2005), 544.

10. Ernest Best, *The Temptation and the Passion: The Markan Soteriology*, 2nd ed. (Cambridge: Cambridge University Press, 1990), 97.

11. Darrell Bock, *Mark* (New York: Cambridge University Press, 2015), 370. Cf. Best, *The Temptation and the Passion*, 127; Davies, *Matthew*, 227; Robert H. Stein, *Mark* (Grand Rapids, MI: Baker Academic, 2008), 715.

pronounced.¹² But it is possible to reach even further back into the Old Testament in order to grasp the significance of the darkness of Christ's passion. Might we perceive in the Evangelists' reference to darkness a description of creation's return to—or, perhaps better, eschatological actualisation of—the situation of Genesis 1, when "the earth was formless and empty, [and] darkness was over the surface of the deep" (Gen. 1:2)?

Barth, unlike most modern commentators, does in fact make a connection between Mt. 27:45/Mk. 15:33 and Gen. 1:2.¹³ He does so in his doctrine of creation in *CD* III/1. A quick glance at Barth's exegesis of Gen. 1:2 in this part-volume will helpfully set the stage for the kind of three-agent account of the cross (and the resurrection) on display in *CD* IV/1. Three features of this exegesis are particularly germane to the present discussion.

The first of these features is Barth's refusal to find any intrinsic value or potentiality in the formlessness and darkness of the earth, a refusal engendered by a "three-agent" reading of this biblical text. According to Barth, the situation in which the earth finds itself in Gen. 1:2 "is the very opposite of promising. It is quite hopeless."¹⁴ It is hopeless because it is a situation not of latent fecundity but of thoroughgoing enmity. We are confronted here with the realm of the third agent, of nothingness, of chaos. And the chaos which reigns must not receive "a positive qualification." Rather, "The earth as *tohu wa-bohu* is the earth which is nothing as such, which mocks its Creator and which can only be an offence to the heaven above it, threatening it with the same nothingness."¹⁵ The same is even more true, Barth argues, with respect to the "darkness" hovering over the face of the deep. This darkness is

> the darkness in which there is no knowledge and therefore no objectivity; the darkness in which man cannot be man or can be only sleeping, intoxicated, dreaming man; the darkness of which it cannot later be said that God created it, but that God separated from it the light which He had created and which He found to be good.¹⁶

---

12. C. S. Mann, *Mark: A New Translation with Introduction and Commentary* (New York: Doubleday, 1986), 650; Adela Yarbro Collins, *Mark: A Commentary*, ed. Harold W. Attridge (Minneapolis, MN: Fortress Press, 2007), 751; Craig A. Evans, *Matthew* (New York: Cambridge University Press, 2012), 463.

13. James Edwards very briefly suggests a connection between the darkness at the crucifixion and Gen. 1:2. See James R. Edwards, *The Gospel According to Mark* (Grand Rapids, MI: Eerdmans, 2002), 475. For a more extensive exploration of this connection, see Dane C. Ortlund and G. K. Beale, "Darkness over the Whole Land: A Biblical Theological Reflection on Mark 15:33," *Westminster Theological Journal* 75 (2013): 221–38.

14. *CD* III/1, 104.
15. *CD* III/1, 105.
16. *CD* III/1, 105.

The darkness of Genesis 1, then, is no "natural" darkness but an enemy of creation and covenant, an agent thoroughly opposed to the gracious will of God for light and life. This first feature of Barth's exegesis thereby places the motif of conflict at the foundation of the biblical story.

A second feature of Barth's exegesis is the connection he makes between the situation of the cosmos in the beginning and the judgment executed at the end of time. Following Scripture's lead (Jer. 4:23 and Is. 34:11), he interprets the *tohu* and *bohu* of the earth as effects of a divine judgment and concludes that "the condition of the earth depicted in v. 2 is identical with the whole horror of the final judgment."[17] Note again that this eschatological event, like its protological counterpart, is intrinsically one of "horror" or "terror" (*Schrecken*). Why is the judgment so terrifying? An answer to this question can be found in Barth's description of the world of chaos and darkness as a "world without the Word of God."[18] Here we have judgment in its most terrifying form: not a Word of God against the world, but no Word at all. A Word of God against the world might be taken to be a form of grace, a moment of loving chastisement. But the silence of God, the separation of the world from the Word? This is a moment of chaos, of darkness, of Satan's reign.

A third feature of Barth's exegesis is its christological orientation. Like all other judgments in the Old Testament, the dark judgment of Gen. 1:2 points to "the divine judgment and the end of the age which took place in His death on the cross." The darkness that descends on Calvary is in fact "the darkness of all darkness."[19] While Barth appears to render this shadowy world of chaos utterly impotent by asserting that God will not permit "the actual realisation of the dark possibility of Gen. 1:2,"[20] he finds this dark possibility to have been "executed" at a singular point in history: the cross of Christ.[21] He writes,

> This—the moment of darkness in which His own creative Word, His only begotten Son, will cry on the cross of Calvary: "My God, my God, why hast thou forsaken me?"—will be "the small moment" of His wrath (Is. 54:7) in which all that is indicated in Gen. 1:2 will become real. For all the analogy of other kinds of darkness, there is no other moment such as this.[22]

Developing further a line of thought indicated above in Chapter 3, in the crucifixion of Jesus as the "last word" of the cosmos there can be heard a (momentarily successful) attempt to "return to its essential past," to a state of chaos.[23] In crucifying Jesus, the cosmos has actually managed to "conjure up the

---

17. *CD* III/1, 104–5.
18. *CD* III/1, 108.
19. *CD* III/1, 167.
20. *CD* III/1, 109.
21. *CD* III/1, 109.
22. *CD* III/1, 109.
23. *CD* III/1, 108.

shadow of Gen. 1:2."[24] As Johannes Schreiber portrays the matter, "The powers of darkness and the primeval flood, banished into the underworld at creation, break out again and threaten sinners."[25] This, for Barth, is what the arrival of darkness signifies in the Gospels, with the qualification that the powers of darkness threaten sinners only as they threaten "the one great sinner": Christ.[26] Turning now to *CD* IV/1 and to themes of a cosmic destruction (*Vernichtung*) and God's "covenant with death," we will see how the three-agent view of the cross already sketched in §41 is fleshed out in §59.

4.2. Subverting Forensicism

That "destruction" is a key term in Barth's account of the atonement has been recognised by various scholars.[27] Moreover, that in Barth's conception of the cross as an event of destruction we are confronting an *apocalyptic* theme has recently been highlighted.[28] In much of this analysis, however, a basic forensicism on the part of Barth is assumed. There are solid reasons to view the destruction of the

---

24. *CD* III/1, 109.

25. Johannes Schreiber, *Theologie des Vertrauens: Eine redaktionsgeschichtliche Untersuchung des Markusevangeliums* (Hamburg: Furche-Verlag, 1967), 33. Similarly, Dominic Rudman, by associating the darkness that descends on Jerusalem in the hour of Christ's death with the powers of darkness present throughout His life, has argued that the Synoptic Gospels present the crucifixion of Christ "as a *Chaoskampf*, but one in which the powers of chaos are victorious." Dominic Rudman, "The Crucifixion as *Chaoskampf*: A New Reading of the Passion Narrative in the Synoptic Gospels," *Biblica* 84, no. 1 (2003): 102–7. Rudman concludes that "The crucifixion as depicted in the synoptic gospels ... demonstrates the unravelling of the old created order prior to the its renewal or, better, replacement, heralded by Jesus' resurrection" (107).

26. *CD* IV/1, 239. Cf. Luther's description of Christ as "the highest, the greatest, and the only sinner" in Martin Luther, *Lectures on Galatians 1535: Chapters 1-4*, ed. and trans. Jaroslav Pelikan, Luther's Works 26 (Saint Louis: Concordia Publishing House, 1963), 281.

27. David L. Mueller, *Foundation of Karl Barth's Doctrine of Reconciliation: Jesus Christ Crucified and Risen* (Lewiston: Edwin Mellen Press, 1990), 329; Jeannine Michele Graham, *Representation and Substitution in the Atonement Theologies of Dorothee Sölle, John Macquarrie, and Karl Barth* (New York: Peter Lang, 2005), 230; Garry J. Williams, "Karl Barth and the Doctrine of the Atonement," in *Engaging with Barth: Contemporary Evangelical Critiques*, ed. Daniel Strange and David Gibson (London: T&T Clark, 2008), 246; Matthias Grebe, *Election, Atonement, and the Holy Spirit: Through and Beyond Barth's Theological Interpretation of Scripture* (Cambridge: James Clarke, 2015), 170; David C. Chao, "Cur Deus homo? Reflections on Divine Power and Ontology in Barth's Doctrine of Reconciliation, Church Dogmatics IV/1, §59," *Zeitschrift für Dialektische Theologie* 32, no. 1 (2016): 125–6.

28. Joseph L. Mangina, *Karl Barth: Theologian of Christian Witness* (Burlington: Ashgate, 2004), 120, 127; Williams, "Karl Barth and the Doctrine of the Atonement," 241;

alienated cosmos in Christ within a forensic framework. McCormack, for instance, has drawn attention to Barth's repeated description of God's negating judgment as a "sentence," a term that seems to place the drama of salvation within the setting of a courtroom.[29] As demonstrated in this book thus far, however, military imagery is by no means absent from Barth's soteriology, certainly not from *Church Dogmatics* as a whole, and not even from as ostensibly forensic a section as §59.2. Barth's description of God's saving work as a "battle against sin" is no throwaway line; it is a description that gets to the core of his understanding of reality.[30]

Without seeking to deny or neglect Barth's steady use of forensic terminology, the aim of this second part of the current chapter is to expose a certain subversion in Barth's account of the atonement of some of the key tenets of forensicism, a subversion demonstrative of the fact that he does not operate completely within a juridical frame of reference. I do this by interrogating two classically forensic concepts that show up in Barth's doctrine of the atonement: the concepts of forgiveness and substitution. In both cases, there can be spied a subversion of these concepts as Barth seeks to grasp the full—and catastrophic—meaning and effect of the cross for the cosmos and its human inhabitants.

Beyond Forgiveness

That the Christian doctrine of salvation is chiefly concerned with the legitimate pardon of sinners is a hallmark of forensic accounts of this doctrine. In this light, the forensic reading of Barth's soteriology receives perhaps its most weighty support from his claim that "the forgiveness of sins [*Sündenvergebung*] is the central meaning of the divine action in the passion of Jesus Christ."[31] Such a claim appears to put Barth at odds with "apocalyptic" doctrines of salvation learned from the apostle Paul. Lou Martyn, for instance, argues that forgiveness (along with repentance) is "largely foreign to Paul's theology" and is replaced by Paul's own conviction that God in Christ has *liberated* humanity from its enslavement to anti-God powers.[32]

McCormack, "Can We Still Speak of 'Justification by Faith'?," 180; Smythe, *Forensic Apocalyptic Theology*, 130.

29. McCormack, "Can We Still Speak of 'Justification by Faith'?," 181. McCormack cites *CD* IV/1, 219, 221, 223.

30. *CD* IV/1, 254.

31. *CD* IV/1, 256 rev. For a recent treatment of Barth on forgiveness, see Jon Coutts, *A Shared Mercy: Karl Barth on Forgiveness and the Church* (Downers Grove: IVP Academic, 2016).

32. J. Louis Martyn, "The Apocalyptic Gospel in Galatians," *Interpretation* 54, no. 3 (2000): 254n23. Cf. Martyn, *Galatians*, 273. Similarly, Martinus de Boer observes that "the term *aphesis* (forgiveness) is notably absent from the undisputed Pauline Letters." Martinus C. de Boer, *Galatians: A Commentary*, The New Testament Library (Louisville, KY: Westminster John Knox Press, 2011), 30n42. Rudolf Bultmann, not always considered a friend to apocalyptic readings of Paul, had drawn the same conclusion in his *Theology of the*

Where does Barth's soteriology stand in relation to these readings of Paul? While he evidently does not surrender the concept of forgiveness, a "cosmological" impulse can be seen to guide his understanding of it.[33] In the course of explaining the death of Jesus as "the victory that has been won for us, in our place, in the battle against sin,"[34] Barth enlists a collection of New Testament texts that connect that death with God's combat against sin, death, and the devil: Rom. 6:10, 8:3; 2 Cor. 5:14; Eph. 2:16; Col. 2:14; Heb. 2:14.[35] Part of Barth's reason for collating these New Testament texts is to demonstrate that the concept of the forgiveness of sins, a concept connected with the death of Christ most pointedly in Mt. 26:28, is "brought into surprisingly little direct relation to the death of Jesus Christ" elsewhere in the New Testament.[36] When he turns briefly to the theme of forgiveness in §59.2, his aim is thus to interpret it in the light of the more radical (and more dominant) strand of the New Testament witness. Whatever forgiveness of sins means, Barth urges, it "cannot mean anything less radical" than "the abolishing, the taking away, the executing, the killing of sin which takes place in the death of Christ."[37]

Fundamentally, for Barth, the death of Christ is not an event that resets a prescribed legal framework. It is an event that shatters "a legal relationship fatal to the human being."[38] A particular strength of forensic language is that it speaks

---

New Testament. There he called attention to Paul's "avoidance" of the concept of forgiveness, explaining this avoidance on the basis that the apostle was interested not in release from guilt but in release from "the power of sin." Bultmann, *Theology of the NT I*, 287.

33. Barth's understanding of forgiveness shares remarkable similarities with that of Albert Schweitzer in *The Mysticism of Paul the Apostle*, trans. William Montgomery, 2nd ed. (London: Adam & Charles Black, 1953). Like Barth, Schweitzer gives a central place to forgiveness within the doctrine of salvation, claiming that "Paul regards the forgiveness of sins by God as the most essential thing in the bringing about of redemption" (217). Yet in an argument that anticipates Barth's theological moves, Schweitzer contends that "It is not so much a matter of a forgiving of sin as of an annulling [*Vernichtung*] of sin, which in point of fact becomes the same thing as forgiving it" (222). Schweitzer calls this doctrine of the forgiveness of sins a doctrine of the "annihilation of sin [*Sündenvernichtung*]" (223) and rightly calls attention to the importance of the resurrection for Paul's distinct doctrine of forgiveness. Also worth mentioning at this juncture is E. P. Sanders' argument that "acquittal" and "participation in [Christ's] death to the power of sin" are conceived by Paul "not as two different things, but as one." Sanders, *Paul and Palestinian Judaism*, 507. Put otherwise, the "forensic" concept of forgiveness is transfigured as it is incorporated into Paul's cosmological account of God's saving activity.

34. *CD* IV/1, 254.

35. *CD* IV/1, 255 rev.

36. *CD* IV/1, 255.

37. *CD* IV/1, 256.

38. *CD* IV/1, 256 rev. Here I disagree with Günter Thomas's Anselmian reading of §59.2, particularly when he claims that "the substitution of the Son allows God to maintain the legal system oriented to distributive [justice] [*die distributiv orientierte Rechtsordnung*] and *at the same time* to be merciful to the sinners." Günter Thomas, "Der für uns 'gerichtete

to the legal relationship in which the human being is imprisoned—and all too willingly imprisoned. Often absent from forensicism as a system, however, is the notion that existence in this legal relationship is part of what it means to live under the powers of darkness, under the power of Satan the accuser, under the power of sin, under the power of the law as it is itself under the power of sin and the devil. "As the subject of sin, sins and transgressions," Barth states, "man finds himself in this fatal relationship, under this intolerable commitment, in this imprisonment. He cannot release himself from it."[39] But Christ can and does. Within this conception of the human plight, divine forgiveness takes the form not of a pardoning of the old human but of a division and conflict between an old human and a new.[40] The kind of forgiveness Christ accomplishes does not amount to the renewal of a fatal legal relationship; rather, Christ renders this relationship old precisely as he renders the human entangled in this relationship old. And "*to that extent*," Barth states, "the forgiveness of sins is the central meaning of the divine action in the passion of Jesus Christ."[41]

Barth's claim later in *CD* IV/1 regarding what happens (and does not happen) to the "old human" on the cross invites further reconsideration of the meaning of forgiveness. He writes:

> The old man could not be co-ordinated [*zugeordnet*] with the new, nor the new with the old. The new could only live, and the old yield and die. The divisive [*schneidende*] No of the wrath of God, which is the consuming fire of His love, lay

Richter': Kritische Erwägungen zu Karl Barths Versöhnungslehre," *Zeitschrift für Dialektische Theologie* 18, no. 2 (2002): 212.

39. *CD* IV/1, 256.

40. Here it is finally apparent how misguided is Wingren's critique that Barth makes little of the old human–new human contrast (Gustaf Wingren, *Theology in Conflict: Nygren, Barth, Bultmann*, trans. Eric H. Wahlstrom [Edinburgh: Oliver and Boyd, 1958], 115). Barth, in a sub-section on "The Pardon of Man" in his doctrine of justification, finds a parallel between God's division between creation and nothingness and God's division between the old human and the new human. See *CD* IV/1, 568–9. On the "falling out" between the old human and the new that is constitutive of Christian conversion, see *CD* IV/2, 573–4. For an account of the meaning of the death of Christ that fuses juridical language with death–life language, see Gerhard O. Forde, *Justification by Faith: A Matter of Death and Life* (Eugene, OR: Wipf and Stock, 2012). What Barth emphasises more strongly than Forde is that, in the words of Robert Tannehill, "Dying and rising with Christ is … related to two dominions or aeons and their rulers, and indicates release from one and transfer to the other." Robert C. Tannehill, *Dying and Rising with Christ: A Study in Pauline Theology* (Berlin: Alfred Töpelmann, 1967), 7. Death-language can thus be paired not only with forensic language but also with cosmological language. For an account of Forde's doctrine of justification that mobilises it in the service of an apocalyptic theology attuned to the discontinuity and transcendence of divine grace, see Ziegler, *Militant Grace*, 3–15.

41. *CD* IV/1, 256 rev. (emphasis added).

on the old man, destroying [*zunichte gemacht*] and extinguishing [*ausgelöscht*] him
.... No compromise was made, no armistice arranged, no pact of non-aggression concluded at the place where he and all men were helped, but to an unequivocal and intolerable and definitive enemy of God and of man there has befallen what he has deserved: his destruction [*Untergang*]. This enemy is the sin of man; it is he himself as the old man who wills and does this sin. He was *not* tolerated at that place. *No* pardon [*Pardon*] was given him. An *end* was made of him.[42]

This passage brings to light several crucial features of Barth's soteriology. First, there is contained within it a hint of the broader, biblical view of judgment discussed in Chapter 3. The cross deals not only with an enemy of God but also an enemy of humanity, the third agent intent on humanity's destruction. Second, the language used here is quite in keeping with a military view of salvation. Barth depicts salvation as a war between God and God's enemies. Moreover, this is a war that is not ended peaceably but with a destruction.[43] Third, and following on from the second, this passage shows up the limits of viewing forensicism as the framework that holds together Barth's soteriology. Barth claims that *no* pardon is given to the old human being.[44] Essentially, the old human is not forgiven, but ended, destroyed, erased (more on which below). While on the one hand Barth

---

42. *CD* IV/2, 400 rev.

43. In view of the fate of this enemy of God, Hunsinger's claims that "Enemy-love in Karl Barth's theology is the heart of the gospel" and that enemy-love is "a decisive category for understanding God's love as revealed in the cross of Christ" are potentially misleading if the apocalyptic-eschatological dimension of Barth's thought is suppressed. George Hunsinger, "The Politics of the Nonviolent God: Reflections on René Girard and Karl Barth," *Scottish Journal of Theology* 51, no. 1 (1998): 77. Equally, however, Barth's violent imagery—if indeed it is mere imagery—might be called into question for clouding the purported non-violence of God's saving act in Christ (see J. Denny Weaver, *The Nonviolent Atonement*, 2nd ed. (Grand Rapids, MI: Eerdmans, 2011); T. Scott Daniels et al., *Atonement and Violence: A Theological Conversation*, ed. John Sanders (Nashville, TN: Abingdon Press, 2006). Richard Hays criticises Lou Martyn along these lines. Martyn's persistent use of the language of "invasion" is potentially misleading, Hays claims, because it suggests violence instead of nonviolence as the mode of God's saving activity. Richard B. Hays, "Apocalyptic Poiesis in Galatians: Paternity, Passion, and Participation," in *Galatians and Christian Theology: Justification, the Gospel, and Ethics in Paul's Letter*, ed. Mark W. Elliott et al. (Grand Rapids, MI: Baker Academic, 2014), 217.

44. Barth's use of the German *Pardon* in this passage is his only use of this term in *Church Dogmatics*. In the German translation of a conversation Barth held in Princeton, the word is used as a virtual synonym for *Sündenvergebung*. Barth had said: "Perhaps it would be a sign of more than political weight and importance if in that very place, Jerusalem, this person Eichmann would not be executed and something like pardon [*Pardon*], forgiveness of sin [*Sündenvergebung*], would take place—significant, symbolic, so to say, over against this whole terrible thing that happened." Karl Barth, "Gespräch in Princeton I," in *Gespräche*

holds up forgiveness as the core meaning of what God has done in Christ, on the other hand he proceeds to call into question the adequacy of divine forgiveness in itself as a solution to the cosmic plight.

Following on from the discussion of the cosmic plight in Chapter 3, it can be submitted that the plight of the cosmos is far too severe for forgiveness (in its strictly forensic sense) to be the solution.[45] For this is a world that crucifies the One who extends divine forgiveness. For this reason, Christ's death need not be thought of as an event that makes it possible for God to forgive sinners.[46] Christ's death, precisely as an event of cosmic destruction, puts an end to a world that refuses to live by divine forgiveness. If the language of forgiveness is to be retained— and Barth manifestly thinks it ought to be—then the almost violent division and discontinuity between the old and the new accomplished in the destructive event of the cross must be allowed to interpret the very meaning of divine forgiveness.[47] Also in need of correction, however, is a "cosmological" view of salvation that understands salvation to consist solely in an exchange of lordships occurring above our heads. While Barth certainly construes reconciliation along the line of an exchange of lordships, he is insistent, as we will see in the next section, that the human does not come out of this exchange unscathed.

Beyond Substitution

Alongside forgiveness, a second and related forensic theme in Barth's soteriology is substitution. One of the questions that has occupied interpreters of Barth's soteriology is whether his is a doctrine of the atonement in accord with a typically Protestant theory of substitution.[48] Much depends, of course, on what is meant by "substitution." Paul Nimmo has stated that Barth's account of the crucifixion is "unhesitatingly a *substitutionary* account."[49] It is so, he argues, because Jesus

---

1959–1962, ed. Eberhard Busch, *Gesamtausgabe*, IV.25 (Zürich: TVZ, 1995), 507–8 (304 for the German translation of the conversation).

45. On account of the fact that "Sin is a power which holds man in bondage," Reginald Fuller contends that forgiveness is too "weak" a concept for grasping the saving event. Reginald H. Fuller, *Interpreting the Miracles* (Philadelphia, PA: Westminster Press, 1963), 51n1.

46. On this see Gerhard O. Forde, "Caught in the Act: Reflections on the Work of Christ," *Word & World* 3, no. 1 (1983): 22–31.

47. Thomas Altizer expresses the apocalyptic logic of Christ's forgiveness as follows: "the forgiveness of sin is an apocalyptic forgiveness, one only possible and real in an absolutely new world, and if that world is the consequence of an absolute ending, it is thereby the ending of everything that is humanly or interiorly knowable as forgiveness." Altizer, *Godhead and the Nothing*, 95. Altizer thus calls the forgiveness of sins a "profoundly antinomian" act (96). In contrast to Barth, however, Altizer speaks not of sin's "destruction" but of its "transfiguration."

48. On this see Johnson, *God's Being in Reconciliation*, 93–4, and the literature there cited.

49. Nimmo, *Barth*, 116.

"takes our place" on the cross.⁵⁰ By this Nimmo means to indicate that, in Barth's view, Jesus does what we are unable to do.⁵¹ "Substitution" so conceived acts as a short-hand description of salvation as *God's* work, a work to which humanity's only "contribution" is its futile resistance. If this is what substitution means, there can indeed be "little question that Barth's account is substitutionary."⁵²

There is, however, a direction in which the concept of substitution can be taken that does not sit entirely comfortably with Barth's doctrine of reconciliation. Justyn Terry identifies Barth (along with Martin Luther) as a theologian "who endorses substitutionary atonement."⁵³ By "substitutionary atonement" Terry signifies the following reality: "Sin led to death as divine justice demands (Gen. 2:17; Rom. 6:23), but it led to Jesus' death rather than ours as divine mercy desired (Eph. 2:4)."⁵⁴ It is with a view to this understanding of substitution that Barth's account of atonement can be interpreted as less "substitutionary" than appearances suggest.

Barth's apocalyptic portrayal of the death of Christ in §59.3 is instructive in this regard. Rather than immediately thinking of the event of cosmic destruction in Christ on the cross as a *restitutio ad integrum*, Barth first contemplates the possibility that this event is nothing less than a catastrophic reversal of creation. He writes:

> There is indeed every reason to fear that the being and activity of Jesus Christ for us can be understood only as the ending of all other human beings, the reconciliation of the world with God accomplished in Him only as the reversal [*Rückgängigmachung*] of its creation, only as its end.⁵⁵

Put otherwise, there is reason to fear that we now exist "in the nothingness to which we are delivered by that which Jesus Christ has done in our place."⁵⁶ Barth

---

50. Nimmo, *Barth*, 116. Cf. IV/1, 216: "*Deus pro nobis* means that God in Jesus Christ has taken our place when we become sinners;" *CD* IV/1, 222: "What took place is that the Son of God fulfilled the righteous judgment on us men by Himself taking our place as man and in our place undergoing the judgment under which we had passed."

51. That this is indeed Barth's primary meaning is demonstrated in the following claim:

> "Jesus Christ for us" means that as this one true man Jesus Christ has taken the place of us men, of many, in all the authority and omnipotence and competence of the one true God, in order to act in our name and therefore validly and effectively for us in all matters of reconciliation with God and therefore of our redemption and salvation, representing us without any co-operation on our part. (IV/1, 230)

52. Johnson, *God's Being in Reconciliation*, 95n7.

53. Justyn Charles Terry, "The Forgiveness of Sins and the Work of Christ: A Case for Substitutionary Atonement," *Anglican Theological Review* 95, no. 1 (2013): 17.

54. Terry, "The Forgiveness of Sins and the Work of Christ," 14.

55. *CD* IV/1, 294.

56. *CD* IV/1, 294.

will eventually suggest that this fear ultimately has no grounds, but his journey to this position is worth tracking.

The journey involves considering a series of counterfactual hypotheses. They run as follows:

> It might have pleased God to execute His good and holy will with the world in this way. This did not have to include either the continuance of the world or a further being of man. His grace might have consisted in the fulfilment of a final judgment. The mission and way of the Son of God into the far country might have been for the purpose of setting a term to this foreign being by simply abolishing [*Aufhebung*] its existence. The judgment executed on Him in the place of all might have meant the end of all things.[57]

This is an unnerving set of suggestions which ought not to be passed over lightly or explained away. While Barth maintains that the negative possibility—the destruction of the cosmos—has been powerfully "surpassed" or "outdone" (*überboten*), he does not think that in itself this possibility has been excluded or arrested. In fact, Barth insists in §59.2–3 that the end of humanity, the end of the cosmos, is included in God's act of reconciliation. We really are confronted here with an *apocalyptic* act in the more popular sense of the term, with a "*catastrophe breaking on man.*"[58] Thus, Barth writes:

> If God in Jesus Christ has reconciled the world with Himself this *also* means that in Him He has made an end, a radical end, of the world which contradicts and opposes Him, that an old aeon, our world-time (the one we know and have of ourselves) with all that counts and is great in it, has been brought to an end.[59]

The self-giving of God in Christ is in the truest sense an apocalypse, making actual and revealing to us "that our hour has struck, our time has run its course, and it is all up with us."[60] If Barth can be said to have a "substitutionary" doctrine of reconciliation, then we must not think that, for him, substitution means that humanity is let off the hook or removed from harm's way. On the contrary, the death of Jesus under the divine judgment means "that we have died in and with Him, that as the people we were we have been done away and destroyed [*abgetan und erledigt*], that we are no longer there and have no more future."[61]

Far from saving us "from the impending loss and destruction,"[62] as Barth misleadingly contends at one point in *CD* IV/1, the overwhelming impulse of his

---

57. *CD* IV/1, 294 rev.
58. *CD* IV/1, 296.
59. *CD* IV/1, 294.
60. *CD* IV/1, 294.
61. *CD* IV/1, 295.
62. *CD* IV/1, 223.

theologia crucis is insistent—if not consistently so—that the Son of God became a human "to redeem and save us *by our destruction*."⁶³ By understanding the human being as the subject of sin—subject in the sense of both agent *and* prisoner (see Chapter 3)—Barth resists the softer analogy of a patient who is helped by the intake of medicine, or by surgery. The patient, Barth claims, must be killed if they are to be helped.⁶⁴ Their salvation is contingent on their destruction (*Vertilgung*): "There is no question that he should be separated from his sin, or his sin from him. He stands and falls with it. If it disappears [*verschwinden*], he disappears. And that is what happened on Golgotha."⁶⁵

The set of counterfactuals highlighted above, then, need not be read as counterfactuals at all. Rather, we are in truth confronted in the cross of Christ with nothing less than "the end of the world" (*das Weltende*).⁶⁶ As Barth soberly acknowledges, "Judgment is judgment. Death is death. End is end." And "In His person, with Him, judgment, death and end have come to us ourselves once and for all."⁶⁷ It is Christ and not the world who is obedient unto death. In this sense, Barth thinks of Christ as the substitute, as the One who stands in the place that the world refuses to stand. But what happens in this place is understood by Barth to be not so much a legal transaction—the punishment of one instead of the many—but an apocalyptic ending of the many in this One human, an apocalyptic ending that involves the "third agent."⁶⁸

---

63. *CD* IV/1, 222 (emphasis added).

64. One can detect a similar dialectic operative in Martyn's cosmological apocalyptic reading of Paul:

> The motif of invasion is death-dealing in order to be life-giving. To draw a metaphor from 1944, God's redemptive act in Christ must first be compared to the cross-channel invasion as that event was experienced by the Germans. Only as a second step can one compare God's redemptive act to the cross-channel invasion of 1944 as it was experienced by the Germans' captives. (Martyn, *Galatians*, 382)

65. *CD* IV/1, 296 rev.

66. *CD* IV/1, 296.

67. *CD* IV/1, 296 rev.

68. With this apocalyptic subversion—or, perhaps better, redescription—of substitution I am not putting Barth on the side of the "liberal" or "modernist" theologians who, according to F. W. Camfield, rejected the idea of substitution out of hand as immoral or illogical. Camfield's passionate defence of a substitutionary atonement begins, in fact, with a quote from Barth: "I believe that we have to learn anew what the Holy Scriptures say and mean by substitution of Jesus Christ and satisfaction." F. W. Camfield, "The Idea of Substitution in the Doctrine of the Atonement," *Scottish Journal of Theology* 1, no. 3 (1948): 282, quoting *God in Action*, 123. Barth's radical reformulation of the doctrine of substitution (and satisfaction) in *CD* IV/1 is, I submit, of a piece with the "learning anew" recommended by him in the 1930s. What is more, Camfield's own doctrine of substitution is in some ways a departure from more individualist and forensic notions. "Christ," he states, "is the name of a new cosmos which is set for man's faith and trust in place of the old; a new realm of

Berkouwer is for this reason right to observe—though he observes it as a point of criticism—that Barth deploys concepts related to substitution in such a way that their meaning, as put forward in the Reformation confessions, is wholly transformed.[69] "The heart of Barth's idea of substitution," Berkouwer claims, is that God's judgment "*includes our dying*, and, in view of Christ's work, we have no future anymore."[70] The association of Barth with a "substitutionary" view of atonement that thinks of sinful humanity *avoiding* death and destruction by virtue of Christ the Substitute becomes severely strained.[71] The eschatological division of

reality which is given (*note*, given) in place of the old realms of nature, man, and history" (287). With this cosmological rendering of substitution, in which "Christ comes to take the place of the world" (288), Barth would be in agreement. For in this rendering something is "given to [the human] in place of what he has, a new world in place of the old" (288). In the end, while Camfield is critical of Aulén's *Christus Victor* model, he is not as far from certain "cosmological apocalyptic" accounts of salvation as initial appearances suggest.

69. Bertold Klappert, similarly, argues that Barth moves away from a "guilt-and-punishment, merit-and-imputation oriented concept of representation in favour of a Christological-personal concept of representation" and that he does so in response to Socinian critiques of substitution and as a correcting and deepening of this concept. Klappert, *Die Auferweckung des Gekreuzigten*, 207.

70. Berkouwer, *The Triumph of Grace in the Theology of Karl Barth*, 317. In his treatment of the atonement, Bruce Demarest comes to a similar conclusion to Berkouwer: though Barth employs the language of substitution, he "diverges significantly from the orthodox formulation." He does so, according to Demarest, insofar as he denies the notion that on the cross Christ bears the penalty of human sin and thus propitiates the wrath of an offended God. Instead, writes Demarest, "on the cross the punishment of God fell on him and on us." Demarest, *The Cross and Salvation*, 157. See also Klooster, *The Significance of Barth's Theology*, 96, where it is claimed that the "context of discussion" gives to the term "substitution" "a meaning quite different from the historic Reformed conception."

71. A "participatory" account of the atonement suggests itself as an alternative to a "substitutionary" account. Paul Tillich, for example, suggests that "The replacement of the concept of substitution by the concept of participation seems to be a way to a more adequate doctrine of atonement, in which the objective and the subjective sides are balanced." Paul Tillich, *Systematic Theology, Volume II: Existence and The Christ* (London: University of Chicago Press, 1957), 173. Yet two cautions ought to be heeded with respect to considering Barth's soteriology in light of this suggestion from Tillich. First, the meaning of "substitution" outlined by Nimmo—that it refers to salvation as a divine work alone—must not be jettisoned. Second, and following on from this, the idea of "participation," if it is to be applicable to Barth at this point, must not signal a requirement for the human agent *actively* "to partake in the event" (contra Grebe, *Election, Atonement, and the Holy Spirit*, 192). Human participation is not first a product of human decision and agency but an inescapable implicate of the fact that Christ is the Second Adam who alone has taken humanity to Himself. Understood in this way, Barth can indeed be seen to bring "participation and substitution together in such a way that neither can be described apart from the other." Adam Neder, *Participation in Christ: An Entry into Karl Barth's* Church

"the human" into "old" and "new" tends to be obscured by this "substitutionary" view, and while Barth is not immune from statements reminiscent of this position, Bertold Klappert correctly concludes that Barth's understanding of substitution/representation is ultimately at some remove from any understanding "oriented on the identity of the ego." Instead, Klappert asserts that, for Barth, "the death of Jesus Christ is about the 'hominem auferri' ['human destroyed'] (Luther) which shatters the identity of the human."[72] As we observed earlier, it is about the apocalyptic ending of a world inseparable from sin. Barth connects this apocalyptic ending with a "covenant with death." It is to this strange covenant that I turn in what follows.

4.3. A Covenant with Death

Barth, as discussed previously, reads the wilderness temptations as a prefiguration of Christ's passion and Christ's passion as the climax of the way that began with Christ's baptism and the subsequent wilderness temptations.[73] The victory in the wilderness leads directly to the anguish of Gethsemane. But there is in Barth's view a decisive difference between the two narratives. In the wilderness he finds no evidence of any "hesitation or questioning on the part of Jesus."[74] There is an absoluteness and resoluteness to the resistance to Satan offered there. Gethsemane,

---

Dogmatics (Louisville, KY: Westminster John Knox Press, 2009), 23. As Hendry, summing up Barth's doctrine of atonement, rightly observes, "The Passion of Christ is not only our judgment, but our annihilation; since he went to the cross in our place, we are crucified with him; we are done away with; our existence has now no object and no future." Hendry, *The Gospel of the Incarnation*, 125. For further discussion of participation in Barth's theology, see also Grant Macaskill, *Union with Christ in the New Testament* (Oxford: Oxford University Press, 2013), 92–9 and Keith L. Johnson, "Karl Barth's Reading of Paul's Union with Christ," in *"In Christ" in Paul: Explorations in Paul's Theology of Union and Participation*, ed. Michael J. Thate, Kevin J. Vanhoozer, and Constantine R. Campbell (Tübingen: Mohr Siebeck, 2014), 453–74.

72. Klappert, *Die Auferweckung des Gekreuzigten*, 219. Luther, in his early lectures on Romans, discusses the "removal" of the human in the context of the contest between metaphysical-moral reasoning on one side and apostolic thinking on the other. The metaphysicians and moralists, who stand on the side of human righteousness, have it as their goal "to remove and to change the sins and to keep man intact" (194). The apostle, by contrast, declares "that it is man rather than sin that is taken away, so that sin continues as something that remains and man is cleansed from sin rather than that the opposite is the case" (193–4). See Martin Luther, *Lectures on Romans*, ed. and trans. Wilhelm Pauck, The Library of Christian Classics (Louisville, KY: Westminster John Knox Press, 2006).

73. *CD* IV/1, 264.

74. *CD* IV/1, 265.

however, tells a different story.⁷⁵ It tells of the anguish of Christ as the definitive hour approaches, of His asking after some other potential alternative to what is about to happen, of a momentary "stumbling," of a "pause and trembling."⁷⁶ In the light of this stark difference, Barth is led to ask, "What is the frightful thing which, according to these passages, He foresaw in His suffering and dying, which now forces Him to this terrified and shaken halt, to this question whether it really has to be, as had not been the case in the wilderness?"⁷⁷ The third part of this chapter seeks to grapple with Barth's answer to this question, and to tease out some of its potential consequences.⁷⁸ I will do so by elaborating Barth's notion of God's "covenant with death."

First, I outline the theological resonances that Barth's notion of a "covenant with death" has with the sole biblical use of this phrase in Isaiah 28 and examine Barth's shift from Isaiah's notion of *humanity's* covenant with death to his own notion of *God's* covenant with death. Second, I critically examine "the hidden God" who emerges in §59.2 and whose identity with the revealed God cannot be presumed. Here, though aware that I am venturing into theological territory Barth sought to leave behind, there is a case to be made that the idea of God's faithfulness to God's "covenant with death" introduces a certain conflict into the divine being.

---

75. It should be emphasised, however, that Gethsemane still tells an *apocalyptic* story. Fleming Rutledge rightly draws attention to the fact that Barth "emphasizes Gethsemane in specifically apocalyptic terms as a 'world-occurrence,' the collision of the aeons, the final and climactic confrontation with Satan." Fleming Rutledge, *The Crucifixion: Understanding the Death of Jesus Christ* (Grand Rapids, MI: Eerdmans, 2015), 374n67. Rutledge, in her understanding of Christ in Gethsemane as a "combatant" operating on an "apocalyptic battleground," is in close proximity to Barth in his reading of this second and decisive temptation narrative. Where Barth will speak of the "coincidence" of the divine and satanic will, Rutledge speak of the coincidence of God's judgment upon the ruler of this world and the judgment that Jesus takes upon himself. There is a subtle difference between these two "coincidences," however. While Rutledge clarifies that "The violence that we see in the crucifixion is the work of the Enemy" (500), Barth, we will discover, finds the true terror of the cross in the fact that in this apocalyptic act of violence Jesus also and primarily has to do with *God*, with the God of a strange "covenant with death."

76. *CD* IV/1, 265.

77. *CD* IV/1, 265.

78. I have learned much from Paul Dafydd Jones's essay "Karl Barth on Gethsemane," *International Journal of Systematic Theology* 9, no. 2 (2007): 148–71, in which the three-agent character of this episode is kept firmly in view. However, where Jones could only briefly broach Barth's "difficult perspective" on Gethsemane—Barth's perspective that in this event the will and work and word of God and the will and work and word of Satan are identical—I seek to offer a more extensive (and more critical) analysis of this perspective and its implications.

A Biblical Allusion?

The term "covenant with death" appears in Barth's claim that "*Gott selbst unverkennbar einen Bund mit dem Tode geschlossen hatte*"[79] but is present nowhere else in *Church Dogmatics*.[80] From where does Barth derive it? Alexander Massmann has identified Luther's 1535 *Commentary on Galatians* as a key influence on Barth's thought at this point.[81] Barth's "covenant with death," according to Massmann, is a variation of Luther's notion of "God's punishment through the law."[82] Though I too take Luther's influence to be important at this point, there is another place to which I propose one might turn for interpretive help.

The precise term "covenant with death" appears in Isaiah 28.[83] I make no claim that Barth had this specific text in mind as he wrote §59.2.[84] But a brief examination of Isa. 28:15-22 helpfully illumines some of the theological moves Barth makes at this crucial juncture of the doctrine of reconciliation, and such illumination renders at least plausible the possibility that Barth had this particular passage in mind when drawing on the provocative phrase. And even if this were not the case, or cannot be demonstrated to be so, Isaiah 28 provides a heuristic hermeneutical lens for grasping Barth's complex formulations at this point in *Church Dogmatics*.

In Isaiah 28, it is the rulers of Jerusalem who boast in verse 15 that "We have entered into a covenant with death" (*Mit dem Tod haben wir einen Bund geschlossen*).[85] The "covenant with death" is entered into for the sake of protection, so that when the "overwhelming scourge" comes, these rulers boast that "it cannot

---

79. *KD* IV/1, 298.

80. That being noted, the roots of the concept, if not the precise terminology, can be traced back to *CD* II/2, in particular to the discussion of Christ being handed over by God to the power of Satan on pp. 480–506. In a 1927 Easter article, Barth uses the term "*Bund mit dem Tode*," though in a different sense to his use of it in *CD* IV/1: there he simply means to signal the pact that human existence has forged with the "necessity" of death. See Barth, *Predigten 1921–35*, 553.

81. Alexander Massmann, *Citizenship in Heaven and on Earth: Karl Barth's Ethics* (Minneapolis, MN: Fortress Press, 2015), 356–59.

82. Massmann, *Citizenship in Heaven and on Earth*, 357.

83. On this covenant see, among others, Alistair C. Stewart, "The Covenant with Death in Isaiah 28," *Expository Times* 100, no. 10 (1989): 375–7; Francis Landy, "Tracing the Voice of the Other: Isaiah 28 and the Covenant with Death," in *Beauty and the Enigma: And Other Essays on the Hebrew Bible* (Sheffield: Sheffield Academic Press, 2001), 185–205.

84. Berkouwer helpfully alludes to the text in Isa. 28 in his discussion of the concepts of alien work and proper work as used by Luther and Barth. See Berkouwer, *The Triumph of Grace in the Theology of Karl Barth*, 241.

85. The German translation comes from the Zürcher Bibel. The Lutherbibel is near identical: *Wir haben mit dem Tod einen Bund geschlossen*. Landy finds the "covenant with death" to be one entered into not only by the Jerusalem leaders of the text but universally: "every post-edenic human endeavour is an attempt to make a deal with death." Landy, "Tracing the Voice of the Other," 186.

touch us."[86] As the passage continues, God promises (or, perhaps better, threatens) the people of Jerusalem that "Your covenant with death will be annulled" (v. 18). This prospective annulment of their covenant with death we might take to be a word of good news. But God declares that the annulment will happen in this way: "When the overwhelming scourge sweeps by, you will be beaten down by it. As often as it comes it will carry you away; morning after morning, by day and by night, it will sweep through" (vv. 18–19).[87] The covenant with death is annulled, we begin to understand, not when God protects the rulers of Jerusalem from the "overwhelming scourge" but when God ushers it in. This is why "it will be sheer terror [*Entsetzen*] to understand the message" (v. 19).

The prophet calls this a "decree of destruction" (v. 22) that he has heard from the Lord. With this decree, Walter Brueggemann comments, the text of Isaiah 28 "nullifies the entire tradition of Yahweh's care for Israel."[88] But it should not go unnoticed that this destructive work is described by Isaiah as a "strange" or "alien" work of God.[89] God is acting strangely here, in a way that seems to contradict the promises that He has made. No wonder this action invokes "sheer terror."

---

86. In his commentary on Isaiah, Walter Brueggemann offers two possible referents for the "death" with which Jerusalem has covenanted, one more likely than the other. The more likely referent is that the covenant is made "with deathly, self-serving, self-indulgent practices, such as those noted in verses 7–8." Walter Brueggemann, *Isaiah 1-39*, Westminster Bible Companion (Louisville, KY: Westminster John Knox Press, 1998), 226. The less likely referent is that the covenant is made with "the god Mot (whose name means 'death')" (225). In this second meaning, the covenant with death does not merely signal perverse human activity but a "religious commitment alternative to Yahweh" (225). Barth, I claim, develops the notion of a "covenant with death" more in keeping with the second (apocalyptic) interpretive possibility put forward by Brueggemann.

87. Willem Beuken proposes that in v. 19, "the perspective moves slightly towards apocalyptic in the sense that the calamity simply swallows time." Willem A. M. Beuken, *Isaiah Part II, Volume 2: Isaiah 28-39*, trans. Brian Doyle (Leuven: Peeters, 2000), 55.

88. Brueggemann, *Isaiah 1-39*, 228.

89. Luther, in his lecture on this text, describes the proper work and alien work of God as follows: "the proper work and nature of God is to save. But when our flesh is so evil that it cannot be saved by God's proper work, it is necessary for it to be saved by His alien work." Martin Luther, *Lectures on Isaiah, Chapters 1-39*, ed. Jaroslav Pelikan, trans. Herbert J. A. Bouman, Luther's Works 16 (Saint Louis: Concordia Publishing House, 1969), 233. Luther, we should note, does not here state that the proper work of God is to save and the alien work is to damn. Rather, both the proper *and* the alien work are distinct forms of the activity by which God saves. As Luther continues, it becomes clear that, in this context, he divides between the proper and the alien work of God not along objective but along subjective lines—the division between these two works corresponds to the difference between faith and unbelief. He writes:

> To the ungodly the Word is scandal, pestilence, and death; but to the godly it is righteousness, refreshment, life, and sweet aroma. This is not the fault of the Gospel

There is one further set of themes in Isa. 28:15-22 that connects with Barth's doctrine of atonement in §59.2, namely, the set that includes lies, falsehood, deception, concealment, and—finally—revelation. Turning to Barth's concluding portrayal of the positive effects of Christ's drinking of the cup of divine wrath, the notion of humanity's covenant with death/Satan lies just below the surface. Humanity has made this deadly covenant for the sake of protection. What humanity does not know, according to Barth, is that its covenant partner is a "deceiver."[90] Far from being their protector and deliverer, their covenant partner is in fact "their destroyer."[91] With humanity's covenant with death in mind Barth presents the following account of the work of the cross: "That the deceiver of men is their destroyer, that his power is that of death, is something that had to be proved true in the One who was not deceived, in order that it might not be true for all those who were deceived."[92] The cross in this way is an unmasking of the truth, an event that reveals Satan for what he truly is.[93]

Isaiah 28 does not speak of *God's* "covenant with death." For Barth, by contrast, it is not fundamentally the rulers of Jerusalem who have made a covenant with death—though it is certainly these also, as it is indeed every human—but *God*. Barth's use of the term thus turns its use in Isaiah on its head, yet only in such a way that it captures the essence of the passage's wider context. For what has God

> but of the ungodly, who by their unfaithfulness turn all good things into evil for themselves. Therefore this work is called God's alien work, to cast down the ungodly, who are themselves to blame, and to save His own godly people, who accept the Word and all the things of God. (234)

It is for this reason the ungodly who "turn God into Satan, light into darkness, and righteousness into offense" (234). As an alternative to the view that the "strange" work of God is either that work which goes "against his will" and "contrary to his nature" or that work which marks a shift in God's dealings with His people—from deliverance to destruction—John Calvin considers "strange" in this context to mean "simply what is uncommon or wonderful." John Calvin, *Commentary on the Book of the Prophet Isaiah*, trans. William Pringle, vol. 2 (Edinburgh: Calvin Translation Society, 1851), 298–9. Calvin, however, does not categorically dismiss those other views. For a modern view similar to Calvin's, see Joseph Blenkinsopp, *Isaiah 1-39. A New Translation with Introduction and Commentary* (New York: Doubleday, 2000), 395, who takes "strange" to be a synonym for "the unanticipated, the sudden, the astounding." For a modern view similar to Luther's, see Brueggemann, *Isaiah 1-39*, 228, who understands God's alien work to be work that "is not what Yahweh has characteristically done nor, we may assume, not what Yahweh would choose to do. But it must be done." In other words, the strangeness of this work, according to Brueggemann, does not make it any less necessary, and its necessity does not make it any less strange.

90. *CD* IV/1, 272.
91. *CD* IV/1, 272.
92. *CD* IV/1, 272.
93. Barth returns to this scriptural trope (Col. 2:15) in §59.3, at *CD* IV/1, 307.

done but aligned Himself with the forces of destruction and employed them in the service of His alien work?

The text from Isaiah is not without reference to what might be called the "proper" work of God, the work of protection and deliverance. God announces: "See, I am laying in Zion a foundation stone, a tested stone, a precious cornerstone, a sure foundation: 'One who trusts will not panic.' And I will make justice the line, and righteousness the plummet" (vv. 16–17). This "summons to faith," Brueggemann argues, "is the only 'safe place' in a world severely under assault."[94]

However, if one were to offer a Christological interpretation of this passage from Isaiah in keeping with Barth's doctrine of atonement, one would be compelled to observe that precisely this foundation stone—the proper work of God—is in fact rejected. Indeed, the world in its covenant with death has, as its own protective measure, put its source of righteousness, Jesus Christ, to death (see Chapter 3 above). And what does Barth's reading of Gethsemane tell us? It tells us that Christ Himself is now the object of the "overwhelming scourge." He faces the "terror" (*Entsetzen*)[95] of God's destructive work, of God's covenant with death. The "safe place," to use Brueggemann's language, is now precisely the place that is "under assault."

The cross is also for Barth an unmasking of human illusion, the illusion most vividly portrayed in his interpretation of the second temptation in the wilderness, namely, the illusion that humanity's covenant with Satan will allow the world to "remain as it had been,"[96] the illusion that the coming of God's Deliverer need not entail an end of the world, a *Weltende*. Christ, by resisting Satan, reveals Himself to be One without illusion. In His resistance of Satan in the second wilderness temptation, Barth portrays Christ as One who resists accomplishing what might at first appear to be the *opus proprium* of God, a *christlich-humanitären* work, a work that may rightly be considered the best work from a "practical" or "realistic" perspective.[97] Christ instead sets His face towards the cross and the strange work that God will perform there. He resists Satan for the sake of obedience to the God who has made a covenant with death. The terror of this paradox is what Barth finds to be the true content of the anguish in Gethsemane.[98]

Satan as the Servant of the Hidden God

As has just been observed, the coincidence of the divine and satanic work and word is "the problem of this hour, the darkness in which Jesus addressed God in Gethsemane."[99] Barth writes:

---

94. Brueggemann, *Isaiah 1-39*, 226.
95. See *KD* IV/1, 291, 296.
96. *CD* IV/1, 262.
97. *CD* IV/1, 262.
98. *CD* IV/1, 266–70.
99. *CD* IV/1, 268.

What shook Him was the coming concealment of the lordship of God under the lordship of evil and evil men. This was the terrible thing which He saw breaking on Himself and His disciples and all men, on His work as the Reconciler between God and man, and therefore on God's own work, destroying everything, mortally imperilling the fulfilment of His just and redemptive judgment.[100]

Christ, to phrase the matter most pointedly, seems to be confronted with the reality of God against God, with the reality of a left-handed work of God that breaks in on the work of God's right hand, a left-handed work that imperils Christ's redemptive activity, a negative form of judgment that contradicts its positive form. And, moreover, the service that this activity of God's left hand might render to the activity of His right is entirely concealed. Christ is not only caught between God and nothingness—"He had nothing but nothingness under and behind and beside Him, and nothing but God before and above Him"[101]—but caught in such a way that there is an identity between the two that renders Him "helpless."[102]

As Barth reads it, Christ's prayer in the garden is a response to the emerging identification of God and nothingness. In keeping with the cosmic apocalyptic thrust of his rendering of Christ's obedience, the content of the prayer that Christ prays is thoroughly apocalypticised by Barth. This passage from *Church Dogmatics* is worth quoting in full:

> Jesus prays that this hour, this cup of wrath might *pass* from Him, might be spared Him. He prays, therefore, that the good will and the sacred work and the true word of God should not coincide [*zusammentreffen*] with the evil will and the corrupt work and the deceitful word of the tempter and of the world controlled by him, the sinners. He prays that God should *not* give Him up to the power the temptation of which He had resisted and willed to resist in all circumstances. He prays that God will so order things that the triumph of evil will be prevented, that the claim of Satan to world dominion will *not* be affirmed but given the *lie*, that a *limit* will be set to him, and with him to the evil course of the world and the evil movement of men. He prays that, directed by God's providence, the facts might speak a different language from that which they are about to speak, that in their end and consequence they should not be against Him, just as He had decided for God and not against Him in the wilderness. He

---

100. *CD* IV/1, 269. Barth's notion of the "concealment of the lordship of God under the lordship of evil" casts some doubt on Wüthrich's claim that, for Barth, God "does not act *hidden* in, with and under nothingness, God does not act sub contrario under a mask of Satan!" Indeed, Wüthrich himself notes that Barth's notion of nothingness as a divine "instrument" and "servant" generates a more complex account of the nature of the relationship between God and nothingness. See Wüthrich, "Das 'fremde Geheimnis des wirklich Nichtigen,'" 403.

101. *CD* IV/1, 458.

102. *CD* IV/1, 458 rev.

prays that for the sake of God's own cause and glory the evil determination of world-occurrence should not finally rage against Himself, the sent One of God and the divine Son. Surely this is something which God cannot will and allow.[103]

Jesus, according to Barth, recognises that what is about to happen is nothing less than "the triumph of evil," the revelation of the cosmos as Satan's possession. His mission has been a prolonged incursion into territory held by the devil for the sake of the lordship of God. The conclusion of this mission now sees Satan reassert his claim to cosmic lordship and—even more terrible—reassert this claim with divine permission and appointment. We cannot miss the exchange that happens: the executor of divine judgment is not Christ, the just Judge, the Saviour and Deliverer—the Judge in the positive, biblical sense of the term (see Chapter 3)—but Satan and the cosmos belonging to him, the judges who operate under the "unbreakable law" of retribution and in accordance with "the irresistible right of might."[104]

We might put it this way: Barth's doctrine of the atonement argues not only that the Judge becomes the judged but also the obverse—that the judged becomes the judge.[105] The three-agent conflict, while somewhat concealed in the title of Barth's doctrine of the atonement, is manifest here in its details. God and Jesus Christ against Satan becomes God and Satan against Jesus Christ.[106]

It is with reference to this complex relationship between divine and satanic activity that the language of concealment and revelation does its work. For the cross does not unmask Satan without masking God. Satan the destroyer only acts in accordance with God's will, as the executor of the divine judgment. God, the God who has kept His covenant with death, is concealed within the revelation of Satan as God's "minister of justice"[107]—more on which below.

There are occasions when Barth speaks as if the concealment on the cross is not really concealment, as if the terror of the "coincidence of the divine and the satanic will and work and word" with which Christ is now faced in prayer to God is always already offset and outflanked by the knowledge that what Satan intends for evil God intends for good. One such occasion arises at the beginning of Barth's exegesis of the Gethsemane episode, as he seeks to bracket the claims and acts of Satan within the claims and acts of God. He underscores at this point,

---

103. *CD* IV/1, 269.

104. *CD* IV/1, 266, 271.

105. *CD* IV/1, 271: "It was a matter of the execution of the divine judgment being taken out of the hands of Jesus and placed in those of His supremely unrighteous judges and executed by them upon Him."

106. It is noteworthy that Barth repeatedly states that Christ puts God in the right *against* Himself (*CD* IV/1, 258, 259, 263, 270).

107. Henry Ansgar Kelly, *Satan in the Bible, God's Minister of Justice* (Eugene, OR: Cascade, 2017).

Above and in and through the event which is now disclosed and works itself out, God rules and does His work, the work which Jesus has to finish and is determined to finish. He is the living Lord even of the world which is in conflict with Him. As such He can never be idle. He can never grow weary, He can never resign. In this world Satan can have only the power which is given and allowed him as he is powerfully upheld by the left hand of God.[108]

According to Barth, it is this knowledge that Satan's power is a power only given to Him by God that constitutes "the self-evident presupposition of everything that happens."[109]

Another occasion in which the concealment appears to be something less than an impenetrable and terrifying concealment arises towards the conclusion of Barth's exegesis. He seeks to clarify the point that Jesus's acceptance of the will of God is "an expression of the supreme and only praise which God expects of man and which is rendered to Him only by this One man in place of all, the praise which comes from the knowledge that He does not make any mistakes, that His way, the way which He whose thoughts are higher than our thoughts actually treads Himself, is holy and just and gracious."[110] But on these occasions, I submit, Barth goes against the grain of his *theologia crucis* in §59.2.

It is Barth's contention that "God will give His answer to the prayer only in this inconceivable, this frightful event, and not otherwise," that is, only in the event of the divine and satanic "coincidence."[111] God's answer is for this reason a non-answer, an answer spoken "in the same language in which Satan now spoke with Him as the prince of this aeon, triumphantly avenging His contradiction and opposition in the wilderness."[112] This language is what Barth calls the "language of facts."[113]

Barth's reference to Satan's triumphant vengeance indicates a new form of Christ's conflict with this adversary. Satan's role in Gethsemane, Barth claims, is quite different to what it was in the wilderness. Or, rather, Satan appears here in a new, different form to that of the wilderness, in the form of the "avenger" of his defeat in the wilderness.[114] Earlier Satan took the form of a cunning counsellor and was quite straightforwardly dismissed by Jesus. Here, however, he comes with the power to act and work, with the power of the one to whom the kingdoms of the world have been given over.

It is in view of this satanic lordship, discussed above in Chapter 3, that Barth understands the self-giving of Christ to the world to have been carried out with "the

---

108. *CD* IV/1, 267.
109. *CD* IV/1, 267.
110. *CD* IV/1, 271.
111. *CD* IV/1, 268.
112. *CD* IV/1, 268.
113. *CD* IV/1, 266–7, 271.
114. *CD* IV/1, 266.

certainty of failure."[115] For in giving Himself to *this* world, He is giving Himself to "the power of the unbreakable *law* to which these men are subject in their willing and doing, to which the world itself is subject, the overwhelming *retribution* which must come upon Him at the hand of these men because He has undertaken and dared to be unique amongst them, to resist temptation, to achieve righteousness in their place."[116] It is as Christ, in Gethsemane, perceives Satan to be "actually triumphant as he necessarily would be in this world," as He is "refuted by him in the hard language of facts," that this moment becomes for Him a moment of pause and trembling. The triumphant decision for the cross in the wilderness now gives rise to the stark reality that the cross speaks the language of Satan's triumph. The one who throughout His life had overpowered the kingdom of darkness must now allow Himself to be overpowered by it. The impossible possibility of Gen. 1:2 has become actualised. This is God's terrifying "answer" to Christ's prayer.

Christ does not continue on His way because He knows that this triumph of evil is in fact salvific, but in the certainty of His own failure. At this moment of tribulation, He is not given a wider vantage point from which to view God's wrath as the hidden fire of His love. As we have observed above, the situation of Gen. 1:2—the situation now realised for the first time in history—is a situation without hope. Christ, therefore, does not proceed as if what is about to happen is anything less than a catastrophe—a divinely willed catastrophe, to be sure, but all the more catastrophic for just that reason. The knowledge of God's providential involvement in this event—Barth speaks of Satan as one who exercises "the right of might" by "divine permission and appointment"[117]—functions not as a source of comfort or empowerment to Christ, but as the true source of His terror. For in the cross, the triumph of God is "completely concealed under that of His adversary, of nothingness, of that which supremely is not [*des Allernichtigsten*]."[118]

The Flight from God to God

The thought of a terrifying concealment of divine lordship under the lordship of Satan leads us, finally, into a nuanced rendering of a "God against God" that can be extrapolated from Barth's three-agent *theologia crucis*, wherein Satan is the executor of the work of God's left hand. The notion that the will of God and the will of Satan are identical in the event of Christ's death is not restricted in *Church Dogmatics* to the exegesis of the episode in Gethsemane in §59.2. This hard saying is further developed in §70.1 ("The True Witness"), where Barth considers together the passion of Christ and the passion of Job. A brief glance at this later portion of *Church Dogmatics* will shed additional light on Barth's account of the atonement in "The Judge Judged in Our Place."

---

115. *CD* IV/1, 262.
116. *CD* IV/1, 266.
117. *CD* IV/1, 271.
118. *CD* IV/1, 271 rev.

For Barth, the similarity between the passions of Job and Jesus lies in the fact that, while Satan is not absent from either scene, both Christ and Job are smitten and afflicted *by God*. It is with God that they have to do, and it is to God that they appeal—the very God who now hides His face from them. As Barth asserts, "continually and with intensified severity there comes upon [Christ] the most bitter thing of all, that He is dealing not merely with the contradiction and opposition of evil, of the man of sin, of his pride and sloth and falsehood, that He is dealing not merely with what we call the devil, but that He has also to wrestle with the good will of God."[119] It is not with some other God that Christ wrestles but with the one God whom He has known and loved. As is the case with Job, He "cannot as it were look behind this God who acts towards him in this manner, or look away to another who gives him no cause for complaint."[120]

But what Job and Jesus must reckon with is a "change" in this God.[121] Job's friends are in the wrong, Barth argues, because they have not reckoned with the change in God with which Job is now confronted. According to Barth, it is "the change in the divine form [*Gestaltwandel*] which found concrete manifestation and expression in the blows of fate which he had suffered" that is the theme of Job's complaint.[122] God, as He has exposed Job to these blows, has "adopted this new form." And so "Where God had previously been the Friend and Helper of His elected and electing servant, He has now become his Enemy and Persecutor." "Wrath and curse" have replaced "blessing."[123] To use Luther's phrase, God has become a devil.

Two things are especially important in relation to what Barth has to say here. First, he clarifies that Job, even in the darkness of this moment, even in this change of the divine attitude towards him, still has to do with God. Not even in these transformed circumstances is there necessarily a "dissolution or removal of the covenant relationship established in the prior free choice of God and the subsequent free choice of man."[124] Second, however, Barth is equally adamant that Job has to do with the electing God who hides Himself. And this means that Job "cannot see to what degree he has to" with this God. Job, unlike his friends, does not cling to an unhistorical God. The God who has not ceased to be Job's God is "unrecognisable as his God."[125] The same, moreover, is true of Christ's God in Gethsemane, the God whose will is now "indistinguishably one [*ununterscheidbar eins*] with the evil will of men and the world and Satan."[126]

---

119. *CD* IV/3, 393–4.

120. *CD* IV/3, 424.

121. Barth, in *CD* IV/1, 271, speaks of a "turning [*Wendung*] and decision *against* [Christ] according to the determined counsel of providence."

122. *CD* IV/3, 422.

123. *CD* IV/3, 422.

124. *CD* IV/3, 405.

125. *CD* IV/3, 405.

126. *CD* IV/1, 271.

This sets up what I take to be Barth's version of "God against God"—though it must be stressed that Barth would recoil at this phrasing.[127] What Barth discerns in the book of Job and in the Garden of Gethsemane is not a metaphysical dualism of one God against another God but an existential, epistemological crisis that overtakes Job (and indeed Christ) and thus a suffering obedience that can be achieved "only in the conflict and unbearable tension of knowledge and ignorance: of knowledge that he has to do with God even in this alien form; of ignorance how far He has to do with God in this form."[128] Beyond matters epistemic, however, Job's crisis does correspond to an objective reality—a real change in the encountered form of God—and in Barth's eyes it leads to his "real complaint": the complaint against the unknown God on the basis of the known God. As Barth clarifies, "it is in the name of God that he complains against God, i.e., against the strange form in which God encounters him, rejects him, disputes against him, and persecutes him as an unjustly disowned and ill-treated servant."[129] Barth, perhaps surprisingly, even accepts the phrase "a flight from God to God," though only to the extent that this is understood as "a flight from the God unknown in His unknowability to the God whom we hope or are sure is known in the same unknowability."[130] The "hard saying" of Roland de Pury, which Barth accepts as one of the most "perspicacious" among modern expositions of the Book of Job, comes to mind here:

> [Job] flees to the God whom he accuses. He sets his confidence in God who has disillusioned him and reduced him to despair .... Without deviating from the violent assertion of his innocence and God's hostility, he confesses his hope, taking as his Defender the One who judges him, as his Liberator the One who throws him in prison, and as his Friend his mortal enemy.[131]

---

127. George Hunsinger points out that "unlike Luther, Barth recoiled from any suggestion that the cross entailed a contradiction or conflict in God's being itself." George Hunsinger, "What Karl Barth Learned from Martin Luther," in *Disruptive Grace: Studies in the Theology of Karl Barth* (Grand Rapids, MI: Eerdmans, 2000), 289. Nevertheless, given the tension Barth posits between the right hand work of God (*opus proprium*) and the left hand work of God (*opus alienum*) in §50.4 (discussed in Chapter 2), and given the key role that Satan has as the executor of *divine* judgment in §59.2, it seems that talk of some kind of contradiction or conflict internal to God can be scarcely avoided.

128. *CD* IV/3, 405.

129. *CD* IV/3, 405.

130. *CD* IV/3, 424.

131. *CD* IV/3, 424. Quoted from R. de Pury, *Hiob, der Mensch in Aufruhr*, 1957, 23-4. This "hard saying" is reminiscent of some of Barth's own scorching pronouncements in his monumental commentary on Romans. In Barth's exegesis of Rom. 5:3-5 in *RII*, 157, for instance, he writes:

> When we recognize that in suffering and brokenness it is God whom we encounter, that we have been cast up against Him and bound to Him, that we have been dissolved by Him and uplifted by Him, then tribulation worketh *probation* of faith,

There are strategies that might seek to attenuate the starkness of the language and conceptuality at play here. For example, one might protest to Barth that God is love, or even "the One who loves in freedom," and therefore that the *Anfechtung* Job and Christ experience has nothing to do with God but only with God's enemy. Barth, as his treatment of the miracles of Christ in *CD* IV/2 demonstrates, has room for such a view in certain contexts. But with regard to the singular, apocalyptic event of the cross, to which Job is a witness, Barth is insistent that the battle lines of the cosmological conflict cannot be so neatly drawn. Alternatively, one might wish to mitigate the terror of *Anfechtung* with the renewed affirmation that God's wrath is only the fire of His love. The mistake here, however, would be—as noted above—to imply that God's hiddenness, what Barth even describes as God's *enmity*, becomes humanly penetrable and dispersible, simply one temporary episode in a discernibly continuous process, and not the site of an epistemological crisis.[132]

Job is ultimately a witness to the way in which the tension between knowledge of God and "ignorance how far [Job] has to do with Him" is not only theologically upheld but actually lived.[133] As someone who knows the faithfulness of God, Job's complaints and protests are not necessarily benign or passive presumptions of ultimate divine mercy; by contrast, they could well be the exercising of "the liberty of the child of God which may and must cling to the possession promised and assigned to it."[134] For as Barth asks,

> Is not his very freedom as a child of God revealed in the stubborn impatience by which he most seriously jeopardises it? Is it not the true children of God who even at best can be patient only with great impatience? Reaching after God, what can he do but declare himself dissatisfied, and thus assert and reach beyond himself, reprehensible though this may be?[135]

Christ's prayer, similarly, is understood by Barth to be the opposite of speculation concerning the question of theodicy. Instead, it enacts Christ's lively engagement

---

and faith discovers God to be the Originator of all things, and awaits all from Him. Our particular situation proves this general proposition, and the gate at which all hope seems lost is the place at which it is continually renewed.

132. Dogmatics cannot determine in advance, on the basis of a doctrine of the divine love, what God will say, and least of all can it actually say what God alone can say. Instead, Barth argues that the one who is elected by God, like Job, "must follow with complete openness the change in God's attitude [*Verhalten*] towards him, and thus look to the point where God finds Himself here and now in relation to him on the basis of this change. He must thus look steadily into and not past the hostility with which God encounters him" (*CD* IV/3, 426). And from this point, the elected one can only wait for God to speak His (resurrecting) Word.

133. *CD* IV/3, 458.

134. *CD* IV/3, 406.

135. *CD* IV/3, 407 rev.

with the living God. God against God is not a theological construct that solves the problem of evil but an experience of the God who hides Himself in Satan's schemes. The issue of the justice or justification of God as such is not off the table. In §59.3, as the next chapter will demonstrate, this is precisely the issue at hand. What Barth is warning against here, however, is turning this into an issue that can be "contemplated" from afar, and thus solved from afar. At the heart of Barth's doctrine of the atonement is the speech of Jesus Christ directed to the God whose sovereignty is presently aligned with a power intent on the destruction of Jesus Christ and the subjection of creation to chaos.[136]

Barth's interpretation of Moses's protest to God in Ex. 32 in a later section in *CD* IV/1 further illuminates the dynamics of this dialogue. What Moses is doing here, according to Barth, is daring "to remind God of His own promise, to appeal to His faithfulness, to reproach [*vorzuhalten*] Him 'pleadingly,' but with the utmost firmness."[137] And in the light of this daring reproach, Barth, somewhat surprisingly, asks: "Is not this to flee from God to God, to appeal from God to God? And is it not the case that in this flight, this appeal of Moses, God finds Himself supremely and most profoundly understood and affirmed, that in a sense Moses has prayed, or rather demanded, from the very heart of God Himself?"[138] Barth's reading of this episode from the Old Testament encourages us to think of an activity of God that *contradicts* the promises of God. It is precisely this kind of activity that occurs on Calvary.

Returning to §59.2, undoubtedly Barth takes Christ's prayer to be, in the end, a prayer of acceptance in the face of this terrible event.[139] Barth insists, however, that this obedience, this acceptance of—or, better, persistence in the face of—God's

---

136. As Massmann writes, "In this situation, God seems not to be on Jesus' side, but on Satan's." Massmann, *Citizenship in Heaven and on Earth*, 355.

137. *CD* IV/1, 425 rev.

138. *CD* IV/1, 426.

139. The obedience of Christ, as understood by Barth, can be seen to have parallels with Abraham's obedience. In an interpretive move that differs to other readings of this complex biblical text (see, for example, Wilhelm Vischer, *The Witness of the Old Testament to Christ*, trans. Arthur B. Crabtree [London: Lutterworth Press, 1949], 142–43), Christ is thought to be cast not only in the role of Isaac, or the goat, but in the role of Abraham. He is confronted by a command of God that opposes the promise of God. He is confronted by— we might say—God against God, by a will of God that is one with the not-will of God. And Christ is obedient unto His own death. For a reading of Gen. 22 that can be understood as characterising Abraham as a type of Christ, see Gerhard von Rad, *Genesis: A Commentary*, trans. John H. Marks, 2nd ed. (London: SCM Press, 1963), 232–40. The narrative, von Rad argues, has to do with Abraham's journey on the road to "God-forsakenness," a journey during which it appears "that Yahweh often seems to contradict himself" and that He wants "to remove the salvation begun by himself from history" (239). On God-forsakenness as a key aspect of Christ's experience of temptation, see Bonhoeffer, *Creation and Temptation*, 103.

terrifying will "is not a resignation before God."[140] Going beyond Barth's claims, we might finally say that Christ accepts the presupposition represented by the left hand of God—the fact that Satan is upheld by the permissive power of God. But He accepts it only in the hope that this presupposition can be finally removed, in the hope that there will be an unforeseen persistence on God's part, on God's right hand. This means that the cross, far from being the event in which accounts are neatly settled, or the event in which the wrath and love of God are equally satisfied, is an event of the most profound disequilibrium and destabilisation, full of interruption and dislocation, yet void of resolution. As Barth wishes to say, God is indeed "satisfied" in the event of atonement, but He is satisfied only as His love triumphs over His wrath, as the work of His right hand *ends* that of His left. What I will argue in the next chapter is that this satisfaction is not achieved here on the cross: it is only achieved when God raises Christ from the dead.

Conclusion

We have been exploring that singular moment in history when the possibility kept at bay in Gen. 1:2 is permitted to become a reality. At his crucifixion, Christ is confronted with the hopeless reign of chaos and darkness in a world judged by God. Far from operating within a two-agent framework, then, "The Judge Judged in Our Place" intensifies and complexifies the three-agent drama developed elsewhere in *Church Dogmatics*. Typically forensic concepts such as forgiveness and substitution become radically re-worked as they are fitted into Barth's cosmological vision of God's salvific work. Most importantly, however, the very dynamic of the three-agent drama is turned on its head. Barth's allusion to God's "covenant with death" gives expression to that disturbing turn of events. The destruction that befalls the world in Christ leaves open the possibility that Gen. 1:2 is the new reality. To return to Luther's provocative statement, God has become a devil. But even in the midst of this drastic situation, God is not yet God in the fullest sense of that term. What is awaited is an "eschatological difference" in God.[141] It is to this difference that we turn in the next chapter.

---

140. *CD* IV/1, 271. In Heb. 11, Abraham's faith is also understood to be much more than resigned obedience. His readiness to offer up His Son is not undertaken without explicit consideration of "the fact that God is able even to raise someone from the dead" (v. 19).

141. Volker Stümke, "Eschatologische Differenz in Gott? Zum Verhältnis von Barmherzigkeit und Gerechtigkeit Gottes bei Karl Barth und Friedrich-Wilhelm Marquardt," in *Zwischen gut und böse: Impulse lutherischer Sozialethik* (Berlin: LIT Verlag, 2011), 44–68.

Chapter 5

GOD'S ESCHATOLOGICAL JUSTIFICATION

We know that Christ, being raised from the dead, will never die again; death no longer has dominion over him.

—Romans 6:9

If it is true that in humbling Himself in the man Jesus God had to do not only with His creature but with nothingness for the sake of His creature, it is also true ... that in the exaltation of the same man Jesus God has to do only with His creature and no longer with nothingness.

—Karl Barth[1]

Introduction

My argument that Barth's soteriology is best understood in terms of God's defeat of Satan's lordship in the cosmos has thus far considered the doctrine of election (Chapter 2), the key theme of divine judgment and its relation to the plight of the cosmos (Chapter 3), and the theology of the cross (Chapter 4). In each chapter, it was shown how prominent the "third agent" is in Barth's various accounts of what God does in Christ. In the course of this study, however, I have also had cause to critique elements of Barth's three-agent soteriology and to seek out alternative avenues that take us beyond some of his conclusions. This climactic chapter, on the resurrection, represents both the source and the culmination of that critical venture.

In the first volume of his systematic theology, Robert Jenson remonstrates with theologians for too often constructing their systems "as if Christ fully accomplished our salvation at Golgotha."[2] Few theological systems appear to be as

---

1. *CD* III/3, 362.
2. Robert W. Jenson, *Systematic Theology, Volume 1: The Triune God* (New York: Oxford University Press, 1997), 179. A half-century before Jenson, Walter Künneth expressed a similar judgment. "It is a remarkable feature of dogmatic study of the doctrine of salvation," Künneth observed, "that in formulating it the resurrection of Christ is either completely disregarded or treated only incidentally as a point that might have marginal relevance and

susceptible to Jenson's rebuke as that of Karl Barth. The dominant idea in Barth's mature theology of the resurrection is that the resurrection is the revelation of a salvation—a victory—that has been completed on the cross.[3] This account of the relationship between cross and resurrection is on sharp display in *CD* IV/3, where it is argued that Christ's being and action were "not augmented by His resurrection. How could they be? His work was finished."[4] The resurrection, of course, is by no means adjudged superfluous by Barth: it is certainly thought of as a "necessary" occurrence in some sense. But its necessity is tied to the predominantly—though, as will be demonstrated below, not exclusively—noetic question of concealment and revelation, as elsewhere it is tied to the question of the presence and contemporaneity of the history of Christ that was culminated in His death on the cross.[5] Will the reconciliation achieved on the cross remain something "shut up" in Christ or will it invade the anthropological sphere? This, for Barth, is the primary question answered by the resurrection. Within this schema, then, the cross "effects" or "executes" salvation/victory; the resurrection "proclaims" or "declares" or "reveals" it.[6] Scholars, with varying degrees of criticism attached, have noted Barth's tendency to think of the resurrection along these lines.[7]

be mentioned in conclusion." Walter Künneth, *The Theology of the Resurrection*, trans. James W. Leitch (St Louis: Concordia Publishing House, 1965), 156.

3. The link between resurrection and revelation is certainly not unique to Barth. Lutheran dogmatician David Hollaz, in his *Examen Theologie Acroamaticiae*, claims that "Christ rose again in order to manifest the victory which he had obtained over death and the devil …; and to offer and apply to all men the fruits of his passion and death." Quoted in Heinrich Schmid, *The Doctrinal Theology of the Evangelical Lutheran Church*, trans. Charles A. Hay and Henry E. Jacobs (Philadelphia, PA: Lutheran Publication Society, 1889), 407. In another compendium of Protestant orthodoxy, this time from a Reformed perspective, Heinrich Heppe comments that "The three stages of Christ's exaltation are the resurrection from the dead, the ascension into heaven and the session at the Father's right hand. This triple exaltation was imparted to Christ not to complete his work of redemption (which did not need fulfilment), but in order that it might be revealed, glorified and appropriated to the elect, and in order to uphold Christ's name thereby, which is above every name, so that all lips should confess that he is the Lord to the glory of God the Father." Quoted in Heinrich Heppe, *Reformed Dogmatics*, ed. Ernst Bizer, trans. G. T. Thomson, Revised ed. (Eugene, OR: Wipf & Stock Pub, 2008), 497.

4. *CD* IV/3, 282.

5. *CD* IV/1, 313-18.

6. See *CD* IV/1, 661, 725, 730; *CD* IV/2, 356, 585.

7. Among many who have made this observation, see G. C. Berkouwer, *The Triumph of Grace in the Theology of Karl Barth*, trans. Harry R. Boer (London: Paternoster, 1956), 134; Wolfhart Pannenberg, *Jesus: God and Man*, trans. Lewis L. Wilkins and Duane A. Priebe, 2nd ed. (Philadelphia, PA: Westminster Press, 1977), 111; Gerald O'Collins, "Karl Barth on Christ's Resurrection," *Scottish Journal of Theology* 26, no. 1 (1973): 93, 98; George Hunsinger, "Karl Barth's Christology: Its Basic Chalcedonian Character," in *The Cambridge Companion to Karl Barth*, ed. John Webster (New York: Cambridge University Press,

Without denying that this is indeed the dominant pattern of thought in Karl Barth's theology of the resurrection, in this chapter I want to explore a second pattern of thought that is also evident at points in *Church Dogmatics* and that funds the kind of robust *theologia resurrectionis* that Jenson finds lacking in many systematic theologies, yet whose presence in Barth's work has largely been overlooked by scholars.[8] In keeping with the argument already advanced towards the end of Chapter 2, this chapter ultimately aims to shift theological attention from the crucifixion to the resurrection of Christ as the decisive event of divine victory. What I will try to uncover in *Church Dogmatics* in general and in §59.3 in particular is the sense in which Barth might be able to affirm, as others have said, that "The Crucifixion is God's salvific action just in that God overcomes it by the Resurrection,"[9] or that "The resurrection alone saves from death,"[10] or that "the resurrection of Jesus is ... the saving event itself."[11]

I make this shift towards an understanding of the resurrection as *the* saving event with some degree of caution, for to make it is to go against the grain of Barth's soteriology, which, as noted above, is overwhelmingly weighted towards the cross, even when the resurrection is in view. Yet I will do so for three reasons. First, the New Testament can be seen to offer a soteriologically robust view of the resurrection, one that does not limit it to the status of a hermeneutical event

---

2000), 137–8; Günter Thomas, "Chaosüberwindung und Rechtsetzung: Schöpfung und Versöhnung in Karl Barths Eschatologie," *Zeitschrift für Dialektische Theologie* 21, no. 3 (2005): 262–3; R. Dale Dawson, *The Resurrection in Karl Barth* (Aldershot: Ashgate, 2007), 119; Adam Eitel, "The Resurrection of Jesus Christ: Karl Barth and the Historicization of God's Being," *International Journal of Systematic Theology* 10, no. 1 (2008): 38–9; Hans Vium Mikkelsen, *Reconciled Humanity: Karl Barth in Dialogue* (Grand Rapids, MI: Eerdmans, 2010), 215–16; Nathan Hitchcock, *Karl Barth and the Resurrection of the Flesh: The Loss of the Body in Participatory Eschatology* (Eugene, OR: Pickwick, 2013), xiii.

8. Though it has not received significant attention, this second pattern of thought has not been entirely overlooked by scholars. Dale Dawson, for example, comments that "Jesus Christ's passive reception of the Father's gracious verdict is a constitutive element of the objective accomplishment of reconciliation," Dawson, *The Resurrection in Karl Barth*, 119. Hans Mikkelsen also gestures towards this strand in his suggestion that the resurrection, as Barth conceives of it, could be understood as the second defeat of death (the first being the cross). Mikkelsen, *Reconciled Humanity*, 245. Finally, Thomas notes a "clear transgression" of the dominant strand in Barth's theology of the resurrection in the fact that "Barth can recognize in the Easter event a new, total, universal, and definitive determination of the world." Thomas cites Barth's description of the resurrection as a "seed" planted in the world (*CD* IV/3, 306) as one instance of transgression. Thomas, "Chaosüberwindung und Rechtsetzung," 264.

9. Jenson, *Systematic Theology 1*, 182.
10. Forde, "The Work of Christ," 60.
11. Georg Strecker, *Theology of the New Testament*, ed. Friedrich Wilhelm Horn, trans. M. Eugene Boring (Louisville, KY: Westminster John Knox Press, 2000), 109.

disclosive of the cross's hidden meaning.[12] Second, there is a narrow strand of Barth's *theologia resurrectionis* that sits somewhat uncomfortably alongside his primary notion of resurrection as the manifestation of an already-completed salvation/victory. This other strand, which explicitly emphasises the salvific efficacy of the resurrection, ought to be recognised and given a hearing. Third, the broad trend of Barth's *theologia resurrectionis* cannot fully account for the difference it makes that Christ is no longer dead but alive, nor can it resolve certain tensions in Barth's account of the "third agent" (Satan or nothingness) and this agent's role in the death of Christ.

The remainder of this chapter proceeds in four parts. The first part briefly uncovers the "secondary," narrow strand in Barth's *theologia resurrectionis* as it is found in *Church Dogmatics*. The subsequent three parts concentrate on §59.2-3, a key portion of Barth's doctrine of reconciliation in *CD* IV/1. In part two, I examine Barth's understanding of the potential status of God in God's relationship to the cosmos "if Christ had not been raised." In part three, I unfold the more tensive character of the cross-resurrection dialectic when the secondary strand of Barth's *theologia resurrectionis* is accented. Finally, I find in §59.3 the rudiments of a three-agent account of the resurrection wherein the resurrection can be conceived as the justification of God insofar as it is the decisive, eschatological event of divine redemption in the face of the powers of death and nothingness—powers that Barth, as observed in previous chapters, understands to be terrifyingly upheld and used by the left hand of God.

5.1. Resurrection as Redemption in Church Dogmatics

In this first part, I sketch the secondary strand of Barth's theology of the resurrection by taking stock of those moments in *Church Dogmatics* when "declaration" or "revelation" is not the sole word on the resurrection and when the cross is perhaps not the exclusively dominant feature on Barth's soteriological landscape.

Barth's understanding of the relationship cross and resurrection have to the eschatological concepts of the "new aeon" and the "new human" does not only bespeak a cross-dominated soteriology. While one can certainly point to passages claiming that it is in the cross, and not in the resurrection, that the new beginning occurs,[13] there are others that state the opposite. In *CD* I/2, the cross is said to

---

12. For a study which accents the cosmological-soteriological aspects the New Testament doctrine of the resurrection, see the account of the resurrection by Markus Barth in Markus Barth and Verne H. Fletcher, *Acquittal by Resurrection* (New York: Holt, Rinehart and Winston, 1964), 2-96. See also Richard B. Gaffin, Jr, *Resurrection and Redemption: A Study in Paul's Soteriology* (Phillipsburg: Presbyterian and Reformed, 1987).

13. Thomas, "Chaosüberwindung und Rechtsetzung," 262. Thomas cites *CD* IV/2, 291, a text which has Barth at his most crucicentric. The cross, Barth argues there, is the coronation of the royal human.

accomplish the end of the old age, with the resurrection accomplishing the beginning of the new.[14] In *CD* II/1, similarly, the death of Christ is the slaying and burying of the "the old man of the first sphere," while it is in his resurrection that Christ brings to life "the new man of the second sphere."[15] And in *CD* III/1, Barth argues that "the beginning of the coming new age" is something "which took place typically in the resurrection of Jesus," whereas the death of Christ on the cross is where the end of the old age took place.[16]

What difference, one might ask, does this second way of thinking of the cross and resurrection in their relationship to the old age and the new make? If the cross and the resurrection are not to be collapsed into one another, and if, as Barth suggested in his early lectures on Schleiermacher, the idea of "a direct and continuous identity between him who died and him who was raised again" is to be avoided,[17] the pause or distinction between the end of the old and the beginning of the new indicated by this second set of texts is not trivial; it serves to avoid that collapse and to sound a crucial note of discontinuity.[18]

Noted in Chapter 1 of this study was Barth's claim that the concentration of theological thought on the resurrection of Christ reinforces the notion of "the work of Christ as the work of our *redemption* from Satan and death," thereby shifting the theologian's language from that of "law" and "ethics" to that of "war" and "power."[19] This connection between the resurrection and a "military" view of salvation is on display at various points in *Church Dogmatics*. Barth describes the resurrection as the "overcoming" of death,[20] as the "conquest of death,"[21] as the effective shattering of the power of death.[22] If the miracles of Christ are the "signs" of Christ's triumph, it is in the resurrection of Christ that "the overcoming of demons and death" takes place "once and for all."[23] As Barth writes,

---

14. *CD* I/2, 56.

15. *CD* II/1, 626. Cf. III/1, 27–8; III/4, 490.

16. *CD* III/1, 167. Cf. III/4, 490.

17. Karl Barth, *The Theology of Schleiermacher: Lectures at Göttingen, Winter Semester of 1923/24*, ed. Dietrich T. Ritschl, trans. Geoffrey W. Bromiley (Edinburgh: T&T Clark, 1982), 100.

18. Cf. Jürgen Moltmann, *The Way of Jesus Christ: Christology in Messianic Dimensions*, trans. Margaret Kohl (London: SCM Press, 1990), 214: "If we look at the christological statements in the creed—'suffered, crucified, dead' and 'on the third day he rose again from the dead'—what belongs between them is not an 'and' at all. It is a full stop and a pause. For what now begins is something which is qualitatively different: the eschatological statements about Christ."

19. Barth, *Unterricht in der christlichen Religion 3*, 83–4.

20. *CD* I/2, 240.

21. *CD* II/1, 404.

22. *CD* II/2, 264.

23. *CD* II/2, 448.

In Him God, the Lord of death, has already put death behind and beneath us. For He did not merely give this One to suffer in our stead and on our behalf. He caused Him, again in our stead and on our behalf, to triumph over death, not merely dying, but also rising again for us, so that we can now contemplate the prospect of death as something which is really behind and beneath us.[24]

Moreover, Barth identifies Christ as the one who is "rescued from perdition and death" in his resurrection[25] or as the One "delivered from judgment" as he is "snatched from the host of the dead."[26] And citing Rom. 6:9, Barth can describe the raising of Christ from the dead as his being "taken from the dominion of death."[27] The resurrection is thus Christ's transition from being "under the threat of death" to being "under God."[28] He is under God, moreover, as one who has been "reinstated" (*aufgerichtet*) in his resurrection having previously been "delivered up" (*hingerichtet*) in his death.[29] And with this reinstatement the human injustice that had been displaced by the cross is now replaced by the divine justice of the resurrection.[30] Christ, in sum, has been "made the Victor in His resurrection from the dead."[31]

Finally, Barth relates the resurrection to the divine election and rejection in such a way that the resurrection can be conceived as *more* than an act that repeats the pattern of election-rejection. The rejection Christ took to himself in his death, Barth claims, is "left behind" in his resurrection.[32] Any notion of Christ as the eternally Rejected, and of a No of God that infinitely extends into the future, is dispelled by this understanding of what actually happens in the resurrection. I examine the character of and relationship between the divine Yes and No—or, to use the terminology predominant in §50, the right and left hands (or proper and alien works) of God[33]—more fully at the close of this chapter, but with this idea of a No or rejection that is "left behind," the resurrection becomes the decisive event in the history of the work of God's right and left hands.

What is one to make of this second strand of Barth's *theologia resurrectionis*? Can it be squared with the dominant strand of Barth's understanding of the resurrection outlined above? Or do we have in these two strands a dialectical

---

24. *CD* III/2, 614.
25. *CD* II/2, 762.
26. *CD* III/2, 276. On Luke's conception of Christ as "the saved Savior," see Neyrey, *The Passion According to Luke*, 141.
27. *CD* IV/1, 313.
28. *CD* IV/1, 334. Cf. Gaffin, Jr, *Resurrection and Redemption*, 116, where the resurrection is described as Christ's "transition from wrath to grace."
29. *CD* IV/1, 550.
30. *CD* II/2, 607.
31. *CD* IV/1, 557.
32. *CD* II/2, 428.
33. *CD* III/3, 351–63.

pair that permits no easy synthesis of the resurrection as the self-interpretation of the cross and the resurrection as the overcoming of the cross? Rather than presuppose or pursue a systematic coherence to what Barth says across the various volumes of *Church Dogmatics*, the aim in what follows is to interrogate and develop the second strand of his thought in view of the path we have thus far taken.

At the heart of this strand, I claim, is a more tensive relationship between cross and resurrection than is generally permitted in *Church Dogmatics*, the above exceptions notwithstanding. By aggravating this tension, moreover, we begin to loosen the "nail" on which Barth's mature doctrine of reconciliation can be seen to hang.[34] This nail, Thomas correctly observes, is the Christological statement that the "the double movement of the humiliation of the Son of God and the exaltation of the Son of Man" are completed on the cross—a statement that excludes the resurrection from this double movement.[35] Grappling with this Christological claim, Thomas critically asks: "Does not the resurrection belong to the dynamics of exaltation and humiliation, to the history, to the event of Jesus Christ?"[36] If this question cannot be answered in the affirmative—and Thomas is convinced that

---

34. Cf. Thomas, "Chaosüberwindung und Rechtsetzung," 274. See also Berkouwer, *The Triumph of Grace in the Theology of Karl Barth*, 314: "Barth's fundamental idea in his doctrine of reconciliation is that God's glory is revealed *in* the humiliation, His power in weakness, His life *in* death."

35. Thomas, "Chaosüberwindung und Rechtsetzung," 274. For a clear expression of this statement, see *CD* IV/2, 290: "The definitive form of the elevation and exaltation of this man, of His identity with God's eternal Son, was that in which He gave human proof of His humility and obedience to the Father, of His humiliation, in His human suffering and dying as a rejected and outcast criminal on the wood of curse and shame." In making this claim, Barth departs from the traditional identification of Christ's *status exaltationis* with his resurrection and ascension. His departure, he explains, is based on an interpretation of the New Testament: "If we have read the New Testament aright," Barth proposes, "the *datum* of both the humiliation and the exaltation of Jesus Christ is the whole of His human life including His death." Much depends, then, on whether Barth has read the New Testament aright. Indeed, it is arguable that the New Testament itself does not present a unified front on this issue. In his theological commentary on the Fourth Gospel, Herman Ridderbos observes that the decent-ascent schema of John's Gospel "differs from the familiar (cf. Philippians 2) and much employed distinction between Jesus' 'humiliation' and 'exaltation,' for the glory of the Son of man is no less central in his descent than in his ascent (cf. 1:50, 51)." Herman Ridderbos, *The Gospel According to John: A Theological Commentary*, trans. John Vriend (Grand Rapids, MI: Eerdmans, 1997), 429. On the issues involved in John's apparent identification of crucifixion and exaltation and on how these issues pertain to Barth's account of the cross and resurrection, see Massmann, *Citizenship in Heaven and on Earth*, 369–74.

36. Thomas, "Chaosüberwindung und Rechtsetzung," 275–6.

Barth, as one who "abstracts from the corporeality of the Risen One,"[37] cannot so answer it—then there is "no eschatology that can seriously promise *life*."[38] There is only eternal life as "perpetuation" and "uncovering," which, in Thomas's view, may actually be a description not of heaven but of hell.[39] What we have seen emerge in this second strand of Barth's *theologia resurrectionis*, however, is a soteriology whose telos is the event of resurrection understood as an event of redemption or deliverance, an event of "judgment" in what Barth understands to be its fundamental form, an event of life.[40] It is on this understanding of the resurrection that the remainder of the chapter will focus.

5.2. The Unjustified God

An account of the resurrection as the decisive redemptive event entails a view of the cross as an event generative of the very conditions that make a resurrection necessary for there to be any salvation at all. For Richard Gaffin, central to this view of the cross is the apocalyptic idea that the death of Christ represents the triumph of Satan. According to Gaffin, "To Paul's way of thinking, as long as Christ remains dead, Satan and sin are triumphant, or, more broadly, the dominion of the old aeon remains unbroken."[41] Is this also Barth's way of thinking? The dominant strand of Barth's *theologia resurrectionis* suggests that it is not. The secondary strand, however, may suggest otherwise.

To see further why this might be the case, I will consider what the situation would have been, according to Barth, "if Christ has not been raised" (1 Cor. 15:14), as portrayed in §59.2–3. If self-interpretation or declaration alone were the meaning of the resurrection, we might expect this situation to be one of mere concealment. In one sense, this is precisely how Barth understands the matter. As we will see below, however, the language of "concealment" takes on a somewhat demonic resonance.

---

37. Thomas, "Chaosüberwindung und Rechtsetzung," 275. For a work which attends to the promise, but also the shortcomings, of Barth's doctrine of the resurrection of the flesh, see Hitchcock, *Karl Barth and the Resurrection of the Flesh*.

38. Thomas, "Chaosüberwindung und Rechtsetzung," 276.

39. Thomas, "Chaosüberwindung und Rechtsetzung," 268. For a similar critique, see Hitchcock, *Karl Barth and the Resurrection of the Flesh*, 89.

40. On Barth's understanding of the fundamental form of judgment, see the discussion in Chapter 3.

41. Gaffin, Jr, *Resurrection and Redemption*, 116. For other arguments that this is indeed a New Testament pattern of thought, see Neyrey, *The Passion According to Luke*; Vincent P. Branick, "The Sinful Flesh of the Son of God (Rom 8:3): A Key Image of Pauline Theology," *Catholic Biblical Quarterly* 47, no. 2 (1985): 246–62; James D. G. Dunn, *The Theology of Paul the Apostle* (Grand Rapids, MI: Eerdmans, 1998), 237–45.

5. God's Eschatological Justification

For Barth, the annihilation of the sin-controlled world effected in the death of Christ—a major theme in §59.2—is not a "frightful possibility" that the resurrection mercifully obliges us to discount. Barth, in §59.2–3, is clear: the divine judgment is nothing less than an end of the world carried out by the forces of nothingness.[42] The "frightful possibility" to which Barth gives serious consideration in the form of counterfactual statements is the possibility that the *Weltende* brought about by the crucifixion of the Son of God is the final act of God vis-à-vis the cosmos. The frightful possibility, in other words, would be a cross without a resurrection, a cross that would be God's ultimate word and work. This, we recall from the previous chapter, would be a word and work that not only momentarily "actualises" but eternalises the hopeless situation of Gen. 1:2: the situation of a world without the Word of God.[43]

Confronted with this frightful possibility, Barth does not claim that God would have been in the wrong should God have permitted the last word of the old age truly to be the last word. Even if God had "given death and nothingness the last word in relation to the creature," even if God had "repented of having created [the world] (Gen. 6:7), and carried this repentance to its logical conclusion," Barth suggests that God "would still have been in the right."[44] How are we to make sense of this unsettling claim?

The *Weltende* executed in the cross is the negative form of judgment discussed in §59.2; it is judgment in the form of destruction (*Vernichtung*). This death-dealing judgment has been examined in Chapters 3 and 4. Barth's claim in §59.3 is that God is "right" in this form, but that God is right "only in complete concealment."[45] For in this form, according to Barth, death and nothingness as God's instruments of judgment are granted a "right" in relation to the creature. And if this were the sole and ultimate form of God's judgment, death and nothingness would be granted a final right. The cross as *Weltende* thus throws the relationship of God to creation into question. How could it not, if it is the event which opens the doors to nothingness's assault on the cosmos? If the cross alone was God's final word, then it can be concluded that God would have surrendered "His own right in relation to the creature" to death and nothingness or concluded a lasting alliance with them.[46] For in the cross, as the event of the coincidence of the divine and satanic will, the "original choice between heaven and earth on the one hand and chaos on the other"—and, indeed, God's being as "Creator of the world and humanity"—are not "confirmed" but utterly, terrifyingly concealed.[47] The frightful possibility, to

---

42. *CD* IV/1, 306.
43. *CD* IV/1, 268.
44. *CD* IV/1, 306.
45. *CD* IV/1, 306.
46. *CD* IV/1, 306. Günter Thomas is thus right when he states that "Barth knows well that … the cross—without the resurrection—would have been a disastrous triumph of nothingness." Günter Thomas, "Der für uns 'gerichtete Richter': Kritische Erwägungen zu Karl Barths Versöhnungslehre," *Zeitschrift für Dialektische Theologie* 18, no. 2 (2002): 216.
47. *CD* IV/1, 306.

put it most starkly, is that God would be not-God, that is to say, the God who does *not* justify Godself. Returning to Luther's dramatic claim, the frightful possibility is that God "becoming" the devil would be the end of the story. This is the terrible notion that Barth seeks to convey by speaking of the God who "would not have justified Himself" if the *Weltende* of the cross were God's ultimate word. The unjustified God is the God who is "in the right only in and for Himself," the God of wrath, the concealed God.[48]

It is crucial to recognise, as discussed in Chapter 4, that the language of "concealment" is here caught up in Barth's three-agent soteriology. The concealed right of God is virtually indistinguishable from the right of nothingness. It is the "right" of the left hand of God.[49] It is to this right of God, representing the left hand and alien work of God, that Christ bows his head. Christ surrenders himself to the power of death and nothingness as they are taken up by the left hand of God and used "as instruments in His conflict with the corruption of the world and the sin of man."[50] Their being used by God does not blunt their force. Rather, in fulfilment of the will of God, nothingness and death are allowed to "triumph over [Christ]—and in and with Him over the whole of the human race represented by Him."[51] They triumph over Christ and humanity "in all their perverse and destructive power!"[52] Moreover, as instruments in the *left* hand of God they are instruments of wrath, with wrath here understood as God's leaving room for these powers, as God's judging of the wicked person/the evil one/evil (*das Böse*) by evil (*durch das Übel*).[53] Ultimately, Christ surrenders himself to this wrath, to the permission divinely granted to the powers of death and nothingness to have lordship over this one human—the permission for their seizure of power over this one human and thereby over all humans. This is God's "covenant with death" elaborated by Barth in §59.2 and examined in the previous chapter.[54]

Though it transpires on different theological territory, the discussion of concealment and revelation in §64.4 may shed some light on this complicated position that Barth is staking for himself in §59.2–3.[55] In this later text from *CD* IV/2, Barth insists that the concealment that happens on the cross is not like a covering that by its very shape reveals what is beneath it, so that there is no breakthrough required. "If this were so," Barth claims, "the concealment of Jesus Christ and our being in Him could easily be mastered because He, and we in Him,

---

48. *CD* IV/1, 306–7.

49. On the intimate connection between the power of nothingness and the work of the left hand of God, see *CD* III/3, 351, 361–3. Cf. I *CD* V/1, 267.

50. *CD* IV/1, 306.

51. *CD* IV/1, 306.

52. *CD* IV/1, 306 rev.

53. *CD* IV/1, 306.

54. *CD* IV/1, 271 rev.

55. §64.4 is the second of the three transitional sections—together with §59.3 and §69.4—across *CD* IV.

could really be known even in this concealment."⁵⁶ But it is not so. The radicality of this concealment is that that which conceals "gives to what is concealed by it the form of its opposite, to the Yes the form of a No."⁵⁷ Barth describes this as the "*Erschreckende*"—the alarming, disconcerting, even horrifying aspect of the concealment.⁵⁸ He goes on: "That which conceals [*Das Verbergende*] is *not* the analogy of what is concealed, but its *Katalogon*; *not* its parable, but its unlikeness; not a witness of it, but a protest against it."⁵⁹ This, indeed, is disconcerting. *Das Verbergende* "does not prove, but *denies*, the being of Jesus Christ and our being in Him." In fact, it proves precisely the opposite: "What it proves and what is seen here is this: that Jesus Christ is *not* the Lord, that with his kingship there is *nothing*, that we are *not* therefore His, and that we are *not* elevated and exalted to be the saints of God in Him."⁶⁰

This language of hiddenness and concealment from §64.4 picks up from where Barth's *theologia crucis* in §59.2 ends. The earlier section ends with "the coming of the night 'in which no man can work.'"⁶¹ It ends with God's faithfulness to God's "covenant with death,"⁶² with God's will and Satan's will becoming "indistinguishably one."⁶³ This indistinguishability, as noted in Chapter 4, is not unimportant. Christ, in his anguish in the Garden of Gethsemane, has not seen through the event to its true intention. He has not received an answer that lessens the severity of the situation. The only answer to Christ's prayer, Barth insists, is the non-answer of Satan's triumph. God's word is "identical" with Satan's work.⁶⁴ Barth's theology of the cross in §59.2 terminates with Satan as God's appointed judge, executing the "right of might."⁶⁵

There is, further, a completeness and finality to this divine decision and act that Barth insists ought not to be explained away. The *Weltende* that has happened in Christ "is something that we have to see and read like an opened page which we have no power to turn, like a word which we cannot go beyond dialectically, making it equal with some other word, and thus depriving it of all its force."⁶⁶ At this point, the temptation is to use Barth's doctrine of election, or perhaps his understanding of wrath as the fire of divine love, precisely as a dialectical theological construction

---

56. *CD* IV/2, 286.

57. *CD* IV/2, 287.

58. The language used in §64.4 echoes that of §59.2, where Barth asks after the "*Schreckliche*" (the "dreadfulness" or the "terror") of that which confronts Christ in Gethsemane. See *CD* IV/1, 265.

59. *CD* IV/2, 287 rev.

60. *CD* IV/2, 287 rev.

61. *CD* IV/1, 271.

62. *CD* IV/1, 271.

63. *CD* IV/1, 271.

64. *CD* IV/1, 271.

65. *CD* IV/1, 271.

66. *CD* IV/1, 296.

that allows one to turn the page immediately and thus to see past the apocalypse, so to speak, and in this way to contain its catastrophic effects, or even to neutralise it before it occurs. But this is a temptation that runs up against some of Barth's own instincts. As he bluntly states, "Judgment is judgment. Death is death. End is end." And "In [Christ's] person, with Him, judgment, death and end have come to us ourselves once and for all."[67] Barth, it should be clarified, does not intend to present here an "abstract" cross. What he does present, however, is a cross that cannot be caught up by us into some wider worldview or theological scheme, a cross that is truly the rupture and end of such schemes.

5.3. The Dialectic of Cross and Resurrection Reconsidered

If the *Weltende* that occurs in the cross seems to hold open the possibility that God's relationship to creation could terminate in its being eternally under the power of death and nothingness, the resurrection, as the free, sovereign, and inconceivable grace of God, is the negation of this possibility. I discuss this further in the next part. Without ceasing to think of the *Weltende* in the cross as anything other than the "worst," as anything less than the catastrophic triumph of Satan, Barth refuses to think of it as an end in itself. It is not an event willed simply for its own sake. "The Judge Judged in Our Place" already indicates as much. Barth's telling claim is that "*for the sake of the best* the worst had to happen,"[68] with "the best" understood by Barth as "a new peace with God," as the "victory" in the battle against sin, as the bringing into being of a "new human," as the founding of a "new world" and a "new aeon."[69]

What I am arguing is that this indication of hope and resolution in §59.2 comes too soon when it is linked to the cross, as occurs in the dominant strand of Barth's thinking. The language of new peace, of victory, of the new human, of the new world and the new aeon—this is best understood as resurrection language, as the language of the third day, or, better, as the language of "the first day of the week" (Mt. 28:1; Lk. 24:1; Jn 20:1). To apply this language to the event of the cross risks collapsing the resurrection into the cross and identifying the *Weltende* with new creation. The mistake that Barth is seeking to avoid is an abstract view of the cross, a view of it that has not been lit up by the resurrection. But the presumption at work here is that the relationship between cross and resurrection is a relationship of event and interpretation. This presumption undermines the notion of the cross

---

67. *CD* IV/1, 296 rev. Cf. Alan E. Lewis, "The Burial of God: Rupture and Resumption as the Story of Salvation," *Scottish Journal of Theology* 40, no. 3 (1987): 344: "Resurrection is not permitted to verge back upon the cross, modifying its finality, cancelling instantaneously its negativity. Death is given space and time to be itself, to be termination, unabbreviated in its malignancy and infernal horror."

68. *CD* IV/1, 254 (emphasis added).

69. *CD* IV/1, 254.

as being "the worst," for it only *appears* to be the worst to the unenlightened, to those who do not possess what Emil Brunner calls the "spiritual point of view."[70] Indeed, if the resurrection merely unfolds the meaning of the cross, if it does not add anything new, then the worst is no longer something that had to happen for the sake of the best. Instead, the worst *is* the best. Death *is* life. Satan's triumph *is* God's triumph. Hell *is* heaven. Judgment as cosmic negation *is* judgment as cosmic redemption, the covenant with death *is* the covenant of grace, the crucifixion *is* the resurrection.[71]

The hint of a caesura between cross and resurrection goes against the grain of some of Barth's highly dialectical instincts. He wants to say that the wrath of God poured out *is* an act of love, the death of God *is* the scene of God's life, and all because the cross *is* the event of reconciliation, the event whose meaning is disclosed in the resurrection.[72] There are notable gains to be had in this highly dialectical and crucicentric understanding of the atonement. Chief among these is that it makes good sense those New Testament texts that testify to the power (1 Cor. 1:18), the wisdom (1 Cor. 1:24), the glory (Jn 12:27-8), the victory (Col. 2:15), and the sufficiency (Jn 19:30) of the cross, not to mention those texts that identify the death of Christ with the love of God (Jn 3:16; Rom. 5:8; Gal. 2:20; 1 Jn 3:16).

Yet there are also potential problems attending this dominant strand in Barth's account—and in letting it serve as the dominant interpretation of Scripture. These can be raised in the form of various interrelated questions. First, has Barth, by seemingly relegating the resurrection to the status of a predominantly hermeneutical event, underestimated its salvific import, placing a burden on the cross that it alone is not able to bear?[73] Second, is the coincidence Barth posits between the triumph of God and the triumph of Satan in the event of the cross interminable, and if it is not, how will the triumph of God continue after the end of Satan's triumph, if the former is so bound up with the latter? Third, by apparently identifying wrath with love, death with life, and the activity of the left hand of God with the activity of the right, has Barth avoided the notion of "God against God" at the cost of collapsing the distinction between God and nothingness, such that the victory of love in the midst of death is indistinguishable from what Linn Tonstad has called "the victory of death in love"?[74]

---

70. Emil Brunner, *The Christian Doctrine of Creation and Redemption: Dogmatics, Vol. II*, trans. Olive Wyon (Philadelphia, PA: Westminster Press, 1952), 372.

71. Massmann correctly remarks that Barth's "coincidence of opposites is in danger of collapsing the opposites." Massmann, *Citizenship in Heaven and on Earth*, 374.

72. *CD* IV/1, 268.

73. One can think here of Paul's claim in 1 Cor. 15:17 that "if Christ has not been raised, your faith is futile; you are still in your sins."

74. Linn Marie Tonstad, *God and Difference: The Trinity, Sexuality, and the Transformation of Finitude* (New York: Routledge, 2017), 136. The collapse of the distinction between God and nothingness comes to expression in Thomas Altizer's apocalyptic theology. In the full actuality of apocalypse, Altizer writes, "an absolute No and an absolute Yes wholly coincide. Thus even the dead body of the Godhead, or that body of abyss which is a consequence

It may be countered that to ask these questions betrays a failure to think dialectically—to think of the cross as the triumph of God *in* the triumph of Satan—or to understand the cross as an event that brings about "a crisis in the way one sees and perceives."[75] These questions may also be taken to signify that inevitable human offense at the scandal of the cross, that refusal, through pride or wisdom, to hear in the word of the cross the word of salvation. It is arguable in response, however, that it is only when the salvific efficacy of the resurrection is emphasised that the scandal of the cross can be preserved, the scandal that it is our end, the scandal of the alien work of God that is truly alien.[76] For who, in the end, is the God of the New Testament if not the God who raised Christ from the dead? And what could be more unbearably scandalous than that this God makes and keeps a covenant with death and nothingness and Satan, a covenant that results in catastrophic destruction?

5.4. *The Resurrection as the Justification of God*

The endeavour up to this point has been to push beyond a fundamentally noetic understanding of the resurrection's significance. While this endeavour generates some tension with the dominant strand of Barth's *theologia resurrectionis*, I have drawn attention to certain elements in Barth's thought—elements which represent a second strand of his *theologia resurrectionis*—that motivate this endeavour. This second strand comes to particularly explicit expression in §59.3. Here, going against the grain of his own thought, Barth states the resurrection is not only the "noetic reverse-side" of the cross but also the "revelation and declaration of its positive significance and relevance."[77]

Continuing the focus on §59.3, this final part of the chapter explores the salvific import of the resurrection in greater depth, seeking to elaborate and build on Barth's decisive claim that "the resurrection is the *justification of God Himself*."[78] I develop this notion of justification in its cosmological dimension, paying

---

of absolute sacrifice itself, is not simply and only a dead body, but an absolutely abysmal body truly necessary to absolute apocalypse, and wholly inseparable from the absolute Yes of that apocalypse." Altizer, *Godhead and the Nothing*, 156. For Barth, I demonstrate, the resurrection is the great disturbance of this coincidence; it is the reality that has no other reality to balance it (*CD* II/2, 174). The crucifixion is not the resurrection *concealed* nor is the resurrection the crucifixion *revealed*. That Barth can speak as if this is the case is scarcely contestable. But to show that another way of thinking the resurrection is undertaken by Barth is the burden of the present chapter.

75. J. Louis Martyn, "From Paul to Flannery O'Connor with the Power of Grace," in *Theological Issues in the Letters of Paul* (Nashville, TN: Abingdon Press, 1997), 284.

76. This argument is advanced in Forde, *On Being a Theologian of the Cross*, 18.

77. *CD* IV/1, 304.

78. *CD* IV/1, 309.

particular attention to Barth's discussion of the resurrection as *new* act and this act's relationship to the powers of death and nothingness.

Resurrection as New Act

Barth's key claim in respect of the second strand of his *theologia resurrectionis*, one which requires careful attention if it is to be understood fully, is that the resurrection is a "*new* act of God."[79] Intended in this description is an indication of the distinction between the crucifixion and the resurrection as divine acts. The resurrection is not simply "enclosed" in the death of Christ "but follows on it as a different happening."[80] There are at least two aspects to this "difference." The first concerns the agency involved; the second is simply the fact that it occurs *after* the cross and as some form of "answer" to that first act.

Regarding the issue of agency, Barth insists that only of the resurrection can it be said that it is a divine work and a divine work alone, "a free pure act of divine grace."[81] In the work of the cross there is the work of the Son of God and the man Jesus in his identity with the Son. There is also the work of the human beings complicit in the execution of Jesus.[82] And though Barth neglects to mention it at this point, there is perhaps most crucially of all the work of the powers of darkness, the powers which in fact execute the judgment of God in its alien, death-dealing form. None of this means that the cross is not wholly an act of God. Barth is quite clear that the cross is an event of *divine* judgment. Unlike in other doctrines of the atonement, God is not absolved of any responsibility for the darkness that descends at Golgotha.[83] But the resurrection, as an act of pure divine grace, is "marked off" from the events at Golgotha "by the fact that it does not have in the very least this component of human willing and activity"[84]—and, again adding to what Barth states, by the fact that it has no component of satanic willing and activity. According to Barth, the will of God and the will of Satan are identical on the cross, and God's lordship is concealed under Satan's lordship.[85] This is not true

---

79. *CD* IV/1, 304.

80. *CD* IV/1, 304. As Bertold Klappert helpfully puts it, the resurrection, for Barth, is "not yet contained" in the cross. Klappert, *Die Auferweckung des Gekreuzigten*, 308.

81. *CD* IV/1, 304.

82. *CD* IV/1, 300.

83. An example of a doctrine of the atonement that distances God from the events of Christ's crucifixion can be found in Weaver, *The Nonviolent Atonement*. Despite superficial similarities, Weaver's "narrative *Christus Victor*" and Barth's three-agent soteriology betray vastly different theological sensibilities.

84. *CD* IV/1, 300. When Barth denies the "historical" character of the resurrection, he is simply insisting on the fact that it "takes place quite outside the pragmatic context of human decisions and actions" (*CD* IV/1, 300).

85. *CD* IV/1, 268-9.

of the resurrection. The resurrection is "distinct" to the cross as "only God's act."[86] I will explore the theological difference this makes with respect to the dialectic of the divine Yes and No presently.

Regarding the distinctive character of the resurrection as a divine "answer" to Golgotha, Barth places a typical (and typically enigmatic) emphasis on its character as a free act. For Barth, the resurrection of Christ is "an *act* of divine *grace* which follows the crucifixion but which is quite *free*."[87] Barth's attempt to hold together the fact that the resurrection both "follows" the cross as an appropriate—and even in some sense *necessary*—response to it and yet is also a truly free act whose occurrence cannot be presumed gives to his *theologia resurrectionis* a tensive dynamic. Though it places severe pressure on his doctrine of God, part of the reason Barth does not immediately close down the "frightful possibility" of the identification of reconciliation with annihilation is to protect the interruptive, gratuitous, and novel character of the resurrection in its relationship to the cross. The resurrection breaks the deathly silence of the cross; or, put otherwise, the God who is right "for us" breaks out of the God who is right "in Himself."[88] What is more, the freedom God exercises in raising Christ from the dead prevents the end of the world effected in the event of the cross from being a page that we suppose ourselves capable of turning. As Barth writes, the resurrection of Christ "did not follow from His death, but sovereignly on His death. It was not the result [*Konsequenz*] of His death. Its only logical connexion with it was that of the sovereign and unmerited faithfulness, the sovereign, free, and again and again newly decisive [*immer wieder neu entscheidenden*] mercy of God."[89]

Barth has not forgotten the doctrine of election and the reality of the electing God. The resurrection, like the cross, can be described as something that "had to happen," as something "according to the Scriptures" (1 Cor. 15:4), that is, as an event in accordance with the "continuity of the divine will and plan."[90] Yet

---

86. *CD* IV/1, 301. To use Jürgen Moltmann's phrase, it is an "apocalyptic happening" in the strictest sense. See Moltmann, *The Way of Jesus Christ*, 214.

87. *CD* IV/1, 303.

88. It is with this dynamic or "evental" understanding of God for us in mind that Barth defends the seemingly metaphysical talk of God "in Himself" in the Christology of *CD* I/2. As he writes there, the speech of God is a speech "which arises out of the silence of God." The "knowledge of faith" is thus the knowledge of the "coming forth" of God. *CD* I/2, 421. Barth's contention is that to do away with theological discussion of "God in Himself"—as much an original Protestant impulse (Melanchthon) as a modern one (Ritschl)—is to surrender the eventfulness and novelty of grace.

89. *CD* IV/1, 304. As Adam Eitel explains, the second reason for the non-necessity of the resurrection is that "it was not grounded in the natural rhythm of world-occurrence." Eitel, "The Resurrection of Jesus Christ," 39.

90. *CD* IV/1, 303–4. It is with a view to the reality of the electing God that John Flett states that "The resurrection declares the very nature of God from all eternity." John G. Flett, "The Resurrection from the Dead as the Declaration of God's Eternal Being and the Christian Community's Eschatological Reality," *Princeton Seminary Bulletin* 31 (2010): 17.

what binds this first act and second act is not a logic by which God is somehow comprehended. The possession of such a logic would place one on an "upper level" that transcends the crucifixion of the world that occurs in the death of Christ (Gal. 6:14).[91] As Barth will later argue in *CD* IV/1, referring to the cross in particular in all its severity, "There is no escaping this judgment of God, this sentence and the execution of it, least of all by the consideration which is theologically quite true that at bottom the righteousness of God is that of the gracious God."[92] Human beings cannot simply theologise their way out of the wrath of God. For the very fact that wrath is the fire of divine love "means nothing to man as a wrongdoer. It has no significance for him."[93] What binds the first and second acts of God is the *sovereign freedom* of God. The "sequence" of cross and resurrection is, in fact, an eschatological sequence, the sequence of the ending of one age and the beginning of another, the sequence of a climactic ending of the passing form of divine activity and a definitive inauguration of its coming form. The identity of the God who raised Jesus from the dead with the God who made and kept a covenant with death is found only in the discontinuity that characterises the action of this God, in what Oswald Bayer has called "the overthrow within God himself,"[94] in the new mercy irrupting into the givens of creation—"in this world" the way of Jesus comes to "its necessarily bitter end"[95]—as pure, apocalyptic gift.

This is a somewhat provocative way of putting the matter and might appear to call into question the doctrine of divine immutability, or, in Barth's terms, the constancy of divine faithfulness. Nevertheless, might there be, in Christophe Chalamet's phrase, a way in which even by way of a "mutation or alteration" one could "precisely express faithfulness to oneself and to the other"?[96] Though

---

The resurrection does this, according to Flett, as it makes manifest the fact that God is always already the self-revealing God and thus makes manifest God's "missionary nature" (17). In a similar vein, Adam Eitel writes that "Christ's resurrection was the historical continuation of God's eternal being-in-act. In other words, when God gave Godself to history in this way, nothing 'new' took place in Godself; in fact, God revealed Godself as the One God has always been." Eitel, "The Resurrection of Jesus Christ," 45.

91. *CD* IV/1, 297.
92. *CD* IV/1, 540.
93. *CD* IV/1, 540.
94. Oswald Bayer, *Martin Luther's Theology: A Contemporary Interpretation*, trans. Thomas H. Trapp (Grand Rapids, MI: Eerdmans, 2008), 214.
95. *CD* IV/1, 266.
96. Christophe Chalamet, "Divine Extravagance, or Barth's Challenges to Christian Theology in *Church Dogmatics* IV/1, §59.1 ('The Way of the Son of God into the Far Country')," *Zeitschrift für Dialektische Theologie* 32, no. 1 (2016): 111. It may of course be objected: a mutation or alternation from what? From where do we attain knowledge of God *before* this change that would make the notion of "change" intelligible? Jüngel prefers the language of correspondence-in-contradiction to the language of change or alteration. He writes,

perhaps transgressing some of Barth's own assertions on this point,[97] such a line of thought is arguably in close proximity to some of his more enigmatic claims.[98] One of these is an off-hand remark concerning the "holy mutability" of God, located in his treatment of the "constant" God in *CD* II/1:

> He is above all ages. But above them as their Lord, as the ruler of the ages (1 Tim. 1:17), and therefore as the One who—*lordly* and thus in *His* way—partakes in their alteration [*Wechsel*], so that there is something corresponding to that alteration in His own essence. That He is and remains the same in all change is His constancy.[99]

> The hiddenness of God under its opposite ... cannot however mean that in this particular hiddenness God contradicts himself, but rather must mean that God *corresponds* to himself in this hiddenness. Even in the greatest of all imaginable *contradictions*, even in the contradiction of eternal life and earthly death, God *corresponds* to himself. The *being* of God is capable of this contradiction. Indeed, God's being is realized in this contradiction without being destroyed by it. God endures it. And this endurance of the contradiction of life and death is God himself, it is the *depth* of God's glory. Jüngel, "The Revelation of the Hiddenness of God," 130.

97. For example, against the kenoticists of the nineteenth century, and also against certain Hegelian doctrines of God, Barth declares that "The divine being does not suffer any change [*Veränderung*], any diminution, any transformation [*Verwandlung*] into something else, any admixture with something else, let alone any cessation [*Aufhebung*]." *CD* IV/1, 179.

98. It should be noted that, while Barth is in theory against the notion of an essential change to God, in practice he trespasses into this territory on several occasions. For example, Barth describes God as the One "who has disclosed himself and constantly does so in all the mystery of his Godhead, moving out of naked Godhead and into the human world that was created by him, that is lost without him, and that is to be saved and renewed by him." *TCL*, 13–14. Similarly, he states that in electing Himself as our covenant partner, God ordains "the surrender of something." This "something," according to Barth, is God's "own impassibility [*Unangerührtheit*] in face of the whole world which because it is not willed by Him can only be the world of evil." *CD* II/2, 163. Bruce McCormack, for one, espies the unsettling nature of this claim. See Bruce L. McCormack, "Divine Impassibility or Simply Divine Constancy? Implications of Karl Barth's Later Christology for Debates over Impassibility," in *Divine Impassibility and the Mystery of Human Suffering*, ed. James F. Keating and Thomas Joseph White (Grand Rapids, MI: Eerdmans, 2009), 155.

99. *CD* II/1, 496 rev. As Barth proceeds to explain,

> His consistency is not as it were mathematical, the consistency of a supreme natural law, more specifically, a natural mechanism. The fact that He is one and the same does not mean that He is bound to be and say and do only one and the same thing, so that all the distinctions of His being, speaking and acting are only a semblance, only the various refractions of a beam of light which are eternally the same. (II/1, 496 rev.)

Taking seriously the cross and—in particular—the resurrection as an apocalyptic-eschatological turning of the ages, it seems undeniable that God Himself, precisely in faithfulness, does in fact turn with this turning, or, rather, that this turning of the ages is in fact initiated by God's own turning, "where the old aeon begins to pass in face of the coming of God and His new work."[100] Or, stated otherwise, it seems clear that we have to do in the resurrection, above all, with a "*new being and action* of God,"[101] with God's "new presence, action, and declaration,"[102] with the fact that "the hour of God's new rule has dawned."[103]

Resurrection, New Creation, and Cosmic Lordship

The pure, apocalyptic gift in question in the resurrection is *God* in God's eschatological act and presence.[104] The power that death and nothingness exert over the creature—the power, we recall, given to them by God—is not an ultimate reality, but a penultimate one. These instruments, and the wrath of God as it is operative in the work of these instruments, do not speak the "last word" over creation.[105] The covenant with death, so it transpires, is a temporary arrangement. It is the destruction that precedes (new) creation. But the destruction itself is not creative. Death and nothingness do not produce life, even in the hand of God. God may be said to judge evil by evil means, but God does not give life by evil means. This is why the restriction of the resurrection to a hermeneutical event is finally inadequate. As Barth writes, "Death is death. End is end."[106]

Far from adding nothing to a salvation event that is completed in God's "covenant with death" as exposited by Barth in §59.2,[107] the resurrection can be understood as the noetic and ontic end of God's covenant with death—a covenant still in effect as long as Christ lies dead in a tomb and the whole cosmos in (and with) him. God was not unjust in making and keeping this covenant. But Barth

---

This, according to Barth, is the Platonist view of God, and he argues that it would be better for theology to think of God in a grossly anthropomorphic way than to think along this Platonist line.

100. *CD* I/2, 89.

101. *CD* IV/3, 909. Barth uses this phrase in the context of his discussion of Christian hope, which he describes as "simple and concrete expectation of a *new being and action* of God."

102. *TCL*, 78.

103. *TCL*, 14.

104. As Ernst Käsemann puts it, "Salvation never consists in our being given something, however wonderful. Salvation, always, is simply God himself in his presence for us." Ernst Käsemann, "Justification and Salvation History in the Epistle to the Romans," in *Perspectives on Paul*, trans. Margaret Kohl (Philadelphia, PA: Fortress Press, 1971), 74.

105. *CD* IV/1, 307.

106. *CD* IV/1, 296.

107. *CD* IV/1, 271.

posits that God, though He would have been justified "in and for Himself," would have been unjust as the God of the gracious covenant if God had made this covenant with death God's final word.[108] God would have denied Godself as creation's electing Partner and Lord. It is in raising Christ from the dead that God does not "resign as Creator and Lord of the creature," as God would have done had Christ not been raised.[109]

It is to the language of election, creation, and lordship that Barth returns when seeking to describe the significance of the resurrection. "To raise the dead, to give life to the dead, is," according to Barth, "like the creative summoning into being of non-being, a matter wholly and exclusively for God alone, quite outside the sphere of any possible co-operating factors."[110] In the resurrection, God freely acts "to acknowledge Himself the Creator once again and this time in fulness."[111] The justification of God in the resurrection, and the justification of the creature therein, is accomplished by an act of new creation. God, in raising Christ from the dead, has acted to create the human being "afresh with a new: 'Let there be light,' to beget him and to cause him to be born again from the dead."[112]

God has not finally ceded lordship of the cosmos to Satan, as God would have done had Christ remained in the tomb. God has not gone back "on His choice between chaos and the world which He created good."[113] The end of the world that happens in the cross is for the sake of a new world. In sum, the freedom of God enacted and manifest in raising Christ from the dead is for Barth God's freedom "to enforce, prove and reveal Himself as God and Lord of the world," to "actuate and confirm" Godself as creation's ruler,[114] and to exercise God's "right" *for* the world in such a way that this right is no longer bound up with Satan's right. Having served their purpose in the event of the cross, the deadly instruments are "thrown aside"[115] in the event of the resurrection and the creature is "liberated from the right and power which death and nothingness and chaos necessarily had over him in his former corrupted form."[116] All of this gives to Barth's description of the resurrection as the Father's "verdict" (*Urteil*) a distinctly cosmological and apocalyptic content. The *Urteil* actualised in the resurrection can be understood as a kind of a repetition of the "primal separation" of creation from nothingness.

---

108. *CD* IV/1, 306–7.
109. *CD* IV/1, 307.
110. *CD* IV/1, 301.
111. *CD* IV/1, 307.
112. *CD* IV/1, 307.
113. *CD* IV/1, 307.
114. *CD* IV/1, 307 rev.
115. *CD* IV/1, 307.
116. *CD* IV/1, 307 rev.

God's Second Yes

But is the eschatological newness effected by the resurrection fully grasped if it is understood as a mere repetition of a protological event? Thomas argues that, by virtue of Barth's peculiar understanding of nothingness as that which lives by the wrath and rejection of God, any attempt to triumph over nothingness by a repeat of God's electing Yes and rejecting No can only prolong nothingness's strange existence. "Barth," he states, "cannot make it clear how the rejection of nothingness can be so directed at nothingness that it no longer is.'"[117] And so if the resurrection were only the confirmation of an original Yes, an echo of God's decision for creation, redemption would take the form of a restitution to the original state of affairs, with the implication that the cycle would simply repeat itself. Redemption would be an iterative concept fundamentally determined by protology.

Barth's appeal to the language of creation and election throughout his treatment of the resurrection in §59.3 may suggest the notion of redemption as restitution. But appeal to these doctrines, as they are developed in *CD* II and *CD* III and taken up again in *CD* IV, need not be read as an appeal to protology, to a pristine, original state of affairs that must be recovered. Barth's doctrines of election and creation are not developed within a salvation-historical framework that moves from paradise to paradise lost to paradise regained. Rather, these doctrines are essentially iterations of the doctrine of salvation.[118] Election and creation are conceived by Barth to be divine activities patterned after God's redemptive act in Christ. Yet while creation is for Barth a kind of redemption—it represents the victory of God over the menacing force of chaos—it is not the full-fledged redemption that is to come. And the redemption to come, moreover, is not a mere repetition or even a climax of the "redemption" achieved in creation. When Barth states that the resurrection confirms the being of God as Creator, then we can clarify that it confirms this only as God surpasses Godself in this act, for this act is itself an act that surpasses all that came before, since in it there is given "the presence of the *eschaton* in all its fulness."[119] The resurrection gives to the cosmos God in *God's*

---

117. Thomas, "Der Für Uns 'Gerichtete Richter,'" 217n14.

118. Gerhard von Rad has observed this pattern of thinking with respect to Israel's doctrine of creation. He writes of the Old Testament's "soteriological understanding of Creation" wherein "Creation itself was regarded as a saving work of Jahweh's." Gerhard von Rad, *Old Testament Theology, Volume I: The Theology of Israel's Historical Traditions*, trans. D. M. G. Stalker (Edinburgh: Oliver and Boyd, 1962), 138–39.

119. *CD* IV/1, 13. As Barth states at the outset of his doctrine of reconciliation, in the salvation-event we have to do with "an absolutely unique being and attitude and activity on the part of God" (*CD* IV/1, 12). For this reason, the salvation-event must be understood as "much more than the restoration of the *status quo ante* ... more than a *restitutio ad integrum*, more than the preserving and assuring to us of our creaturely being and this as our opportunity for salvation" (*CD* IV/1, 13). Indeed, God in God's saving activity "cannot be understood except as the One who constantly surpasses Himself in His constancy and faithfulness" (*CD* IV/1, 82).

eschatological act and presence, God in God's proper work alone, God who raises the dead. There is divine faithfulness manifested here. But it must be emphasised that the faithfulness of God enacted in the resurrection takes place only in an apocalyptic ending and new beginning. It is a faithfulness revealed to humans only "after their destruction in their old and corrupted form of life," only when God "has spoken a second Yes which creates and gives them new life: a Yes which He did not owe them, but which He willed to speak."[120]

This description of the resurrection as a "second Yes" is crucial. The notion of a non-dialectic second Yes calls for an understanding of the "throwing aside" of the powers of death and nothingness that goes beyond the notion of a re-rejection. The logic of the old age—grace and wrath, election and rejection, life and death—is not repeated but superseded by this new act of God. The resurrection, as the singular, novel, divine act of grace, is the triumphant moment in the three-agent drama precisely because it "does not engage in the contest in keeping with the terms and conditions provided by the world of enmity, but rather by dissolving those very terms and conditions and displacing them sovereignly and lovingly with its own."[121] The defeat of Satan occurs not in a demonstration of brute strength but in an act of gratuity against which there is no law.

The notion of a second Yes thus calls for a step beyond Barth's conception of wrath as the fire of love or of a Yes wholly contained in the cross.[122] The Yes of God spoken in the resurrection is not yet contained in the cross. As the event of the cross is not the event of the resurrection, so the No of God is not the Yes of God, and so the wrath of God cannot finally be the reverse side of God's love. Barth himself gestures towards a more oppositional view of the relationship of wrath to love when he describes the freedom of God actuated in the resurrection as the freedom "to be in the right not only in and for Himself in His wrath, but over and above that: to love [creation] in an inconceivable love, enforcing [*geltend zu machen*] His right to it and in it."[123] The resurrection, it can be ventured, *is* the justice or the "right" of God. It is the judgment of God in its fundamental form—"the omnipotence of God creating order, which is 'now' ... revealed and effective as a turning from this present evil æon ... to the new one of a world reconciled with God."[124] It is, we

---

120. *CD* IV/1, 308. Berkouwer is right to suggest that the triumph of grace in reconciliation "was prefigured in creation." But, he also recognises, this does not imply that reconciliation "is not a *new* triumph in distinction from that of creation." Berkouwer, *The Triumph of Grace in the Theology of Karl Barth*, 123.

121. Philip G. Ziegler, "'While We Were Yet Enemies': Some Particularly Protestant Reflections on Grace," *Journal of Reformed Theology* 14, no. 1 (2020): 50.

122. Cf. *CD* II/1, 394, where Barth writes that the "event of Good Friday embodies the divine No, which contains in itself the divine Yes."

123. *CD* IV/1, 307, my translation.

124. *CD* IV/1, 256. That Barth includes this description of the judgment of God in his *theologia crucis* in §59.2 and not in his *theologia resurrectionis* in §59.3 is, as argued above, premature.

recall, the "conquest of death" and the "rightful end" (*rechtmäßige Ende*) of the judgment executed on the cross.[125]

This does not necessarily mean that the cross, or rather, the Crucified, is left behind. Barth certainly does not think that the resurrection cancels Christ's faithfulness (as was discussed at the conclusion of Chapter 4). He describes the resurrection as the Father's "judicial sentence" (*richterliche Feststellung*) on the efficacy of the Son's obedience unto death.[126] This sentence is one of "approval" and "acknowledgement" of the history of Christ. This history, which journeys to the darkness of the cross, is itself the advent of faith (Gal. 3:23-5). Yet the "approval" is not an element in a "legal"—or, to use a term that is pejorative in Barth's hands, "religious"—relationship. The steadfastness of the Crucified and the steadfastness of the One who raised the Crucified from the dead are actions unconformable to any moral or religious order. As observed in Chapter 4, even where God seems to be unfaithful, Christ is faithful; even where God is most hidden, Christ exposes Himself to Him. This is no meritorious piety on Christ's part. The irony is that the "steadfast" Christ stands for and in the place of the "ungodly" (Rom. 4:5). When God raised Christ from the dead (Rom. 4:24) and when God justifies the ungodly (Rom. 4:5), God is doing the same thing. One event is being described (Rom. 4:25).

In what sense might the Crucified be identified not only with but *as* the "ungodly" who is raised from the dead? Certainly not in the sense that Christ is a wicked man, or an immoral man, or one who fails to keep covenant with God. Two ways of making sense of this identification of Christ recommend themselves. First, an "apocalyptic" grasp of Christ's assumption of flesh (see Chapter 3) can support the identification of Christ as the "ungodly." In an essay on Paul's concept of "flesh," Vincent Branick presents the "flesh" as a cosmic force and Christ's assumption of flesh to mean His "subjugation … to the forces of the aeon."[127] "When Paul speaks of Christ's 'sinful flesh,'" according to Branick, "he is thus pointing to a dimension which is more 'cosmic' than ethical, expressing especially the *situation of Christ*."[128] For Branick, this apocalyptic doctrine of the incarnation secures the claim—against those who seek to protect an abstract "sinlessness" of Christ and so to separate Christ from human creatures—that "Sinful flesh is fully visible in the flesh of Christ."[129] This visibility has nothing to do with personal morality or virtue and everything to do with issues of power and dominion. The Christ who is sent in the likes of sinful flesh is subject to sin's power and dies "under

---

125. *CD* II/1, 404.

126. *CD* IV/1, 305.

127. Branick, "The Sinful Flesh of the Son of God," 248. On the theme of flesh, see the discussion of the temptations in Chapter 3.

128. Branick, "The Sinful Flesh of the Son of God," 251.

129. Branick, "The Sinful Flesh of the Son of God," 250. The doctrine of the incarnation has not been the focus of this book, but material from each of the preceding three chapters could be drawn together to make a similar argument to the one Branick is making. This is not entirely coincidental, however, since references to Karl Barth bookend Branick's essay.

its claim."¹³⁰ Given this concept of flesh, Branick suggests that the resurrection is "Christ's own redemption from sin."¹³¹ Christ is the "primary beneficiary" of God's redemptive activity; He is, in Barth's words, the "pure object and recipient of the grace of God."¹³² For the apostle Paul, Branick argues, Christ is not so much the agent of redemption as the location of redemption.¹³³ This is not to imply that Christ is totally passive. Branick mentions the obedience of Christ as "a key aspect of redemption," citing Rom. 5:19 in support of this.¹³⁴ But Branick urges us not to think of this obedience as meritorious: "the image of Jesus somehow meriting the redemption by the goodness of his life is not a real component of Paul's theology."¹³⁵

This leads into a second way of making sense of the identification of Christ as the "ungodly." Ernst Käsemann's observations on the faith of Abraham are instructive in this regard. Abraham's ungodliness, according to Käsemann, consists in the fact that "he lays claim to no religious achievements and merits" and that "he cannot be called 'good'" as this term was understood in Jewish and Greek worlds. Abraham is ungodly, in other words, because "he does not deal in works."¹³⁶ Understood in light of the faith of Abraham, the faith or steadfastness of Christ is "approved" because "it allows God to act on it instead of wanting to be and do something in itself and thereby seeking a ground of boasting. It lets itself be placed by the word in the possibility of standing outside self before God."¹³⁷

It should finally be clarified that this approval of Christ does not necessarily entail that the end of the world effected on the cross is eternalised or that the deadly work of nothingness that brought Christ to the cross can now be seamlessly integrated into the history of reconciliation.¹³⁸ If we take the redemptive aspect of the resurrection with full seriousness, the "approval" of Christ in the resurrection is nothing less than the redemption of Christ from the realm of the dead. God does not abandon Christ to chaos in order to reveal the justice of this abandonment.

---

130. Branick, "The Sinful Flesh of the Son of God," 259.

131. Branick, "The Sinful Flesh of the Son of God," 259. Cf. Beverly Roberts Gaventa, "Interpreting the Death of Jesus Apocalyptically: Reconsidering Romans 8:32," in *Jesus and Paul Reconnected: Fresh Pathways into an Old Debate*, ed. Todd D. Still (Grand Rapids, MI: Eerdmans, 2007), 139: "God's resurrection of Jesus from the dead not only frees Jesus Christ from the powers, but it sets in motion the defeat of Sin and Death that will culminate when all of God's enemies are placed in subjection."

132. *CD* IV/1, 304.

133. Branick, "The Sinful Flesh of the Son of God," 260.

134. Branick, "The Sinful Flesh of the Son of God," 260.

135. Branick, "The Sinful Flesh of the Son of God," 260.

136. Ernst Käsemann, "The Faith of Abraham in Romans 4," in *Perspectives on Paul*, trans. Margaret Kohl (Philadelphia, PA: Fortress Press, 1971), 85.

137. Käsemann, *Commentary on Romans*, 113.

138. The criticism that Barth has eternalised damnation, or at least the damnation of Christ, is conveyed in Hitchcock, *Karl Barth and the Resurrection of the Flesh*, 89. In the light of what Barth states in *CD* IV/1, 313–14, it is a criticism not without some justification. For there it is claimed that

God does so in order to "snatch" Christ from chaos, and in snatching him from it, to "make a show of it."¹³⁹ It is this snatching, this deliverance, that happens in the resurrection. The resurrection is not the justification of God's instrumentalising of death and nothingness. The death with which God made a terrible covenant is no secret friend, a "negation" that can be "integrated in the all-embracing nexus or system of a harmony of being."¹⁴⁰ Rather, it is the "last enemy" (1 Cor. 15:26) to be defeated. The resurrection does not "justify" or eternalise the alien work of the left hand of God. The alien work can only be apocalyptically ended by the proper work.¹⁴¹

Referencing Acts 2:27, Barth claims that God does not "acknowledge" that the Holy One would see corruption. The "doors of death," which "necessarily closed behind" Christ, were again "opened up."¹⁴² The resurrection "came in the midst of His real death and delivered Him from death."¹⁴³ When, in the resurrection, God "confirmed the verdict which, according to Mk 1:11, He had already pronounced at Jordan when He entered on the way which led Him to Golgotha: 'Thou art my beloved Son, in whom I am well pleased,'" God does so by an act of deliverance, of rescue, of redemption. The love between Father and Son has concrete content: the raising of Christ from the dead. If it did not have this concrete content it would be for us a terrifyingly concealed love, and the danger would exist that God could be considered as identical with Satan.

God's No, we must finally hazard, is not in need of an unveiling of the secret Yes contained within it. God's No is in need of termination, for this is a No by which nothingness, perversely, lives.¹⁴⁴ Given Barth's account of the nature of nothingness, a re-rejection of nothingness would be only a perpetuation of the "old" world, since it would be a perpetuation of the "perishing" work of God. The resurrection, for this reason, must not be understood as a repetition of God's protological

> He not only did bear the sin of the world, He does bear it. He not only has reconciled the world with God, but as the One who has done this, He is its eternal Reconciler, active and at work once and for all. He not only went the way from Jordan to Golgotha, but He still goes it, again and again. His history did not become dead history. It was history in His time to become as such eternal history—the history of God with the men of all times, and therefore taking place here and now as it did then.

It is not clear that these claims can easily be squared with the claim that the grace of the resurrection leaves behind the judgment of the cross as its presupposition (*CD* IV/1, 300) or the claim that "The One who has done this, who in and with Himself has delivered us up to death, reigns and lives to all eternity and dies no more" (*CD* IV/1, 344–5).

139. *CD* IV/1, 307.
140. *CD* IV/2, 397.
141. See *CD* III/3, 362: "The purpose of [God's] *opus proprium* is the termination of His *opus alienum* and therefore the elimination of its object."
142. *CD* IV/1, 307.
143. *CD* IV/1, 305.
144. *CD* III/3, 351–2.

electing Yes and rejecting No.[145] Unlike God's electing Yes, the resurrection is an eschatological Yes that does not "create" its own shadow-side; it is a Yes without a corresponding No—a No that gives "reality" to its object. If the resurrection is to be thought of as an act of new creation[146]—and this is the kind of language which does attend Barth's treatment—it must not be understood to repeat the "technique" of the first creation.[147] This technique involved the dissolving dualism of God's *opus proprium* and *opus alienum*.[148] In the resurrection, the promised dissolution of this dualism is accomplished. As the definitive act of divine grace, the resurrection ends God's *opus alienum* and thus ends the usurped power that Satan exercises in the process of being upheld by this alien work (the left hand of God). God is justified as the One who delivers Christ from death, as the One who says a second Yes that lacks any corresponding No. The resurrection not only reveals but also puts into effect the fact that the life of God, the life of Christ, and the life of the world is "an event *beyond* death."[149] Death is not life. The lordship of God is not identical with the lordship of Satan. The left hand of God is not equal to God's right hand. The Christ elected for suffering and death had his shadow in the rejected devil.[150] The resurrected Christ has no shadow.

Conclusion

Barth's call for a renewed emphasis on the cosmological apocalyptic scope and meaning of salvation ultimately finds its counterpart, I propose, in his call for the Western Church to "proclaim not merely the legitimacy but the indispensability of a *theologia gloriae* in which the *theologia crucis* attains its goal."[151] It is the effort of this chapter, thinking with Barth and beyond Barth, to reconsider in the light of the apocalyptic gospel what it might mean to state that 'The Christian community is the *Easter* community. Our preaching is *Easter* preaching, our hymns are *Easter* hymns, our faith is an *Easter* faith'.[152]

The main line in Barth's theology of the resurrection, as has been frequently observed, is guided by a domineering *theologia crucis*. This would appear to number

---

145. Contrary to the claim of Eitel, "The Resurrection of Jesus Christ," 39, it is in the event of the resurrection, and not the cross, that Barth sees an "exact correspondence with what [God] did as Creator when He separated light from darkness and elected the creature to being and rejected the possibility of chaos as nothingness" (*CD* IV/1, 349).

146. Cf. Berkouwer, *The Triumph of Grace in the Theology of Karl Barth*, 136: "The resurrection of Christ is a deed which stands in a class with creation."

147. See Thomas, "Der für uns 'gerichtete Richter,'" 214; "Chaosüberwindung und Rechtsetzung," 271.

148. On Barth's notion of a "dualism which is dissoluble," see *CD* III/1, 384–5.

149. *CD* IV/1, 309.

150. *CD* II/2, 122.

151. *CD* IV/2, 356.

152. *CD* IV/2, 355.

Church Dogmatics among those theologies that proceed "as if the Crucifixion were by itself the encompassing burden of the message, as if 'Jesus died for us' were itself the defining claim"[153] and among those (Western) soteriologies that exhibit "no very profound sense of the salvific significance of the resurrection."[154] By examining a secondary strand of Barth's theology of the resurrection, a strand that can be seen to accent the distinction of the resurrection from the cross, I have brought forward an aspect of Barth's thought that exhibits a profound sense of the resurrection's salvific significance. Barth's notion of concealment as concealment *under the lordship of Satan* calls for a more soteriologically robust theology of the resurrection, the beginnings of which I have explored across *Church Dogmatics* in general and in §59.3 in particular. While it involves pushing Barth to be more explicit, I hope to have shown that his remarks on the resurrection can be amplified—and in such a way that bolsters my reading of his three-agent soteriology

---

153. Jenson, *Systematic Theology 1*, 179.

154. David Bentley Hart, "A Gift Exceeding Every Debt: An Eastern Orthodox Appreciation of Anselm's *Cur Deus Homo*," *Pro Ecclesia* 7 (1998): 334.

Chapter 6

CONCLUSION

Barth's distinctive and groundbreaking contributions to various doctrinal loci have been long recognised. His doctrine of revelation, his doctrine of God, his doctrine of election, his Christology, and his ecclesiology have each been seen to offer quite radical transformations of—or, even departures from—traditional formulations. His soteriology, by contrast, has tended to be viewed as "robustly orthodox,"[1] a modern development of Protestantism's juridical account of salvation, perhaps, but one that makes sense within its assumed two-agent schema. If the argument of this book is correct, the picture according to which Barth shows himself to be quite traditional in his doctrine of the atonement is painted on a canvas too narrow to accommodate the complexity of his theology. Through a close reading of key sections of *Church Dogmatics*, this study has displayed and elaborated the fundamentally three-agent character of Barth's soteriology, bringing to the fore the clear yet unsettling way in which he conceives of the work of salvation as the defeat of Satan, and it has also identified and elucidated—in tension with Barth's central argument—the resurrection of Christ as the decisive event in that defeat.

Schleiermacher, as noted in this book's introduction, did not think that the exclusion of the devil made any material difference to the Christian doctrine of salvation. Barth does not merely dispute Schleiermacher's position; he argues that the existence and activity of the "third agent" conditions the very undertaking of doctrinal theology, ensuring the fragmentariness of theological thought and utterance.[2] The doctrine of salvation, it follows, is no less unscathed. At the heart of that doctrine we find no grand harmony but a contest that marks the very being of God, a contest from which even God Himself does not emerge unscathed.

The Theologian and the Resurrection

In even talking about that contest in rational terms, theology risks constructing the very thing Barth thought was forbidden in the present age—a system. This book, by carrying forward Barth's conceptions of the alien and the proper work of

---

1. Anthony Thiselton, *Systematic Theology* (Grand Rapids, MI: Eerdmans, 2015), 226.
2. *CD* III/3, 293–5.

God, and of the left and the right hands of God, cannot claim to have fully avoided a problematic systematicity. Those parts of *Church Dogmatics* I have found to be in need of fixing may well be salutary signs of the necessary brokenness of theology and its character as a *theologia crucis*, and the attempt to repair them may ultimately be deemed no less problematic than the original.

What is more, a soteriology geared towards the resurrection as an event of "undialectical" grace—as recommended here—seems particularly susceptible to over-enthusiasm and overreaching on the part of the theologian. After all, what can one who remains on this side of the general resurrection know of a "pure act of grace," of a yes that is simply a yes, of an unmediated act of God? Theology risks forgetting its limitations, its creatureliness, and the scandal of the truth to which it witnesses when it grasps at pure divinity. Indeed, in so doing, it appears to take flight from the only place where God is encountered by sinful people: in the body of the Christ who became obedient to the point of death, even death on a cross. Again, this work cannot plead total innocence in the face of these critical observations.

Nevertheless, in spite of such risks and dangers, Gerhard Forde exemplifies the possibility of emphasising the salvific efficacy and eschatological newness of the resurrection without deflating the scandal of the cross. Indeed, Forde argues that only when the efficacy and newness of the resurrection is emphasised can the scandal of the cross be upheld. This is so not because the resurrection simply makes known the hidden meaning of the cross, as Barth tends to suggest, but because "it is only the resurrection that snatches victory from defeat, brings about something really new, and consequently enables us to look on the cross as a real death."[3] That is not to imply that cross and resurrection are unrelated. The Yes of the resurrection, Forde argues, is the presupposition of the No of the cross. "Without the resurrection," he claims, "theologians will always be tempted to tone down the attack in order to leave room for at least some optimism, some hope for the survival of the old self."[4]

It should not be supposed, then, that the resurrection, understood as an event of pure grace, is the "inoffensive" or "soft" conclusion after the harsh reality of the cross has taken its course. According to John's Gospel, the plot to kill Jesus takes concrete form only after he raised Lazarus from the dead. And as Käsemann reminds us, "the first impression given by a man coming out of the grave is one of terror."[5] Rightly understood, the resurrection is as much a barrier to misplaced theological assurance and stability as the cross. Christ was raised for the defeat of Satan, but the resurrected Christ does not permit us to hold His victory in our grasp or dispose over it in our thinking as a comfortable, observable, brute fact. The

---

3. Gerhard O. Forde, *Where God Meets Man: Luther's Down-to-Earth Approach to the Gospel* (Minneapolis, MN: Augsburg, 1972), 38.

4. Forde, *On Being a Theologian of the Cross*, 18.

5. Ernst Käsemann, *Jesus Means Freedom*, trans. Frank Clark (Philadelphia, PA: Fortress Press, 1969), 83.

resurrection—or, better, the resurrected Christ—is a wholly disruptive reality, an interruptive novum that exceeds and surpasses the present form of this world, ever-calling us to forget what is behind and strain towards what lies ahead (Phil. 3:13).

That theology will fall short of thinking of it as such is inevitable. It might reach for the language of "creation" to make the newness of the resurrection conceivable. Or it might concentrate its attention on the One identified by Barth as the novum, on the One who was raised from the dead and determined to be the Son of God with power.[6] But theology must be careful not to conform Christ, and specifically His resurrection, simply to the pattern of this world in the name of its inability to think of a thing over which death no longer has mastery (Rom. 6:9). To do so risks turning the resurrection into a positive outcome immanent to history and forgetting that it is the site of God's apocalyptic act of redemption, the source of a hoping against hope (Rom. 4:18).

The Demythologising Power of Apocalyptic

Talk of the defeat of Satan in the events of cross and resurrection also exposes the theologian to a further line of critique. The apparently "mythical" depiction of salvation as the defeat of Satan has come in for criticism from various quarters, with Gustav Aulén serving as the lighting rod. For all the potential strengths of the "classical" view of the atonement elaborated and embraced by Aulén, there is perceived in it a failure to give "an explicit statement of the doctrine itself in a form free from all mythical reference."[7] According to this school of thought, the *Christus Victor* motif in its New Testament form can only be unintelligible and unconvincing to people who, unlike the authors of the New Testament, "no longer think along mythical lines."[8] This does not mean that the *Christus Victor* motif is reckoned beyond saving. What is needed, according to this perspective, is a modern, demythologised form of *Christus Victor*.

Expressing the critique of the *Christus Victor* motif in this way means that Rudolf Bultmann, far from being the enemy of the classical theory, can be understood as its modern proponent—albeit in a significantly revised form.[9] Indeed, John

---

6. *CD* IV/2, 157.

7. John Macquarrie, "Demonology and the Classic Idea of Atonement," *Expository Times* 68, no. 1 (1956): 4.

8. Macquarrie, "Demonology and the Classic Idea of Atonement," 4.

9. On the possibility of including Bultmann within the "apocalyptic" fold, see David W. Congdon, "Eschatologizing Apocalyptic: An Assessment of the Present Conversation on Pauline Apocalyptic," in *Apocalyptic and the Future of Theology: With and beyond J. Louis Martyn*, ed. Joshua B. Davis and Douglas Harink (Eugene, OR: Cascade, 2012), 118–36; "Bonhoeffer and Bultmann: Toward an Apocalyptic Rapprochement," *International Journal of Systematic Theology* 15, no. 2 (2013): 172–95; "Apocalypse as Perpetual Advent: The Apocalyptic Sermons of Rudolf Bultmann," *Theology Today* 75, no. 1 (2018): 51–63.

Macquarrie adjudges Bultmann's doctrine of the atonement to be, in its essence, a "modern version of … the so-called classic view of the Atonement."[10] It is classic insofar it understands the death of Christ as a liberation from the powers of this world. It is modern insofar as it interprets these powers existentially.[11] "With Bultmann," Maquarrie announces, "the classic idea has made a powerful come-back."[12]

Bultmann's demythologising program provokes critical questions of any genuinely three-agent soteriology.[13] It also represents an important foil for Barth's soteriology. In the forward to the first part-volume of his doctrine of reconciliation, Barth identifies one of the theological contexts of that part-volume as his ongoing "debate" with Bultmann.[14] One point of that debate is the question of what theology ought to do with the New Testament's "mythological" construal of the saving event. Bultmann, we have noted, has been read as offering a demythologised *Christus Victor* account of salvation. Is the soteriology developed in this book then best characterised as a remythologised classic theory? Given Barth's resistance to "myth" as a useful theological category, that would be a misleading characterisation.[15] Put simply, Barth does not assume that the New Testament's apocalyptically charged witness to Christ's triumph over the powers manifests a "mythical" mode of thinking or worldview that is not "a real option for us now" in the first place.[16] It would for this reason be misguided to suggest that

---

10. John Macquarrie, "Demonology and the Classic Idea of Atonement (Continued)," *Expository Times* 68, no. 2 (1956): 62.

11. For a modern form of the *Christus Victor* motif which interprets the powers politically, see James Cone, *God of the Oppressed*, revised (Maryknoll, NY: Orbis Books, 1997), 212–13.

12. Macquarrie, "Demonology and the Classic Idea of Atonement (Continued)," 63.

13. The manifesto of that demythologising programme is Bultmann, "New Testament and Mythology."

14. *CD* IV/1, ix.

15. See, for example, *CD* I/1, 328–9:

> The verdict that a biblical story is to be understood as a myth is necessarily an attack on the substance of the biblical witness. This is because "myth" does not intend to be history but only pretends to be such. Myth uses narrative form to expound what purports to be always and everywhere true. It is an exposition of certain basic relationships of human existence, found in every time and place, in their connexions to their own origins and conditions in the natural and historical cosmos, or in the deity. These are given narrative form on the assumption that man knows all these things and can present them thus or thus, that he controls them, that in the last resort they are his things. (*CD* I/1, 327)

For this reason, Barth concludes that "the interpretation of the Bible as the witness to revelation and the interpretation of the Bible as the witness to myth are mutually exclusive."

16. Troels Engberg-Pedersen, *Paul and the Stoics* (Louisville, KY: T&T Clark, 2000), 17.

the present work reflects Barth's ownership or acceptance of Paul's "mythological" worldview or that it repositions the line between "the husk of mythology and the kernel of revelation"[17] or that it finally acknowledges that it is "doubtful whether the human mind can ever dispense with myth."[18] This book proceeds under the conviction that theology need not labour under the assumption that Paul is a "mythmaker"[19] and that the New Testament's apocalyptic idiom is the expression of an antiquated worldview; rather, without any sacrifice of the intellect, theology is permitted to think that this idiom is, in Ziegler's words, "uniquely adequate to discerning the realities of our age."[20]

Theology therefore need feel no immediate pressure to translate the message of the New Testament text. The effort to translate and interpret is necessary, not only by virtue of theology's prayerful orientation to the "contemporary situation"[21] but also by virtue of what the New Testament *is*: it is "not a closed system ... no longer capable of development and change" as Morna Hooker rightly observes, but "a series of photographs of people vigorously engaged in the process of 'theologizing,' trying to work out the significance of their faith."[22] Barth himself was not oblivious to theology's responsibility in this direction. His account of *das Nichtige*—the reality which encompasses sin, death, and the devil—is a case in point. The use of a non-biblical term to denote the third agent indicates neither his desire to do away with the devil, as some feared, nor his willingness to demythologise, as Bultmann recommended, but his sense of theology's responsibility to interpret for the present in fidelity to the scriptural text—or, better, in fidelity to the reality to

---

17. Helmut Thielicke, "The Restatement of New Testament Theology," in *Kerygma and Myth: A Theological Debate*, ed. Hans Werner Bartsch, trans. Reginald H. Fuller (New York: Harper & Row, 1961), 141. Thielicke assumes "a real distinction between the form of the New Testament narratives, a form conditioned by the contemporary mythology, and the actual content which the form enshrines" (157). This is not an assumption shared by Martyn, de Boer, Gaventa, Ziegler, and so on. It is, crucially, also not an assumption shared by Barth. And where Thielicke argues for the indispensability of the mythological husk on the basis of humanity's need to express religious truth in mythological language, Barth justifies talk of the powers, Satan, *das Nichtige*—those "mythological" elements of the Christian faith—on the basis of God's self-revelation in Christ.

18. Julius Schniewind, "A Reply to Bultmann: Theses on the Emancipation of the Kerygma from Mythology," in *Kerygma and Myth: A Theological Debate*, ed. Hans Werner Bartsch, trans. Reginald H. Fuller (New York: Harper & Row, 1961), 47.

19. For an understanding of Paul as mythmaker, see Emma Wasserman, *Apocalypse as Holy War: Divine Politics and Polemics in the Letters of Paul* (New Haven, CT: Yale University Press, 2018).

20. Ziegler, *Militant Grace*, 28.

21. CD I/2, 840.

22. Morna D. Hooker, "The Nature of New Testament Theology," in *The Nature of New Testament Theology: Essays in Honour of Robert Morgan*, ed. Christopher Rowland and Christopher Tuckett (Malden, MA: Wiley-Blackwell, 2006), 77.

which the scriptural text bears witness. Barth is clear from the outset of *Church Dogmatics*: systematic theology is not identical with biblical theology. It is not a matter of repeating what the biblical authors said.[23] Yet it is a matter of really grappling with what they said. Theology has a responsibility to the message of the text that it can never assume to have fulfilled.[24] And if the apocalyptic turn in Pauline studies has taught us anything, it is that the text is always capable of surprising us, taking on a force and significance that had seemed lost to it.

Indeed, Ziegler demonstrates that the tables can be turned when it comes to the relationship between apocalyptic and demythologising. Rather than being the object of a demythologising hermeneutic, the idiom of apocalyptic possesses the "power to demythologize our all-too-human common sense that thinks of us, wrongly and desperately, as the only agents on the field of history."[25] Apocalyptic's relevance to "us," then, lies precisely in its power to strip us of our illusions of autonomy, control, and immunity and in its ability "to describe reality as we find it in the world of struggle at the front line of the incursion of the Kingdom."[26] A three-agent account of the atonement need not be thought to sever the doctrine of salvation from the realm of human willing and choosing and acting, as Schleiermacher and Ritschl feared. Rather, it can be seen to advance a more realistic description of that "twice-invaded" realm.[27] Barth's three-agent understanding of atonement keeps in view the complicity of human beings in their own demise. Yet this complicity, as examined in Chapter 3, is manifested not exclusively or even primarily in monstrously evil activity but in unbelief in the divine Word, an unbelief which is at the same time a belief in the powerful temptations of false gods and which comes to its final expression in the crucifixion of Jesus. What Barth offers is neither a demythologised apocalyptic nor the narration of a drama that happens over our heads but an apocalyptic acutely sensitive to the god(s) of this age as the instigator of unbelief, the opponent of the gospel's liberating word, the original false witness.[28] The wager of a thoroughgoing

---

23. See *CD* I/1, 16: "dogmatics as such does not ask what the apostles and prophets said but what we must say on the basis of the apostles and prophets."

24. On this responsibility see Karl Barth, "Rudolf Bultmann—An Attempt to Understand Him," in *Kerygma and Myth: A Theological Debate*, ed. Hans-Werner Bartsch, trans. Reginald H. Fuller, vol. II (London: SPCK, 1962), 83–132.

25. Ziegler, *Militant Grace*, 68. Cf. Anders Nygren, "Christ and the Forces of Destruction," trans. E. Jerome Johanson, *Scottish Journal of Theology* 4, no. 4 (1951): 372: "What occurs when one attempts to de-mythologise the New Testament, is in reality that one transposes the truth and reality of the Gospel into a modern myth."

26. Ziegler, *Militant Grace*, 69.

27. J. Louis Martyn, "World without End or Twice-Invaded World?," in *Shaking Heaven and Earth: Essays in Honor of Walter Brueggemann and Charles B. Cousar*, ed. Christine Roy Yoder et al. (Louisville, KY: Westminster John Knox Press, 2005), 117–32.

28. Even in Barth's presentation of the Christian life as a life of dramatic warfare with forces inimical to creation—a presentation that owes considerable debt to Calvin—there is a recognition that this life represents an attack on "the dominion of unbelief." *TCL*, 206.

three-agent soteriology is that far from distracting us from reality, the apocalyptic idiom is indispensable for a proper grasp of our drastic situation and its divinely accomplished transformation. Yet while the existential purchase of the "cosmic-dualistic battle" should be recognised, theology would at the same do well not to render its talk of the devil too pragmatic. To paraphrase Gregor Etzelmüller, if we begin to speak of the devil only in the face of specific catastrophes, then this speech always comes too late—and certainly too late for theology.[29]

And this life is only an attack to the extent that it puts into effect "the precedence of the Word of God," the Word "in its dissimilarity from all the other forces that lay claim to man," the Word of eschatological "promise." *TCL*, 175, 177. What is more, unbelief, this time having as its object the forces which seek to enslave the Christian, is also a hallmark of Christian faithfulness.

29. See Gregor Etzelmüller, "'Er kommt und schafft Gerechtigkeit': Perspektiven auf Barths ungeschriebene Erlösungslehre," *Zeitschrift für Dialektische Theologie* 21, no. 3 (2005): 240: "If we begin to speak eschatologically only in the face of catastrophes such as 9/11 or the catastrophic floods in Asia, then this speech always comes too late—and certainly too late for theology."

BIBLIOGRAPHY

Althaus, Paul. *Die christliche Wahrheit: Lehrbuch der Dogmatik*. Gütersloh: Gütersloher Verlagshaus, 1962.

Althaus, Paul. *Gebot und Gesetz: Zum Theme "Getetz und Evangelium."* Berlin: Evangelische Verlagsanstalt, 1953.

Althaus, Paul. *The Theology of Martin Luther*. Translated by Robert C. Schultz. Philadelphia, PA: Fortress Press, 1966.

Altizer, Thomas J. J. *Godhead and the Nothing*. Albany: State University of New York Press, 2003.

Aulén, Gustaf. "Chaos and Cosmos: The Drama of the Atonement." *Interpretation* 4, no. 2 (1950): 156–67.

Aulén, Gustaf. *Christus Victor: An Historical Study of the Three Main Types of the Idea of Atonement*. Translated by A. G. Hebert. London: SPCK, 1970.

Aulén, Gustaf. *The Faith of the Christian Church*. Translated by Eric H. Wahlstrom. 2nd ed. London: SCM Press, 1961.

Bagnato, Robert A. "Karl Barth's Personalizing of 'Juridical Redemption.'" *Anglican Theological Review* 49, no. 1 (1967): 45–69.

Bakker, N. T. "Der Mensch vor und nach dem Nichts: Anthropologische Erkundungen im Niemandsland (über K. Barths Lehre vom Nichtigen)." *Zeitschrift für Dialektische Theologie* 2, no. 1 (1986): 109–27.

Balthasar, Hans Urs von. *The Theology of Karl Barth*. Translated by Edward T. Oakes. San Francisco, CA: Ignatius Press, 1992.

Barth, Karl. *The Christian Life*. Church Dogmatics, vol. IV, part 4, Lecture Fragments. Edinburgh: T&T Clark, 1981.

Barth, Karl. *Church Dogmatics*. Edited by G. W. Bromiley and T. F. Torrance. 4 vols in 13 parts. Peabody, MA: Hendrickson, 2010.

Barth, Karl. *Die Kirchliche Dogmatik*. 4 vols in 13 parts. Munich: Chr. Kaiser, 1932 and thereafter Zürich: EVZ, 1938–65.

Barth, Karl. *Dogmatics in Outline*. Translated by G. T. Thomson. London: SCM Press, 1966.

Barth, Karl. *The Epistle to the Ephesians*. Translated by Ross Wright. Grand Rapids, MI: Baker Academic, 2017.

Barth, Karl. *The Epistle to the Romans*. Translated by Edwin C. Hoskyns. Oxford: Oxford University Press, 1968.

Barth, Karl. *Erklärungen des Epheser- und des Jakobusbriefes, 1919–1929*. Edited by Jörg-Michael Bohnet. *Gesamtausgabe*, II.46. Zürich: TVZ, 2009.

Barth, Karl. *Ethics*. Edited by Dietrich Braun. Translated by Geoffrey W. Bromiley. New York: Seabury Press, 1981.

Barth, Karl. "Gespräch in Princeton I." In *Gespräche 1959–1962*, edited by Eberhard Busch, 496–509. *Gesamtausgabe*, IV.25. Zürich: TVZ, 1995.

Barth, Karl. *The Göttingen Dogmatics: Instruction in the Christian Religion*, vol. 1, trans. Geoffrey W. Bromiley. Grand Rapids, MI: Eerdmans, 1990.

Barth, Karl. *The Knowledge of God and the Service of God According to the Teaching of the Reformation: Recalling the Scottish Confession of 1560*. Translated by J. L. M. Haire and Ian Henderson. London: Hodder & Stoughton, 1938.

Barth, Karl. *Predigten 1913*. Edited by Nelly Barth and Gerhard Sauter. *Gesamtausgabe*, I.8. Zürich: TVZ, 1976.

Barth, Karl. *Predigten 1915*. Edited by Heinrich Schmidt. *Gesamtausgabe*, I.27. Zürich: TVZ, 1996.

Barth, Karl. *Predigten 1916*. Edited by Anton Drewes. *Gesamtausgabe*, I.29. Zürich: TVZ, 1998.

Barth, Karl. *Predigten 1921–35*. Edited by Holger Finze. *Gesamtausgabe*, I.31. Zürich: TVZ, 1998.

Barth, Karl. "Rudolf Bultmann—An Attempt to Understand Him." In *Kerygma and Myth: A Theological Debate*, edited by Hans-Werner Bartsch, translated by Reginald H. Fuller, II: 83–132. London: SPCK, 1962.

Barth, Karl. *A Shorter Commentary on Romans*. Edited by Maico Michielin. Translated by D. H. van Daalen. Aldershot: Ashgate, 2007.

Barth, Karl. *The Theology of Schleiermacher: Lectures at Göttingen, Winter Semester of 1923/24*. Edited by Dietrich T. Ritschl. Translated by Geoffrey W. Bromiley. Edinburgh: T&T Clark, 1982.

Barth, Karl. *Unterricht in der christlichen Religion 3: Die Lehre von der Versöhnung/Erlösung 1925/26*. Edited by Hinrich Stoevesandt. *Gesamtausgabe*, II.38. Zürich: TVZ, 2002.

Barth, Markus, and Verne H. Fletcher. *Acquittal by Resurrection*. New York: Holt, Rinehart and Winston, 1964.

Bayer, Oswald. *Martin Luther's Theology: A Contemporary Interpretation*. Translated by Thomas H. Trapp. Grand Rapids, MI: Eerdmans, 2008.

Bayer, Oswald. "The Word of the Cross." Translated by John R. Betz. *Lutheran Quarterly* 9, no. 1 (1995): 47–55.

Beintker, Michael. *Die Dialektik in der "dialektischen Theologie" Karl Barths: Studien zur Entwicklung der Barthschen Theologie und zur Vorgeschichte der "Kirchlichen Dogmatik."* München: Chr. Kaiser Verlag, 1987.

Beker, J. Christiaan. *Paul's Apocalyptic Gospel: The Coming Triumph of God*. Philadelphia, PA: Fortress Press, 1992.

Beker, J. Christiaan. *Paul the Apostle: The Triumph of God in Life and Thought*. Edinburgh: T&T Clark, 1980.

Bender, Kimlyn J. "The Reformers as Fathers of the Church: Luther and Calvin in the Thought of Karl Barth." *Scottish Journal of Theology* 72, no. 4 (2019): 414–31.

Berkouwer, G. C. *The Triumph of Grace in the Theology of Karl Barth*. Translated by Harry R. Boer. London: Paternoster, 1956.

Berkouwer, G. C. *The Work of Christ*. Translated by Cornelius Lambregtse. Grand Rapids, MI: Eerdmans, 1965.

Best, Ernest. *The Temptation and the Passion: The Markan Soteriology*. 2nd ed. Cambridge: Cambridge University Press, 1990.

Beuken, Willem A. M. *Isaiah Part II, Volume 2: Isaiah 28–39*. Translated by Brian Doyle. Leuven: Peeters, 2000.

Blenkinsopp, Joseph. *Isaiah 1–39. A New Translation with Introduction and Commentary*. Garden City, NY: Doubleday, 2000.

Bloesch, Donald G. *Jesus Is Victor! Karl Barth's Doctrine of Salvation*. Nashville, TN: Abingdon Press, 1976.

Bock, Darrell. *Mark*. New York: Cambridge University Press, 2015.
Boer, Martinus C. de. *Galatians: A Commentary*. The New Testament Library. Louisville, KY: Westminster John Knox Press, 2011.
Boer, Martinus C. de. "Paul and Apocalyptic Eschatology." In *Continuum History of Apocalypticism*, edited by John J. Collins, Bernard McGinn, and Stephen J. Stein, 166–94. New York: Continnuum, 2003.
Boer, Martinus C. de. "Paul and Jewish Apocalyptic Eschatology." In *Apocalyptic and the New Testament: Essays in Honour of J. Louis Martyn*, edited by Marion L. Soards and Joel Marcus, 169–90. London: Bloomsbury, 2015.
Boer, Martinus C. de. "Paul, Theologian of God's Apocalypse." *Interpretation* 56, no. 1 (2002): 21–33.
Boer, Martinus C. de. "Paul's Mythologizing Program in Romans 5–8." In *Apocalyptic Paul: Cosmos and Anthropos in Romans 5–8*, edited by Beverly Roberts Gaventa, 1–20. Waco, TX: Baylor University Press, 2013.
Boer, Martinus C. de. *The Defeat of Death: Apocalyptic Eschatology in 1 Corinthians 15 and Romans 5*. Sheffield: Sheffield Academic Press, 1988.
Boersma, Hans. *Violence, Hospitality, and the Cross: Reappropriating the Atonement Tradition*. Grand Rapids, MI: Baker Academic, 2004.
Bonhoeffer, Dietrich. *Berlin: 1932–1933*. Edited by Larry L. Rasmussen. Translated by Isabel Best and David Higgins. Dietrich Bonhoeffer Works 12. Minneapolis, MN: Fortress Press, 2009.
Bonhoeffer, Dietrich. *Creation and Temptation*. London: SCM Press, 1966.
Borg, Marcus J. *Jesus: Uncovering the Life, Teachings, and Relevance of a Religious Revolutionary*. New York: HarperOne, 2006.
Branick, Vincent P. "The Sinful Flesh of the Son of God (Rom 8:3): A Key Image of Pauline Theology." *Catholic Biblical Quarterly* 47, no. 2 (1985): 246–62.
Bromiley, Geoffrey W. *Introduction to the Theology of Karl Barth*. Edinburgh: T&T Clark, 1980.
Brueggemann, Walter. *Isaiah 1–39*. Westminster Bible Companion. Louisville, KY: Westminster John Knox Press, 1998.
Brunner, Emil. *The Christian Doctrine of Creation and Redemption: Dogmatics, Vol. II*. Translated by Olive Wyon. Philadelphia, PA: Westminster Press, 1952.
Brunner, Emil. *The Christian Doctrine of God: Dogmatics*, vol. 1. Translated by Olive Wyon. Philadelphia, PA: Westminster Press, 1949.
Bultmann, Rudolf. "New Testament and Mythology: The Problem of Demythologizing the New Testament Proclamation (1941)." In *New Testament and Mythology and Other Basic Writings*, edited and translated by Schubert M. Ogden, 1–43. Philadelphia, PA: Fortress Press, 1984.
Bultmann, Rudolf. *Theology of the New Testament: Volume I*. Translated by Kendrick Grobel. New York: Charles Scribner's, 1951.
Busch, Eberhard. "Der Theologische Ort der Christologie: Karl Barths Versöhnungslehre im Rahmen des Bundes." *Zeitschrift für Dialektische Theologie* 18, no. 2 (2002): 121–37.
Busch, Eberhard. *Karl Barth: His Life from Letters and Autobiographical Texts*. Translated by John Bowden. London: SCM Press, 1976.
Calvin, John. *Commentary on the Book of the Prophet Isaiah*. Translated by William Pringle. Vol. 2. Edinburgh: Calvin Translation Society, 1851.
Calvin, John. *Institutes of the Christian Religion: Volume One*. Edited by John T. McNeill. Translated by Ford Lewis Battles. Louisville, KY: Westminster John Knox Press, 2006.

Camfield, F. W. "The Idea of Substitution in the Doctrine of the Atonement." *Scottish Journal of Theology* 1, no. 3 (1948): 282–93.

Chalamet, Christophe. "Barth and Liberal Protestantism." In *The Oxford Handbook of Karl Barth*, edited by Paul T. Nimmo and Paul Dafydd Jones, 132–46. Oxford: Oxford University Press, 2019.

Chalamet, Christophe. "Divine Extravagance, or Barth's Challenges to Christian Theology in *Church Dogmatics* IV/1, §59.1 ('The Way of the Son of God into the Far Country')." *Zeitschrift für Dialektische Theologie* 32, no. 1 (2016): 96–118.

Chao, David C. "Cur Deus homo? Reflections on Divine Power and Ontology in Barth's Doctrine of Reconciliation, *Church Dogmatics* IV/1, §59." *Zeitschrift für Dialektische Theologie* 32, no. 1 (2016): 119–35.

Cochrane, Arthur C. *The Existentialists and God: Being and the Being of God in the Thought of Søren Kierkegaard, Karl Jaspers, Martin Heidegger, Jean-Paul Sartre, Paul Tillich, Etienne Gilson, Karl Barth*. Philadelphia, PA: Westminster Press, 1956.

Collins, Adela Yarbro. *Mark: A Commentary*. Edited by Harold W. Attridge. Minneapolis, MN: Fortress Press, 2007.

Cone, James. *God of the Oppressed*. Revised. Maryknoll, NY: Orbis Books, 1997.

Congdon, David W. "Apocalypse as Perpetual Advent: The Apocalyptic Sermons of Rudolf Bultmann." *Theology Today* 75, no. 1 (2018): 51–63.

Congdon, David W. "Bonhoeffer and Bultmann: Toward an Apocalyptic Rapprochement." *International Journal of Systematic Theology* 15, no. 2 (2013): 172–95.

Congdon, David W. "Eschatologizing Apocalyptic: An Assessment of the Present Conversation on Pauline Apocalyptic." In *Apocalyptic and the Future of Theology: With and beyond J. Louis Martyn*, edited by Joshua B. Davis and Douglas Harink, 118–36. Eugene: Cascade, 2012.

Conzelmann, Hans. *The Theology of St. Luke*. Translated by Geoffrey Buswell. London: Faber and Faber, 1960.

Coutts, Jon. *A Shared Mercy: Karl Barth on Forgiveness and the Church*. Downers Grove: IVP Academic, 2016.

Crysdale, Cynthia S. W. *Embracing Travail: Retrieving the Cross Today*. New York: Continuum, 2001.

Daniels, T. Scott, Thomas N. Finger, J. Denny Weaver, and John Sanders. *Atonement and Violence: A Theological Conversation*. Edited by John Sanders. Nashville, TN: Abingdon Press, 2006.

Davies, J. P. *Paul among the Apocalypses? An Evaluation of the "Apocalyptic Paul" in the Context of Jewish and Christian Apocalyptic Literature*. London: T&T Clark, 2016.

Davies, Margaret. *Matthew*. 2nd ed. Sheffield: Sheffield Phoenix Press, 2009.

Davis, Joshua B. "The Challenge of Apocalyptic to Modern Theology." In *Apocalyptic and the Future of Theology: With and beyond J. Louis Martyn*, edited by Joshua B. Davis and Douglas Harink, 1–48. Eugene: Cascade, 2012.

Dawson, R. Dale. *The Resurrection in Karl Barth*. Aldershot: Ashgate, 2007.

Demarest, Bruce. *The Cross and Salvation: The Doctrine of Salvation*. Wheaton, IL: Crossway, 2006.

Dorner, Isaak A. *A System of Christian Doctrine: Volume III*. Translated by Alfred Cave and J. S. Banks. Edinburgh: T&T Clark, 1882.

Dunn, James D. G. *Romans 1–8*. Dallas: Word Books, 1988.

Dunn, James D. G. *The Theology of Paul the Apostle*. Grand Rapids, MI: Eerdmans, 1998.

Edwards, James R. *The Gospel According to Mark*. Grand Rapids, MI: Eerdmans, 2002.

Eitel, Adam. "The Resurrection of Jesus Christ: Karl Barth and the Historicization of God's Being." *International Journal of Systematic Theology* 10, no. 1 (2008): 36–53.

Engberg-Pedersen, Troels. *Paul and the Stoics*. Louisville, KY: T&T Clark, 2000.

Etzelmüller, Gregor. "'Er kommt und schafft Gerechtigkeit': Perspektiven auf Barths ungeschriebene Erlösungslehre." *Zeitschrift für Dialektische Theologie* 21, no. 3 (2005): 238–58.

Evans, Craig A. *Matthew*. New York: Cambridge University Press, 2012.

Fairweather, Eugene R. "Incarnation and Atonement: An Anselmian Response to Aulen's *Christus Victor*." *Canadian Journal of Theology* 7, no. 3 (1961): 167–75.

Fiorenza, Elisabeth Schüssler. *In Memory of Her: A Feminist Theological Reconstruction of Christian Origins*. New York: Crossroad, 1994.

Fitzmyer, Joseph A. *Romans: A New Translation with Introduction and Commentary*. Garden City, NY: Doubleday, 1993.

Flett, John G. "The Resurrection from the Dead as the Declaration of God's Eternal Being and the Christian Community's Eschatological Reality." *Princeton Seminary Bulletin* 31 (2010): 7–26.

Forde, Gerhard O. "Caught in the Act: Reflections on the Work of Christ." *Word & World* 3, no. 1 (1983): 22–31.

Forde, Gerhard O. *Justification by Faith: A Matter of Death and Life*. Eugene, OR: Wipf and Stock, 2012.

Forde, Gerhard O. *On Being a Theologian of the Cross: Reflections on Luther's Heidelberg Disputation, 1518*. Grand Rapids, MI: Eerdmans, 1997.

Forde, Gerhard O. *Where God Meets Man: Luther's Down-to-Earth Approach to the Gospel*. Minneapolis, MN: Augsburg, 1972.

Forde, Gerhard O. "The Work of Christ." In *Christian Dogmatics: Volume 2*, edited by Carl E. Braaten and Robert W. Jenson, 1–99. Philadelphia, PA: Fortress Press, 1984.

Frey, Jörg. "Demythologizing Apocalyptic? On N. T. Wright's Paul, Apocalyptic Interpretation, and the Constraints of Construction." In *God and the Faithfulness of Paul: A Critical Examination of the Pauline Theology of N.T. Wright*, edited by Christoph Heilig, J. Thomas Hewitt, and Michael F. Bird, 489–531. Tübingen: Mohr Siebeck, 2016.

Fuller, Reginald H. *Interpreting the Miracles*. Philadelphia, PA: Westminster Press, 1963.

Gaffin, Jr, Richard B. *Resurrection and Redemption: A Study in Paul's Soteriology*. Phillipsburg: Presbyterian and Reformed, 1987.

Garrett, Susan R. *The Demise of the Devil: Magic and the Demonic in Luke's Writings*. Minneapolis, MN: Fortress Press, 1989.

Gaventa, Beverly Roberts. "The Cosmic Power of Sin in Paul's Letter to the Romans: Toward a Widescreen Edition." *Interpretation* 58, no. 3 (2004): 229–40.

Gaventa, Beverly Roberts. "God Handed Them Over." In *Our Mother Saint Paul*, 113–23. Louisville, KY: Westminster John Knox Press, 2007.

Gaventa, Beverly Roberts. "Interpreting the Death of Jesus Apocalyptically: Reconsidering Romans 8:32." In *Jesus and Paul Reconnected: Fresh Pathways into an Old Debate*, edited by Todd D. Still, 125–45. Grand Rapids, MI: Eerdmans, 2007.

Gaventa, Beverly Roberts. "Neither Height nor Depth: Discerning the Cosmology of Romans." *Scottish Journal of Theology* 64, no. 3 (2011): 265–78.

Gaventa, Beverly Roberts. "The Rhetoric of Violence and the God of Peace in Paul's Letter to the Romans." In *Paul, John, and Apocalyptic Eschatology: Studies in Honour of*

Martinus C. de Boer, edited by Jan Krans, Bert Jan Lietaert Peerbolte, Peter-Ben Smit, and Arie Zwiep, 61–75. Leiden: Brill, 2013.

Gockel, Matthias. *Barth and Schleiermacher on the Doctrine of Election: A Systematic-Theological Comparison*. Oxford: Oxford University Press, 2006.

Godet, Frédéric. *A Commentary on the Gospel of St. Luke*. Translated by E. W. Shalders and M. D. Cusin. Vol. 1. New York: I. K. Funk, 1881.

Godet, Frédéric. *Commentary on St. Paul's Epistle to the Romans*. Translated by A. Cusin. Vol. 1. Edinburgh: T&T Clark, 1881.

Graham, Jeannine Michele. *Representation and Substitution in the Atonement Theologies of Dorothee Sölle, John Macquarrie, and Karl Barth*. New York: Peter Lang, 2005.

Grebe, Matthias. *Election, Atonement, and the Holy Spirit: Through and Beyond Barth's Theological Interpretation of Scripture*. Cambridge: James Clarke, 2015.

Green, Joel B. *The Gospel of Luke*. Grand Rapids, MI: Eerdmans, 1997.

Green, Joel B. "Theologies of Atonement in the New Testament." In *T&T Clark Companion to Atonement*, edited by Adam J. Johnson, 115–34. New York: T&T Clark, 2017.

Greggs, Tom. "Karl Barth." In *Christian Theologies of Salvation: A Comparative Introduction*, edited by Justin S. Holcomb, 300–17. New York: New York University Press, 2017.

Gunton, Colin E. *The Actuality of Atonement: A Study of Metaphor, Rationality and the Christian Tradition*. London: T&T Clark, 2003.

Haddorff, David. *Christian Ethics as Witness: Barth's Ethics for a World at Risk*. Eugene, OR: Cascade, 2011.

Hailer, Martin. "Karl Barths Nichtiges und Martin Luthers Deus absconditus." In *Die Unbegreiflichkeit des Reiches Gottes: Studien zur Theologie Karl Barths*, 34–91. Neukirchen-Vluyn: Neukirchener Theologie, 2004.

Hall, Charles A. M. *With the Spirit's Sword: The Drama of Spiritual Warfare in the Theology of John Calvin*. Zürich: EVZ-Verlag, 1968.

Harink, Douglas. *Paul among the Postliberals: Pauline Theology beyond Christendom and Modernity*. Grand Rapids, MI: Brazos Press, 2003.

Härle, Wilfried. *Sein und Gnade: Die Ontologie in Karl Barths Kirchlicher Dogmatik*. Berlin: Walter de Gruyter, 1975.

Harnack, Adolf von. *What Is Christianity? Lectures Delivered in the University of Berlin During the Winter-Term 1899–1900*. Translated by Thomas B. Saunders. London: Williams and Norgate, 1902.

Hart, David Bentley. *The Beauty of the Infinite: The Aesthetics of Christian Truth*. Grand Rapids, MI: Eerdmans, 2003.

Hart, David Bentley. "A Gift Exceeding Every Debt: An Eastern Orthodox Appreciation of Anselm's Cur Deus Homo." *Pro Ecclesia* 7, no. 3 (1998): 333–49.

Hart, Trevor. *In Him Was Life: The Person and Work of Christ*. Waco, TX: Baylor University Press, 2019.

Hart, Trevor. "Revelation." In *The Cambridge Companion to Karl Barth*, edited by John Webster, 37–56. New York: Cambridge University Press, 2000.

Hasel, Frank M. "Karl Barth's *Church Dogmatics* on the Atonement: Some Translation Problems." *Andrews University Seminary Studies* 29, no. 3 (1991): 205–11.

Hays, Richard B. "Apocalyptic Poiesis in Galatians: Paternity, Passion, and Participation." In *Galatians and Christian Theology: Justification, the Gospel, and Ethics in Paul's Letter*, edited by Mark W. Elliott, Scott J. Hafemann, N. T. Wright, and John Frederick, 200–19. Grand Rapids, MI: Baker Academic, 2014.

Hendry, George S. *The Gospel of the Incarnation*. London: SCM Press, 1959.
Heppe, Heinrich. *Reformed Dogmatics*. Edited by Ernst Bizer. Translated by G. T. Thomson. Revised ed. Eugene, OR: Wipf & Stock, 2008.
Heron, Alasdair I. C. "The Theme of Salvation in Karl Barth's Doctrine of Reconciliation." *Ex Auditu* 5 (1989): 107–22.
Highfield, Ron. *Barth and Rahner in Dialogue: Toward an Ecumenical Understanding of Sin and Evil*. New York: Peter Lang, 1989.
Hitchcock, Nathan. *Karl Barth and the Resurrection of the Flesh: The Loss of the Body in Participatory Eschatology*. Eugene, OR: Pickwick, 2013.
Hodgson, Leonard. *The Doctrine of the Atonement*. New York: Scribner, 1951.
Holmes, Christopher R. J. "Disclosure without Reservation: Re-Evaluating Divine Hiddenness." *Neue Zeitschrift für Systematische Theologie und Religionsphilosophie* 48, no. 3 (2006): 367–80.
Hooker, Morna D. "The Nature of New Testament Theology." In *The Nature of New Testament Theology: Essays in Honour of Robert Morgan*, edited by Christopher Rowland and Christopher Tuckett, 75–92. Malden, MA: Wiley-Blackwell, 2006.
Horton, Michael S. "Covenant, Election, and Incarnation: Evaluating Barth's Actualist Christology." In *Karl Barth and American Evangelicalism*, edited by Bruce L. McCormack, 112–47. Grand Rapids, MI: Eerdmans, 2011.
Hunsinger, George. "Karl Barth's Christology: Its Basic Chalcedonian Character." In *The Cambridge Companion to Karl Barth*, edited by John Webster, 127–42. New York: Cambridge University Press, 2000.
Hunsinger, George. "The Politics of the Nonviolent God: Reflections on René Girard and Karl Barth." *Scottish Journal of Theology* 51, no. 1 (1998): 61–85.
Hunsinger, George. "What Karl Barth Learned from Martin Luther." In *Disruptive Grace: Studies in the Theology of Karl Barth*, 279–304. Grand Rapids, MI: Eerdmans, 2000.
Jennings, Theodore W. "Apocalyptic and Contemporary Theology." *Quarterly Review* 4, no. 3 (1984): 54–68.
Jenson, Matt. *The Gravity of Sin: Augustine, Luther and Barth on "Homo Incurvatus In Se."* London: T&T Clark, 2007.
Jenson, Robert W. *Alpha and Omega: A Study in the Theology of Karl Barth*. New York: Thomas Nelson, 1963.
Jenson, Robert W. "Apocalyptic and Messianism in Twentieth Century German Theology." In *Messianism, Apocalypse and Redemption in 20th Century German Thought*, edited by Wayne Cristaudo and Wendy Baker, 3–12. Adelaide: ATF Press, 2006.
Jenson, Robert W. *Systematic Theology, Volume 1: The Triune God*. New York: Oxford University Press, 1997.
Jersild, Paul. "Judgment of God in Albrecht Ritschl and Karl Barth." *Lutheran Quarterly* 14, no. 4 (1962): 328–46.
Jewett, Robert. *Romans: A Commentary*. Edited by Eldon Jay Epp. Minneapolis, MN: Fortress Press, 2006.
Johnson, Adam J. *God's Being in Reconciliation: The Theological Basis of the Unity and Diversity of the Atonement in the Theology of Karl Barth*. London: T&T Clark, 2012.
Johnson, Keith L. "Karl Barth's Reading of Paul's Union with Christ." In *"In Christ" in Paul: Explorations in Paul's Theology of Union and Participation*, edited by Michael J. Thate, Kevin J. Vanhoozer, and Constantine R. Campbell, 453–74. Tübingen: Mohr Siebeck, 2014.
Johnson, Luke Timothy. *The Gospel of Luke*. Collegeville, PA: Liturgical Press, 1991.

Jones, Paul Dafydd. "Barth and Anselm: God, Christ and the Atonement." *International Journal of Systematic Theology* 12, no. 3 (2010): 257–82.

Jones, Paul Dafydd. "Karl Barth on Gethsemane." *International Journal of Systematic Theology* 9, no. 2 (2007): 148–71.

Jüngel, Eberhard. "The Revelation of the Hiddenness of God: A Contribution to the Protestant Understanding of the Hiddenness of Divine Action." In *Theological Essays II*, edited by John Webster, translated by Arnold Neufeldt-Fast and John Webster, 120–44. Edinburgh: T&T Clark, 1995.

Käsemann, Ernst. *Commentary on Romans*. Translated by Geoffrey W. Bromiley. Grand Rapids, MI: Eerdmans, 1980.

Käsemann, Ernst. "The Faith of Abraham in Romans 4." In *Perspectives on Paul*, translated by Margaret Kohl, 79–101. Philadelphia, PA: Fortress Press, 1971.

Käsemann, Ernst. *Jesus Means Freedom*. Translated by Frank Clark. Philadelphia, PA: Fortress Press, 1969.

Käsemann, Ernst. "Justification and Salvation History in the Epistle to the Romans." In *Perspectives on Paul*, translated by Margaret Kohl, 60–78. Philadelphia, PA: Fortress Press, 1971.

Kelly, Henry Ansgar. *Satan in the Bible, God's Minister of Justice*. Eugene, OR: Cascade, 2017.

Kerr, Nathan R. *Christ, History and Apocalyptic: The Politics of Christian Mission*. Eugene, OR: Cascade, 2008.

Klappert, Bertold. *Die Auferweckung des Gekreuzigten: Der Ansatz der Christologie Karl Barths im Zusammenhang mit der Christologie der Gegenwart*. Neukirchen-Vluyn: Neukirchener Verlag, 1981.

Klooster, Fred H. *The Significance of Barth's Theology: An Appraisal, with Special Reference to Election and Reconciliation*. Grand Rapids, MI: Baker Book House, 1961.

Kovacs, Judith L. "'Now Shall the Ruler of This World Be Driven Out': Jesus' Death as Cosmic Battle in John 12:20–36." *Journal of Biblical Literature* 114, no. 2 (1995): 227–47.

Krötke, Wolf. "Sin." In *The Westminster Handbook to Karl Barth*, edited by Richard E. Burnett, 202–4. Louisville, KY: Westminster John Knox Press, 2013.

Krötke, Wolf. *Sin and Nothingness in the Theology of Karl Barth*. Edited and translated by Philip G. Ziegler and Christina-Maria Bammel. Princeton, NJ: Princeton Theological Seminary, 2005.

Künneth, Walter. *The Theology of the Resurrection*. Translated by James W. Leitch. St Louis: Concordia Publishing House, 1965.

Landy, Francis. "Tracing the Voice of the Other: Isaiah 28 and the Covenant with Death." In *Beauty and the Enigma: And Other Essays on the Hebrew Bible*, 185–205. Sheffield: Sheffield Academic Press, 2001.

Lange, Johann P. *The Epistle of Paul to the Romans*. Translated by John F. Hurst Hurst. New York: Charles Scribner's, 1869.

Lauber, David. *Barth on the Descent into Hell: God, Atonement and the Christian Life*. Burlington: Ashgate, 2004.

Lewis, Alan E. "The Burial of God: Rupture and Resumption as the Story of Salvation." *Scottish Journal of Theology* 40, no. 3 (1987): 335–62.

Lowe, Walter. "Why We Need Apocalyptic." *Scottish Journal of Theology* 63, no. 1 (2010): 41–53.

Luce, H. K. *The Gospel According to S. Luke*. Cambridge Greek Testament for Schools and Colleges. Cambridge: Cambridge University Press, 1933.

Luther, Martin. *Lectures on Galatians 1535: Chapters 1–4*. Edited and translated by Jaroslav Pelikan. Luther's Works 26. Saint Louis, MO: Concordia Publishing House, 1963.

Luther, Martin. *Lectures on Isaiah, Chapters 1–39*. Edited by Jaroslav Pelikan. Translated by Herbert J. A. Bouman. Luther's Works 16. Saint Louis, MO: Concordia Publishing House, 1969.

Luther, Martin. *Lectures on Romans*. Edited and translated by Wilhelm Pauck. The Library of Christian Classics. Louisville, KY: Westminster John Knox Press, 2006.

Luther, Martin. *Predigten 1533/34*. Luthers Werke: Kritische Gesamtausgabe [Schriften] 37. Weimar: H. Böhlau, 1910.

Luther, Martin. "Psalm 117." In *Selected Psalms III*, edited by Jaroslav Pelikan, translated by Edward Sittler, 1–39. Luther's Works 14. Saint Louis, MO: Concordia Publishing House, 1958.

Luther, Martin. "The Large Catechism." In *The Book of Concord: The Confessions of the Evangelical Lutheran Church*, edited by Robert Kolb and Timothy J. Wengert, translated by Charles P. Arand, Eric Gritsch, Robert Kolb, William Russell, James Schaaf, Jane Strohl, and Timothy J. Wengert. Minneapolis, MN: Fortress Press, 2000.

Luther, Martin. *Tischreden: Volume 5*. Luthers Werke: Kritische Gesamtausgabe [Tischreden; 6 vols]. Weimar: H. Böhlau, 1912–21.

Luz, Ulrich. *Matthew 21–28*. Edited by Helmut Koester. Translated by James E. Crouch. Minneapolis, MN: Augsburg Fortress, 2005.

Macaskill, Grant. *Union with Christ in the New Testament*. Oxford: Oxford University Press, 2013.

MacDonald, Neil B. *Karl Barth and the Strange New World within the Bible: Barth, Wittgenstein, and the Metadilemmas of the Enlightenment*. Carlisle: Paternoster, 2000.

Macquarrie, John. "Demonology and the Classic Idea of Atonement." *Expository Times* 68, no. 1 (1956): 3–6.

Macquarrie, John. "Demonology and the Classic Idea of Atonement (Continued)." *Expository Times* 68, no. 2 (1956): 60–3.

Mangina, Joseph L. *Karl Barth: Theologian of Christian Witness*. Burlington: Ashgate, 2004.

Mann, C. S. *Mark: A New Translation with Introduction and Commentary*. Garden City, NY: Doubleday, 1986.

Martyn, J. Louis. "Afterword: The Human Moral Drama." In *Apocalyptic Paul: Cosmos and Anthropos in Romans 5–8*, edited by Beverly Roberts Gaventa, 157–66. Waco, TX: Baylor University Press, 2013.

Martyn, J. Louis. "The Apocalyptic Gospel in Galatians." *Interpretation* 54, no. 3 (2000): 246–66.

Martyn, J. Louis. "From Paul to Flannery O'Connor with the Power of Grace." In *Theological Issues in the Letters of Paul*, 279–97. Nashville, TN: Abingdon Press, 1997.

Martyn, J. Louis. *Galatians: A New Translation with Introduction and Commentary*. New Haven, CT: Yale University Press, 1997.

Martyn, J. Louis. "World without End or Twice-Invaded World?" In *Shaking Heaven and Earth: Essays in Honor of Walter Brueggemann and Charles B. Cousar*, edited by Christine Roy Yoder, Kathleen M. O'Connor, E. Elizabeth Johnson, and Stanley P. Saunders, 117–32. Louisville, KY: Westminster John Knox Press, 2005.

Martyr, Justin. *Dialogue with Trypho*. Edited by Michael Slusser. Translated by Thomas B. Falls. Washington, DC: Catholic University of America Press, 2003.

Massmann, Alexander. *Citizenship in Heaven and on Earth: Karl Barth's Ethics*. Minneapolis, MN: Fortress Press, 2015.

Matlock, R. Barry. *Unveiling the Apocalyptic Paul: Paul's Interpreters and the Rhetoric of Criticism*. Sheffield: Sheffield Academic Press, 1996.

McCormack, Bruce L. "Can We Still Speak of 'Justification by Faith'? An In-House Debate with Apocalyptic Readings of Paul." In *Galatians and Christian Theology: Justification, the Gospel, and Ethics in Paul's Letter*, edited by Mark W. Elliott, Scott J. Hafemann, N. T. Wright, and John Frederick, 159–84. Grand Rapids, MI: Baker Academic, 2014.

McCormack, Bruce L. "Divine Impassibility or Simply Divine Constancy? Implications of Karl Barth's Later Christology for Debates over Impassibility." In *Divine Impassibility and the Mystery of Human Suffering*, edited by James F. Keating and Thomas Joseph White, 150–86. Grand Rapids, MI: Eerdmans, 2009.

McCormack, Bruce L. "For Us and Our Salvation: Incarnation and Atonement in the Reformed Tradition." *Greek Orthodox Theological Review* 43, nos. 1–4 (1998): 281–316.

McCormack, Bruce L. "Grace and Being: The Role of God's Gracious Election in Karl Barth's Theological Ontology." In *The Cambridge Companion to Karl Barth*, edited by John Webster, 92–110. New York: Cambridge University Press, 2000.

McCormack, Bruce L. "*Justitia aliena*: Karl Barth in Conversation with the Evangelical Doctrine of Imputed Righteousness." In *Justification in Perspective: Historical Developments and Contemporary Challenges*, edited by Bruce L. McCormack, 167–96. Grand Rapids, MI: Baker Academic, 2006.

McCormack, Bruce L. *Karl Barth's Critically Realistic Dialectical Theology: Its Genesis and Development, 1909–1936*. New York: Oxford University Press, 1997.

McCormack, Bruce L. "Karl Barth's Historicized Christology: Just How 'Chalcedonian' Is It?" In *Orthodox and Modern: Studies in the Theology of Karl Barth*, 201–33. Grand Rapids, MI: Baker Academic, 2008.

McCormack, Bruce L. "Longing for a New World: On Socialism, Eschatology and Apocalyptic in Barth's Early Dialectical Theology." In *Theologie im Umbruch der Moderne: Karl Barths frühe Dialektische Theologie*, edited by Harald Matern and Georg Pfleiderer, 135–49. Zürich: TVZ, 2014.

McCormack, Bruce L. "The Passion of God Himself: Barth on Jesus's Cry of Dereliction." In *Reading the Gospels with Karl Barth*, edited by Daniel L. Migliore, 155–72. Grand Rapids, MI: Eerdmans, 2017.

McDowell, John C. "Much Ado about Nothing: Karl Barth's Being Unable to Do Nothing about Nothingness." *International Journal of Systematic Theology* 4, no. 3 (2002): 319–35.

McGrath, Alister E. *Iustitia Dei: A History of the Christian Doctrine of Justification*. 3rd ed. Cambridge: Cambridge University Press, 2005.

McMaken, W. Travis. "Election and the Pattern of Exchange in Karl Barth's Doctrine of the Atonement." *Journal of Reformed Theology* 3, no. 2 (2009): 202–18.

McSwain, Jeff. *Simul Sanctification: Barth's Hidden Vision for Human Transformation*. Eugene, OR: Pickwick, 2018.

Mikkelsen, Hans Vium. *Reconciled Humanity: Karl Barth in Dialogue*. Grand Rapids, MI: Eerdmans, 2010.

Moltmann, Jürgen. *God in Creation: An Ecological Doctrine of Creation*. Translated by Margaret Kohl. London: SCM Press, 1985.

Moltmann, Jürgen. *The Way of Jesus Christ: Christology in Messianic Dimensions*. Translated by Margaret Kohl. London: SCM Press, 1990.

Moltmann, Jürgen. "Zwölf Bemerkungen zur Symbolik des Bösen." *Evangelische Theologie* 52 (1992): 2–6.

Moo, Douglas J. *Epistle to the Romans*. Grand Rapids, MI: Eerdmans, 1996.

Mueller, David L. *Foundation of Karl Barth's Doctrine of Reconciliation: Jesus Christ Crucified and Risen*. Lewiston: Edwin Mellen Press, 1990.
Neder, Adam. *Participation in Christ: An Entry into Karl Barth's Church Dogmatics*. Louisville, KY: Westminster John Knox Press, 2009.
Neyrey, Jerome. *The Passion According to Luke: A Redaction Study of Luke's Soteriology*. New York: Paulist Press, 1985.
Nimmo, Paul T. *Barth: A Guide for the Perplexed*. London: T&T Clark, 2017.
Nimmo, Paul T. "The Divine Wisdom and the Divine Economy." *Modern Theology* 34, no. 3 (2018): 403–18.
Nygren, Anders. "Christ and the Forces of Destruction." Translated by E. Jerome Johanson. *Scottish Journal of Theology* 4, no. 4 (1951): 363–75.
Nygren, Anders. *Commentary on Romans*. Translated by C. Rasmussen. Philadelphia, PA: Fortress Press, 1949.
O'Collins, Gerald. "Karl Barth on Christ's Resurrection." *Scottish Journal of Theology* 26, no. 1 (1973): 85–99.
Ortlund, Dane C., and G. K. Beale. "Darkness Over the Whole Land: A Biblical Theological Reflection on Mark 15:33." *Westminster Theological Journal* 75 (2013): 221–38.
Pannenberg, Wolfhart. *Jesus: God and Man*. Translated by Lewis L. Wilkins and Duane A. Priebe. 2nd ed. Philadelphia, PA: Westminster Press, 1977.
Parker, T. H. L. *The Oracles of God: An Introduction to the Preaching of John Calvin*. London: Lutterworth Press, 1947.
Pedersen, Daniel J. *Schleiermacher's Theology of Sin and Nature: Agency, Value, and Modern Theology*. New York: Routledge, 2020.
Peterson, Robert A. *Calvin's Doctrine of the Atonement*. Phillipsburg: P & R, 1983.
Pfleiderer, Georg. "The Atonement." In *Trinitarian Soundings in Systematic Theology*, edited by Paul Louis Metzger, 127–38. London: T&T Clark International, 2006.
Preus, Robert D. "The Doctrine of Justification and Reconciliation in the Theology of Karl Barth." *Concordia Theological Monthly* 31, no. 4 (April 1960): 236–44.
Price, Robert B. *Letters of the Divine Word: The Perfections of God in Karl Barth's Church Dogmatics*. London: T&T Clark, 2012.
Rad, Gerhard von. *Genesis: A Commentary*. Translated by John H. Marks. 2nd ed. London: SCM Press, 1963.
Rad, Gerhard von. *Old Testament Theology, Volume I: The Theology of Israel's Historical Traditions*. Translated by D. M. G. Stalker. Edinburgh: Oliver and Boyd, 1962.
Reeling Brouwer, Rinse H. *Karl Barth and Post-Reformation Orthodoxy*. Farnham: Ashgate, 2015.
Reeling Brouwer, Rinse H. "Karl Barth's Encounter with the Federal Theology of Johannes Cocceius: Prejudices, Criticisms, Outcomes and Open Questions." *ZDT Supplement Series* 4 (2010): 160–208.
Reeling Brouwer, Rinse H. "The Royal Man: Some Hermeneutical, Dogmatic, Biblical Theological, and Contextual Remarks." *Zeitschrift für Dialektische Theologie* 33, no. 1 (2017): 93–112.
Ricoeur, Paul. "Evil, a Challenge to Philosophy and Theology." Translated by David Pellauer. *Journal of the American Academy of Religion* 53, no. 4 (1985): 635–48.
Ridderbos, Herman. *The Gospel According to John: A Theological Commentary*. Translated by John Vriend. Grand Rapids, MI: Eerdmans, 1997.
Rieske-Braun, Uwe. *Duellum Mirabile: Studien Zum Kampfmotiv in Martin Luthers Theologie*. Göttingen: Vandehoeck & Rupprecht, 1999.

Ritschl, Albrecht. *The Christian Doctrine of Justification and Reconciliation*. Edited by H. R. Mackintosh and A. B. Macaulay. Edinburgh: T&T Clark, 1902.

Ritschl, Albrecht. *A Critical History of the Christian Doctrine of Justification and Reconciliation*. Translated by John S. Black. Edinburgh: Edmonston and Douglas, 1872.

Rodin, R. Scott. *Evil and Theodicy in the Theology of Karl Barth*. New York: Peter Lang, 1997.

Rose, Matthew. *Ethics with Barth: God, Metaphysics and Morals*. Farnham: Ashgate, 2010.

Rudman, Dominic. "The Crucifixion as Chaoskampf: A New Reading of the Passion Narrative in the Synoptic Gospels." *Biblica* 84, no. 1 (2003): 102–7.

Ruether, Rosemary Radford. "The Left Hand of God in the Theology of Karl Barth: Karl Barth as a Mythopoeic Theologian." *Journal of Religious Thought* 25, no. 1 (1968): 3–26.

Rutledge, Fleming. *The Crucifixion: Understanding the Death of Jesus Christ*. Grand Rapids, MI: Eerdmans, 2015.

Sanders, E. P. *Paul and Palestinian Judaism: A Comparison of Patterns of Religion*. Philadelphia, PA: Fortress Press, 1977.

Schleiermacher, Friedrich D. E. *The Christian Faith*. Edited by H. R. Mackintosh and J. S. Stewart. London: T&T Clark, 1999.

Schmid, Heinrich. *The Doctrinal Theology of the Evangelical Lutheran Church*. Translated by Charles A. Hay and Henry E. Jacobs. Philadelphia, PA: Lutheran Publication Society, 1889.

Schniewind, Julius. "A Reply to Bultmann: Theses on the Emancipation of the Kerygma from Mythology." In *Kerygma and Myth: A Theological Debate*, edited by Hans Werner Bartsch, translated by Reginald H. Fuller, 45–101. New York: Harper & Row, 1961.

Schreiber, Johannes. *Theologie des Vertrauens: Eine redaktionsgeschichtliche Untersuchung des Markusevangeliums*. Hamburg: Furche-Verlag, 1967.

Schreiner, Thomas R. "Penal Substitution Response." In *The Nature of the Atonement: Four Views*, edited by James K. Beilby and Paul R. Eddy, 50–3. Downers Grove: IVP, 2006.

Schweitzer, Albert. *The Mysticism of Paul the Apostle*. Translated by William Montgomery. 2nd ed. London: Adam & Charles Black, 1953.

Scott, J. L. "The Covenant in the Theology of Karl Barth." *Scottish Journal of Theology* 17, no. 2 (1964): 182–98.

Smythe, Shannon Nicole. *Forensic Apocalyptic Theology: Karl Barth and the Doctrine of Justification*. Minneapolis, MN: Fortress Press, 2016.

Smythe, Shannon Nicole. "Karl Barth." In *T&T Clark Companion to Atonement*, edited by Adam J. Johnson, 237–55. New York: T&T Clark, 2017.

Smythe, Shannon Nicole. "The Way of Divine and Human Handing-over: Pauline Apocalyptic, Centering Prayer, and Vulnerable Solidarity." *Theology Today* 75, no. 1 (2018): 77–88.

Spence, Alan. "A Unified Theory of the Atonement." *International Journal of Systematic Theology* 6, no. 4 (2004): 404–20.

Stein, Robert H. *Mark*. Grand Rapids, MI: Baker Academic, 2008.

Stewart, Alistair C. "The Covenant with Death in Isaiah 28." *Expository Times* 100, no. 10 (1989): 375–7.

Strecker, Georg. *Theology of the New Testament*. Edited by Friedrich Wilhelm Horn. Translated by M. Eugene Boring. Louisville, KY: Westminster John Knox Press, 2000.

Stümke, Volker. "Eschatologische Differenz in Gott? Zum Verhältnis von Barmherzigkeit und Gerechtigkeit Gottes bei Karl Barth und Friedrich-Wilhelm Marquardt." In *Zwischen gut und böse: Impulse lutherischer Sozialethik*, 44–68. Berlin: LIT Verlag, 2011.

Sturm, Richard E. "Defining the Word 'Apocalyptic': A Problem in Biblical Criticism." In *Apocalyptic and the New Testament: Essays in Honour of J. Louis Martyn*, edited by Marion L. Soards and Joel Marcus, 17–48. Sheffield: Sheffield Academic Press, 1989.
Sumner, Darren O. "Theory and Metaphor in Calvin's Doctrine of the Atonement." *Princeton Theological Review* 13, no. 2 (2007): 49–60.
Tannehill, Robert C. *Dying and Rising with Christ: A Study in Pauline Theology*. Berlin: Alfred Töpelmann, 1967.
Taubes, Jacob. "Theodicy and Theology: A Philosophical Analysis of Karl Barth's Dialectical Theology." In *From Cult to Culture: Fragments Toward a Critique of Historical Reason*, edited by Charlotte Elisheva Fonrobert and Amir Engel. Stanford, CA: Stanford University Press, 2010.
Terry, Justyn Charles. "The Forgiveness of Sins and the Work of Christ: A Case for Substitutionary Atonement." *Anglican Theological Review* 95, no. 1 (2013): 9–24.
Thielicke, Helmut. "The Restatement of New Testament Theology." In *Kerygma and Myth: A Theological Debate*, edited by Hans Werner Bartsch, translated by Reginald H. Fuller, 138–74. New York: Harper & Row, 1961.
Thiessen, Matthew. *Jesus and the Forces of Death: The Gospels' Portrayal of Ritual Impurity within First-Century Judaism*. Grand Rapids, MI: Baker Academic, 2020.
Thiselton, Anthony. *Systematic Theology*. Grand Rapids, MI: Eerdmans, 2015.
Thomas, Günter. "Chaosüberwindung und Rechtsetzung: Schöpfung und Versöhnung in Karl Barths Eschatologie." *Zeitschrift für Dialektische Theologie* 21, no. 3 (2005): 259–77.
Thomas, Günter. "Der für uns 'Gerichtete Richter': Kritische Erwägungen zu Karl Barths Versöhnungslehre." *Zeitschrift für Dialektische Theologie* 18, no. 2 (2002): 211–25.
Thurneysen, Eduard. "Introduction." In *Revolutionary Theology in the Making: Barth-Thurneysen Correspondence, 1914–1925*, edited and translated by James D. Smart, 11–25. London: Epworth Press, 1964.
Tillich, Paul. *Dynamics of Faith*. New York: Harper Torchbooks, 1958.
Tillich, Paul. *Systematic Theology, Volume II: Existence and the Christ*. London: University of Chicago Press, 1957.
Tonstad, Linn Marie. *God and Difference: The Trinity, Sexuality, and the Transformation of Finitude*. New York: Routledge, 2017.
Tseng, Shao Kai. *Karl Barth's Infralapsarian Theology: Origins and Development, 1920–1953*. Downers Grove: IVP Academic, 2016.
Vischer, Wilhelm. *The Witness of the Old Testament to Christ*. Translated by Arthur B. Crabtree. London: Lutterworth Press, 1949.
Wasserman, Emma. *Apocalypse as Holy War: Divine Politics and Polemics in the Letters of Paul*. New Haven, CT: Yale University Press, 2018.
Weaver, J. Denny. *The Nonviolent Atonement*. 2nd ed. Grand Rapids, MI: Eerdmans, 2011.
Weber, Otto. *Foundations of Dogmatics: Volume 2*. Translated by Darrell L. Guder. Grand Rapids, MI: Eerdmans, 1983.
Webster, John. *Barth*. London: Continuum, 2000.
Webster, John. *Barth's Ethics of Reconciliation*. Cambridge: Cambridge University Press, 1995.
Weiß, Johannes. "Die Bedeutung des Paulus für den modernen Christen." In *Zeitschrift für die Neutestamentliche Wissenschaft und die Kunde des Urchristentums*, edited by D. Erwin Preuschen, 127–42. Giessen: Alfred Töpelmann, 1920.
Weiß, Johannes. *Jesus' Proclamation of the Kingdom of God*. Translated by R. H. Hiers and D. L. Holland. Philadelphia, PA: Fortress Press, 1971.

Wendte, Martin. "Lamentation between Contradiction and Obedience: Hegel and Barth as Diametrically Opposed Brothers in the Spirit of Modernity." In *Evoking Lament: A Theological Discussion*, edited by Eva Harasta and Brian Brock, 77–98. London: T&T Clark, 2009.

Westerholm, Stephen. "Righteousness, Cosmic and Microcosmic." In *Apocalyptic Paul: Cosmos and Anthropos in Romans 5–8*, edited by Beverly Roberts Gaventa, 21–38. Waco, TX: Baylor University Press, 2013.

Williams, Garry J. "Karl Barth and the Doctrine of the Atonement." In *Engaging with Barth: Contemporary Evangelical Critiques*, edited by Daniel Strange and David Gibson, 232–72. London: T&T Clark, 2008.

Wingren, Gustaf. *Theology in Conflict: Nygren, Barth, Bultmann*. Translated by Eric H. Wahlstrom. Edinburgh: Oliver and Boyd, 1958.

Winn, Christian T. Collins. *"Jesus Is Victor!": The Significance of the Blumhardts for the Theology of Karl Barth*. Eugene, OR: Pickwick, 2009.

Wisse, Maarten. "Was Augustine a Barthian?" *Ars Disputandi* 7, no. 1 (2007): 54–67.

Wood, John Halsey. "Merit in the Midst of Grace: The Covenant with Adam Reconsidered in View of the Two Powers of God." *International Journal of Systematic Theology* 10, no. 2 (2008): 133–48.

Wrede, William. *Paul*. Translated by Edward Lummis. London: Philip Green, 1907.

Wüthrich, Matthias D. "Das 'fremde Geheimnis des wirklich Nichtigen': Karl Barths einsamer Denkweg in der Frage des Bösen." In *Karl Barth im europäischen Zeitgeschehen (1935–1950): Widerstand—Bewährung—Orientierung*, edited by Michael Beintker, Christian Link, and Michael Trowitzsch, 395–411. Zürich: TVZ, 2010.

Wüthrich, Matthias D. *Gott und das Nichtige: Zur Rede vom Nichtigen ausgehend von Karl Barths KD § 50*. Zürich: TVZ, 2006.

Wüthrich, Matthias D. "Lament for Nought? An Inquiry into the Dismissal of Lament in Systematic Theology: On the Example of Karl Barth." In *Evoking Lament: A Theological Discussion*, edited by Eva Harasta and Brian Brock, 60–76. London: T&T Clark, 2009.

Ziegler, Philip G. "The Adventitious Origins of the Calvinist Moral Subject." *Studies in Christian Ethics* 28, no. 2 (2015): 213–23.

Ziegler, Philip G. "'Bound Over to Satan's Tyranny': Sin and Satan in Contemporary Reformed Hamartiology." *Theology Today* 75, no. 1 (2018): 89–100.

Ziegler, Philip G. *Militant Grace: The Apocalyptic Turn and the Future of Christian Theology*. Grand Rapids, MI: Baker Academic, 2018.

Ziegler, Philip G. "'While We Were Yet Enemies': Some Particularly Protestant Reflections on Grace." *Journal of Reformed Theology* 14, no. 1 (2020): 35–51.

INDEX

Althaus, Paul 2, 15 n.69, 47 n.120
Altizer, Thomas 24 n.9, 91 n.47, 123 n.74
Anselm 48 n.127
apocalyptic
  cosmological 9–10, 12, 71 n.96, 130
  forensic 10–11, 71 n.96, 75 n.111
  turn 5
Aulén, Gustaf 3 n.16, 13, 15 n.69, 17 n.79, 31, 41 n.93

Beintker, Michael 46
Berkouwer, Gerrit 20 n.82, 24 n.9, 39 n.89, 95, 98 n.84, 117 n.34, 132 n.120, 136 n.146
Brueggemann, Walter 99, 101
Bultmann, Rudolf 8, 57 n.26, 75, 87 n.32, 141–2

Calvin, John 11, 14, 15, 16, 45, 71 n.95, 100 n.89, 144 n.28
Camfield, F. W. 94 n.68
Chalamet, Christophe 4 n.19, 29–30, 127
chaos 24 n.9, 37, 60, 62, 64–5, 84–5, 119, 130, 134–5
Christus Victor 9 n.38, 12 n.54, 13, 14, 17, 31, 125 n.83, 141–2
covenant
  with death 96–110, 120, 121, 129, 135
  of grace 24–5, 37, 52–4, 130

De Boer, Martinus 9–10, 58 n.26, 71 n.96, 75 n.110, 87 n.32
demythologising 75 n.110, 141–5
divine
  freedom 126, 127, 130, 132
  grace 35, 43, 45, 47, 69, 125, 126, 134, 136, 140
  handing-over 27–31
  hiddenness (conceal) 40 n.90, 41, 45, 47, 101–5, 108, 120–1, 127 n.96
  holiness 34–5
  love 29, 40 n.91, 43, 57 n.25, 69, 77, 90 n.43, 108, 110, 123, 132, 135
  mutability 127–8
  opus alienum 36, 38–9, 42, 43–8, 99, 116, 120, 124, 135, 136

opus proprium 39 n.89, 42, 43–8, 99 n.89, 101, 132, 135, 136
  risk 24 n.10, 32–3, 69
  steadfastness 31–3, 45–6, 133
  wrath 24, 41–2, 43, 47, 63, 69–70, 105, 108, 110, 120, 123, 127, 132
dualism 35, 37, 107, 136

eschatology 9–10, 44, 45 n.112, 53 n.12, 66, 69, 85, 127, 131–2
ethics 31 n.48, 64
Etzelmüller, Gregor 145

faith 33, 70 n.87, 72 n.96, 110 n.140, 133, 134
flesh 29 n.35, 60–1, 133
Forde, Gerhard 12 n.54, 41, 89 n.40, 91 n.46, 113 n.10, 124 n.76, 140
forensicism 8, 13, 17, 18, 26, 56, 73–4, 86–96
forgiveness 87–91

Gaffin, Richard 114 n.12, 116 n.28, 118
Gaventa, Beverly 26, 27 n.26, 134 n.131
Greggs, Tom 18 n.81

Hart, David Bentley 40, 137 n.154
Hart, Trevor 16 n.74, 17, 30 n.41, 55 n.17
Holmes, Christopher 29–30
Hunsinger, George 90 n.43, 107 n.127

Israel 47, 54, 66 n.70, 74, 99

Jenson, Robert 45 n.111, 111–12, 137 n.153
Jesus Christ
  death of 33, 52, 75–8, 83 n.8, 85–6, 88–91, 92–6, 119, 123, 126, 133–4
  incarnation 28–31, 69, 133–4
  obedience of 31–3, 70–8, 101, 109–10, 133–4
  temptation of 70–8, 101
Jones, Paul Dafydd 13, 97 n.78
judgment 10, 33, 52–7, 67–70, 78, 83, 85, 94–5, 103, 119, 125, 132–3

Käsemann, Ernst 129 n.104, 134, 140 n.5
Klappert, Bertold 45 n.112, 95 n.69, 96, 125 n.80

law 53–4, 74, 76, 79
Luther, Martin 14, 15, 16, 40 n.90, 41 n.93, 52, 70 n.87, 81, 86 n.26, 96 n.72, 98, 99 n.89

Macquarrie, John 141–2
Martyn, J. Louis 58 n.26, 72 n.96, 75 n.110, 87, 94 n.64, 124 n.75, 144 n.27
Massmann, Alexander 82 n.5, 98, 109 n.136, 117 n.35, 123 n.71
McCormack, Bruce 9–12, 13–14, 38 n.83, 40 n.91, 53 n.11, 87, 128 n.98
Moltmann, Jürgen 37 n.78, 115 n.18, 126 n.86
Mueller, David 13, 56 n.21

new creation 129–36
Nimmo, Paul 30 n.41, 65 n.66, 91–2
nothingness 24 n.9, 25, 49, 64, 84, 102
    defeat of 131–6
    as instrument 42–4, 119–20
    ontology of 34–8, 47

prayer 32, 102–3, 108–10

resurrection 12, 32, 45–6
    as hermeneutical event 112, 122–3
    as new act 125–9
    and the new aeon 114–15, 122
    as redemption 114–18, 129–36
Ricoeur, Paul 42, 47 n.121

Ritschl, Albrecht 3, 53 n.11
Rutledge, Fleming 13, 17, 63 n.54, 97 n.75

Schleiermacher, Friedrich 2–3, 139
Schweitzer, Albert 88 n.33
sin
    and grace 67, 69
    of the individual 3, 10
    and nothingness 47, 57
    as power 29, 57–62, 89
    and Satan 6 n.28, 26, 64
Smythe, Shannon Nicole 9–11, 22 n.3, 27 n.26, 75 n.111
substitution 91–6

Taubes, Jacob 43 n.107
Thomas, Günter 88 n.38, 119 n.46
Thurneysen, Eduard 5–6, 56 n.21
Tonstad, Linn 123

Weber, Otto 13, 18 n.81
Weltende 62, 77, 78, 82, 94, 101, 119–20, 121–2
Wingren, Gustav 4, 89 n.40
Wüthrich, Matthias 4 n.23, 39, 42 n.96, 61 n.47, 102 n.100

Ziegler, Philip 16 n.73, 17, 42 n.98, 57 n.24, 89 n.40, 132 n.121, 143–4

www.ingramcontent.com/pod-product-compliance
Lightning Source LLC
Chambersburg PA
CBHW061839300426
44115CB00013B/2442